ABRAHAM

Abraham

The First Jew

ANTHONY JULIUS

Yale

UNIVERSITY

PRESS

New Haven and London

Yale University Press books may be purchased in quantity for educational, business, or promotional use. For information, please e-mail sales.press@yale.edu (U.S. office) or sales@yaleup.co.uk (U.K. office).

Set in Janson Oldstyle type by Integrated Publishing Solutions.
Printed in the United States of America.

Library of Congress Control Number: 2024939686
ISBN 978-0-300-26680-1 (hardcover : alk. paper)

A catalogue record for this book is available from the British Library.

This paper meets the requirements of ANSI/NISO Z39.48-1992 (Permanence of Paper).

10 9 8 7 6 5 4 3 2 1

Frontispiece: Abraham, Sarah, and Isaac. Detail from the Venice Haggadah, 1609, folio 6r, Beinecke Rare Book and Manuscript Library, Yale University

In memory of my teachers:
George Baracs (1914–2001)
Dan Jacobson (1929–2014)

CONTENTS

All citations are in the notes, save for those referencing Maimonides and Freud, which are incorporated in the book's chapters. The Freud citations refer to the twenty-four-volume *Standard Edition*.

My biography posits two periods in Abraham's life, periods so at odds with each other that it makes better sense to think of them as lived by two Abrahams. I call them "Abraham 1" and "Abraham 2," or "the first Abraham" and "the second Abraham."

The first Abraham is born into a pagan, polytheistic milieu. In mid-adulthood, he invents himself as an inquiring, skeptical, independent-minded public intellectual. Daring to know, reasoning himself toward monotheism, and contemptuous of superstition, he addresses the inhabitants of his native Mesopotamian city of Ur, endeavoring to persuade them to think like him. He adopts various adversarial, iconoclastic modes— challenging, mocking, statue smashing.

This noisy, combative activity comes to the attention of the city authorities. Abraham is arrested for advocating doctrines subversive of received religious truths. The city's ruler, Nimrod, debates with him, expecting to win him over. When Nimrod fails to do so, he condemns Abraham to death, dispatching him to a furnace. Standing in this furnace, the temperature rising, Abraham prays for a miracle. "Save me from death; liberate me from this society." The prayer is an acknowledgment of the failure of his project. Nimrod releases him, giving Abraham his miracle, as he believes. Abraham 1's life has come to an end.

He becomes Abraham 2, a man of faith, subordinating himself to God in all His exacting demands and thrilling, unlikely promises. Exiled from Ur by Nimrod, Abraham sets out for Haran, another Mesopotamian city. He lives there for many years with his wife, Sarah, and his nephew Lot, as a member of his father's household. His public activities in Haran differ from his Ur activities. He no longer asks his interlocutors to think for themselves; he invites them to surrender themselves to God. This second Abraham is the leader of an emerging sect.

At a certain moment in this period, he is addressed by God. In this first message, Abraham is instructed to leave Haran and go to another land, leaving his father, Terah, behind. He complies, and after many adventures, God then makes another wrenching demand of Abraham. He must sacrifice on a mountain his son Isaac, the young man on whom the continuation of the familial and national line depends. This story is known in Hebrew as the *Akedah* (the Binding), and as with the furnace, it too brings an Abraham life to an end. But with this second crisis, no further Abraham emerges: there is no Abraham 3. In this sense, the *Akedah* represents an unsurpassed horizon for Abraham and for Jews thereafter, the "master narrative of Jewish memory."[1] It is not a miracle; it is a catastrophe. Abraham's life loses energy thereafter, and his story peters out.

The Scriptural account of the Abraham story begins with God's command to him in Haran and ends with Abraham's death in Hebron. No attention is paid to the Ur period; a good deal of attention is paid to the post-*Akedah* period. My biography in the Jewish tradition, we make choices on what we will write about and what we will pass over. Last, we are all interested in how our figures are received in Jewish life.[13]

In the writing of this book, I have also had in mind the example of Dan Jacobson's *The Story of Stories* (1982), an account of "the Chosen People and its God," composed "as a kind of narrative, in a spirit of critical speculation; not as a work of scholarship."[14] That Dan did not live to subject *Abraham: The First Jew* to searching criticism makes it a poorer work.

I have been thinking about Abraham since childhood days, long enough to accumulate many debts. "Sing every day, sing every day—review your studies like a song that one sings over," advises the Talmud (Sanhedrin 99b). This has been my way. I have sung not only to myself but also to family members, to friends, to colleagues, and to the Yale-appointed reader of the manuscript, all of whom have contributed to this book. Thank you, each one of you. I am also grateful to the general editors of Yale Jewish Lives, Steven Zipperstein and Anita Shapira, for inviting me to contribute to their series.

Last, as readers will notice, I refer to my subject throughout as "Abraham" and never as "Abram." The decision was dictated by reasons of argument and style, but I am happy to invoke rabbinic authority: "Whoever calls Abraham Abram breaks a commandment" (Berakhot 13a).

ABRAHAM

1

Abraham 1's Life

"Abraham"

If one was inclined to find meaning in given names, one would want to make something of Abraham's. It is so rich in implication.

To begin with, consider the first letter, *aleph*. Abraham's name reprises the line that he himself initiates: he is the *aleph* of the Jewish people. The first *two* letters of his name, *aleph* and *bet*, are the first two letters of the Hebrew alphabet. *Aleph* and *bet* are both beginnings. *Bet* is a strong beginning—the Book of Genesis, *Bereishit* in Hebrew, begins with the letter *bet*. Abraham begins, and then he begins again. The Abraham story is the beginning of everything for the Jews, which includes the story of Abraham's own beginnings. He starts (*aleph*) and then starts again (*bet*). A crisis precipitates the second beginning, which a second crisis then ends. Beyond that moment, though he lives on, there are no further beginnings.

Putting the two letters together, *ab* or *av*, we get the Hebrew word for "father"—another pointer, then, to a beginning, here not the beginning of one life but of a family and then of a nation. However, even though Abraham is the father of a nation precisely by being the father of a family, the two are also distinct—not all the members of his family will constitute that nation. Another son will found a second nation; other sons will live their lives unmomentously.

But what of Ab-*raham*? Take a step back. When he first appears in his story, his name is not Abraham; it is Abram. The name is given to him by his father, Terah. *Abram* means "exalted" or "elevated" father. It expresses both a father's vanity and his hope. My son has an exalted father; may he too become such a person. But Ab-ra*ham* means something more opaque. The addition of a *hey* signifies God's name—but there is no word *raham*. We might say, the entry of God into Abraham's life makes the meaning of that life mysterious, opaque. He is now father of—whom? What kind of a father is he? Not lofty anymore. But then what?

Mysterious—not meaningless. On the contrary, two meanings are intimated, or rather, one meaning and a *not*-meaning that hints at a second meaning.

The meaning is given in Genesis 17:4–5. God tells Abram that he will be father of a multitude of nations (*av hamon goyim*) and that his name will henceforth be Abraham. One can just about get to this new role of Abraham's in the new name. *Av*, father; *resh*, the Hebrew letter *r*, which sounds like (and is the first letter of) the word *rosh*, the Hebrew word for "head" or "leader"; and *ham*, the first syllable of the Hebrew word for "multitude."

The not-meaning is the encouragement that the new name gives us to associate Abraham with the quality of mercy (*racham*). But that is *not* a meaning of the name, because it is spelled with the Hebrew letter *hey*, not the letter *chet*. The *hey*, one of the letters that make up God's name, the Tetragrammaton, relates Abraham to God. Putting together the not-meaning and the intimated meaning indicates the choice Abraham makes on Mt. Moriah, favoring God over mercy toward his son.

Within the Torah, Abraham is known as "the Hebrew." The word "Hebrew" appears for the first time in connection with his name: "a fugitive brought the news to Abram the Hebrew [*Avram ha'ivri*]." His Mesopotamian origins and Hebrew identity affirm a difference between contingency of circumstance and essential loyalties. *Ivri* means "the other side." Abraham is the "Hebrew," the person from "the other side," because he is a person who is apart from his native community, first, and for a period, because though he is in it, he is adversarial to it, and then, second, for a longer period, because he leaves it and joins no other community in its place.

In common Jewish parlance, he is known as *Avraham Aveinu*, "Abraham our father"—the father of all Jews. ("Look to Abraham your father," Isaiah tells his fellow exiles.) And this means, among other things, that when he takes his son to sacrifice him, we Jewish sons and daughters are there too. The *Akedah* is a family story. This is what *our* father would be willing to do to us, if asked by God. "Abraham our Father" puts each one of us on Mt. Moriah.

And yet, with all this, the name is *his* name. It is not the name of a general characteristic attached to him. He is not an allegorical figure; he does not stand for something else. Nor is he a "type." In the Christian reading of his life, he anticipates the Jesus story; the meaning of his life is in that anticipation. This is not the Jewish reading. The commentator Ibn Ezra (1089– 1167) insisted that we should not expect an explanation for each and every name,[1] as if to say, "Do not, in your enthusiastic, fanciful, glossing of the man's name, forget the man himself." Sometimes a name is just a name, the designation of a person, which we need to insist on, in order to pay proper respect to the weighty singularity of the person who carries it, in all his or her non-conceptual particularity and individuality.[2]

Abraham before Abraham

The first step, the step taken by this first chapter, is to chart a certain passage, one from "mere being" to "being Abraham." As it turns out, it is the passage to being the *first* Abraham—a passage from one kind of intellectual to another kind, that is, and transacted in Ur, the city of his birth.

Ur of the Chaldees

Ur was a major city in the region. Across the period of Abraham's life, it was the capital of the Sumerian empire; at no other time in its history was it so important.[3] "City possessing all that is vital, water-washed, firm-standing, ox, confident of its power," sang a Sumerian poet.[4] It was maintained by agriculture, by commerce, and by manufacture. It was famous for its textiles. It had ties of trade and diplomacy with other cities. It had overseas trade links with the ports of the Persian Gulf. Raw copper was imported from the Anatolian mountains. It was well defended against attack, though it did not have the appearance of a fortified city.

It had temples and shrines, dwelling houses, schools, and marketplaces. The houses were closely packed, made mostly of mud bricks, with fired bricks for exteriors. Many of them had private chapels, where the family archives were kept, and family vaults under rooms, where the dead of the household were buried. A sacred quarter—a wide, open space—was dedicated to the moon god, Nanna. In the schools, the children learned how to write on clay tablets; they took dictation, often writing out a pious aphorism; they learned their reading by studying temple hymns; there was arithmetic and geometry for the more advanced pupils, as well as conjugation of Sumerian verbs—all this was in the curriculum. Two thousand tablets were discovered in the excavation of a single school.

Much of Ur's sixty-five-thousand-strong population was literate—not just the priests and the professional men but even the majority of the smaller traders and artisans. They took their place in a social organization distinguished for its "elaborate intricacies."[5] At the bottom were slaves. In the middle stratum were traders, agriculturalists, the professions, and their families. At the top, there were the priests, government officials and courtiers, and senior army ranks. Together they maintained a developed economy, an established, functioning bureaucracy, and a legal system. There was considerable patronage of the arts. Support of the craftsmen provided gifted individuals with the opportunity to devote all their imagination and energy to their skill. The concentration of craftsmen in temple precincts promoted a spirit of competitive innovativeness.[6]

Sumerian written culture comprised myths and epic tales, hymns and laments, essays and disputations, proverbs and precepts, all inscribed on tablets.[7] Chaldean society had its own traditions of learning and wisdom. It had skilled mathematicians. The Chaldeans were celebrated as astronomers. During the excavations of Ur made in the 1920s, mathematical tables with formulae for extracting square and cube roots were found. Archives of cuneiform records relating to all aspects of governance survive: legal documents, contracts, land registries, royal correspondence.

Three privileged groups inhabited the Chaldeans' universe.[8]

First, of course, there were the gods. Sumerian religion accommodated hundreds, even thousands, of gods and goddesses. They took an interest in the physical elements, in human activities, in geographical locations, in ranks of society, in phases of human life. They quarreled with each other and got drunk; they were immortal, but they could be killed. Gods were visualized mostly in human form. There were the great gods, to whom city temples were dedicated; there were lesser gods, worshiped at roadside shrines; there were family gods; and there were gods who concerned themselves with the welfare of individuals. All the gods exercised patronage, the lesser gods interceding on behalf of their wards with the greater gods. When the gods battled each other, humans were caught up in the conflict and endured the consequences.

Second, there were demons and guardian spirits. Demons brought disease and misfortune; they stalked people, robbing them of vitality and happiness; they harmed or even stole infants. Guardian spirits brought good fortune. Prayers and rituals kept the demons at bay; other prayers and offerings kept the guardian spirits in line; experts were enlisted for more challenging occasions. These demons and spirits were visualized as hybrids: bull-men, fish-men, scorpion-men.

Last, there were the ancestors of the living. Death meant a spectral existence, joyless and dim; the dead were troubled, as in life, by hunger and thirst. Chaldeans paid a reverential attention to their ancestors. The honoring and placating of ancestors took place in the family home, as did the honoring and placating of lesser gods. Fathers stood at the end of this line in ancestor worship, marking the point at which worshipers and worshiped met. They were ancestors-in-waiting. But perhaps they had to insist on the deference they were due. A Sumerian work of the period reads, "Shuruppak the son of Ubara-Tut gave instructions to his son Zi-ud-sura, let me speak a word to you: you must pay attention! Don't ignore my instructions! Don't transgress my words! The instructions of an old man are priceless; do what I say!"[9]

Religion had a density of presence in the everyday life of the city's inhabitants. Chaldean cosmogony was elaborated in hymns, sung in the many rituals that divided the day. The religion was mostly one of fear; the gods were powerful. They were not admired for their qualities; they were instead courted for

ing by traditional customs, laws, doctrines, and judgments, be-
queathed by his ancestors, deadening the soul and denying him
its freedom. No. The past did not weigh on him as a heavy load;
he did not reject it with wrath and fury.[28] He was not blinded
by tradition because he saw through lenses it provided.

It is at best half right, then, to assert that the educated, literate person, the prototype of the modern intellectual, writer,
teacher, and scholar, was born in the temples and schools of the
cities of Sumer.[29] Only a limited type of educated, literate person was born there: conformist, hierarchical, orthodox, deferential to all established authorities. Priests were representative
of the type then; lawyers are the best examples of the type in
our own times. They are capable of the greatest refinement of
thinking, the most creative use of given concepts, the execution
of an infinite number of tasks and initiatives within the boundaries of their profession. They hold a complacent conviction of
the ordered character of society. They engage in no speculation
concerning fundamental principles; they hold their views on
the basis of traditional authority (Guide, III.51); they are expert
purveyors of the "already-said."[30] They think as they are taught
to think;[31] they share a group mentality. But they are not without resourcefulness or a measure of imagination. They are especially adept at justifying limitations of thought by appeals to
reason.[32] To revert to Ur, there were in the city talented, sensitive individuals, working in and committed to Ur's traditions
and yet not limited to receptivity, passivity, faithful transmission;
they were inventive, even innovative, within inherited limits.[33]

And Abraham's family? His father, Terah, was a manufac-
turer, a retailer, and a trader, the owner of shops in Ur and elsewhere, a person of substantial means and well connected to ruling
circles in the city. He was self-made, resourceful, ambitious, and
civic-minded. He made and sold figures of the gods, products
that brought him into regular contact with the priests. He was
proud of his position in the hierarchy. But he was also guarded,

insecure, sensitive to condescension. He was proud that he had sons in his business and even prouder that he had a son who was equal to the priests, a learned man. His wife was an invisible figure. Abraham too was self-made—a self-made intellectual. He did not acquire the status from his father. But he did not despise his father for being a businessman. He had been competitive with his father, and then he ceased to be competitive. He had a sense that he and his father had collided many times, like rhinos, and neither had given way. That was enough for Abraham; he assumed it was enough for his father. He would still argue with Terah, from time to time, but without passion. Terah took this lack of passion for contempt, which it was not. There was simply nothing rivalrous in Abraham's sense of his father. He was not intimidated by him; he had seen him whole; he had taken his measure; he could do without him. All this Abraham believed.

The part played by Terah later on in Abraham's life could therefore not have been anticipated by either of them. It was a double ignominy. Terah became chief among the despised idolaters and chief among Abraham's betrayers. Though Terah was a widower, his wife's death had had little impact on his household; she had only ever played a shadowy, peripheral part in family life. Let her stand for a certain paradigmatic mother, "the overlooked essential, the witness excluded for millennia, nonetheless bizarrely necessary."[34]

Terah's other sons, Nahor and Haran, supported him in his business affairs. Nahor was smart, business-focused, and a good son; among the brothers, he is the one in whom filial respect and service runs deepest. He was the least imaginative too—not an intellectual but adept at pulling apart a proposal. Haran was the scientist of the family and consulted with the officials concerned with the defense of the city. His family took pride, in equal measure, in his accomplishments and his connections; as much as with Abraham, their hopes for advancement were bound up with him. Haran had three children: Milcah, Iscah, and Lot.

comes from, the influences and circumstances governing the moment of one's entry into the world. We can live and die within the boundaries of these "origins." If we do, we remain defined by our arrival's horizons, inert. "Origin" is passive; "beginning" is active. "Origin" relates to myth; "beginnings" are the material of human history. "Origin" is existence; "beginning" is the promise of essence. A beginning is never "given."[45] We work from our origins toward a beginning; we are a project, if we are anything. In our projects lies our autonomy. Some use the word "growth" to describe this work. It is a sentimentalism. The word denies the creative violence of the process, its repudiations, its leaps, its dismal collapses, its intoxicating elevations.

When does one begin to prize oneself free of origin's grip, a grip as strong as a stranglehold?[46] And what energy of resistance is required to start out? Is it in the energy of the ambition to become one's own person, to shake off the mere circumstances of one's arrival in the world? Is it a recoil from the spectacle of one's own manufacturedness, some sudden, dismaying realization that one has been put together by the people who were already there, before one arrived? The first assertion of this "will," the willing of one's freedom, is not to be taken for granted, though often it is described in simplistic, heroic language.[47] It can be experienced in its first moments as an unchosen extrusion from one's given milieu. Everything that was familiar takes on an alien visage; the very air that was once breathed so thoughtlessly now chokes and stifles.

Abraham's beginning was in his fortieth year. And what was the journey to this beginning, the character of this self-begetting? First, a detaching; then a wandering, followed by a reorienting; and last, a reasoning. Or so the journey might be mapped.

Detaching

The Jewish philosopher Emmanuel Levinas (1906–1995) was asked, "How does one begin to think?" Some pacific answers were proposed to him. "Prompted by a new experience or a person one meets or a book one reads?" "Not quite," replied Levinas. "Thinking—that is, proper, serious thinking, in which some settled belief is at risk—begins with a disturbance to which we cannot give verbal form. It could be a separation, a violent scene, or even a sudden consciousness of the monotony of time."[48]

The first step of Abraham's journey was not what we might expect: say, some grand passion of curiosity, some new boldness of address to the universe. No, not at all. He found himself instead prey to fears. He was afraid that life was going meaninglessly well for him, that he was merely marking time, that his life was living him. He was also afraid that living this life might in time stupefy him. He feared that he would drift into his own background, that his sense of himself as a distinct consciousness, a "self," with its own perspective on the world, might fade to blankness. He was even afraid that what he took to be his thoughts were not "his" at all—that these thoughts did not originate with him, that he did not own them, that he could not play with them, as one might with one's possessions. How did he come to think them? Yes, there were the years of education in Ur's institutions of learning. He had the sense, however, that in every important respect, his mind had been "cast," as a figurine might be, well before his first day in class. He began to feel the oppressive weight of assertive paternal will behind the cultural forms in which he had been educated.[49]

These fears were a great burden to him, but how to dispel them? Was there anywhere else he could go for fresh thoughts, thoughts he could call his own? But there was nothing beyond Ur, no more than what it had to offer, which he had already taken. Perhaps a recommitment to his existing life but with a new vehemence of attachment, a more vigorous embrace, might be the solution.

"I will make a study of our traditional doctrines and practices," Abraham resolved. "I will take them seriously, as invitations to inquiry. On what were they founded? How did they originate? What more can they teach us about the world?" "If I am sunk," he thought, "so be it! I will immerse myself deeper in my given element, my 'near-world.'[50] I will restate my vocation as an exceptional enthusiasm." It led him toward a certain zealotry, even an incipient fanaticism. He distanced himself from his intellectual peers. They now seemed to him to be mere trimmers, accommodating everyday pressures. He grew *over*committed to Ur beliefs and practices; he became a devotee of orthodoxy. He took an unquestioning stance further. He was no longer content with mere submissiveness; only the abject would satisfy him.

This took him, however, to an unanticipated place. He grew contemptuous of established modes of service, with their hierarchies of priests and teachers. These men lacked seriousness. They did not care to look beyond their immediate horizons; they marched in step. And yet they were drunk on self-esteem. They regarded their scientific, theoretical perspectives as markers of their superior status. They were wrong—embarrassingly wrong, Abraham thought. These perspectives were mere versions of that natural attitude that was every sentient being's default perspective. For all their sophistication, the priests and teachers shared with their fellow inhabitants the same fundamental credulousness toward inherited beliefs and practices. They too made no essential distinction between what they believed and what they knew. Their given horizon was for them an unsurpassable one.

This contempt woke him up to fresh possibilities. Prostration turned into an affair of suspicions and doubts, and a space opened up between him and his milieu. Across that new divide, he pondered, "What if my thoughts, even in their most developed form as convictions, are no more than 'takes' on the world?

And what if my society is but one among many societies—even one among an infinite number of *possible* societies?"

His thoughts, his sense of his immediate environment, the universe itself, became objects of reflection. He began to see them "thematically"; he turned his attention to them. And in this movement, he became conscious of being alive in a new sense. He was startled—and embarrassed. There was so much to study. He experienced a sense of elevation, accompanied by a radical alienation from everything that was familiar.[51] He was alone. And so the questions posed themselves to him: "How should I live? In what should I believe?" New fears beset him: "I will not settle these questions. I will not know how to live; I will not be capable of belief."

The detaching was at first a self-impoverishing, a clearing out of everything that lived in him but did not originate with him. He had come to disdain mere belief—even that elaborated belief allowed by Chaldean society.[52] Everything demanded an explanation; no explanation was sufficient. At first, it was all loss: of routine, of what was taken as known, of trust. All this went, though at the price of weakening those ties that bound Abraham to family, friends, coreligionists, fellow citizens. He divested himself of his inherited beliefs. And the first to go? Ur's gods. Abraham was surprised by how easy it was to dismiss them.

To Abraham's new situation, other philosophers have offered their own witness. Take, for example, the early twelfth-century Al-Ghazali's *The Deliverance from Error*, written toward the end of his life. "The thirst for grasping the real meaning of things was habitual for me from my early years," the great Islamic philosopher writes. "It was instinctive, a natural disposition, not something due to my own contriving. The fetters of servile conformism fell away from me; inherited beliefs lost their hold on me. I found loathsome those who restrict the attainment of truth to the uncritical acceptance of the Imam's pronouncements. I wanted to seek out the true meaning of those uncritical beliefs,

imposed from without, by parents and teachers, and then slav-
ishly aped by children and students."[53]

Benjamin Fondane, the twentieth-century Jewish philosopher and poet, had a phrase ideal to describe Abraham's state of
mind at this point: "impertinent disquiet."[54] He was unsettled,
restless; his instinctive respect for institutions and beliefs had
gone; he distrusted all received knowledge, everything that was
proposed as self-evident or consecrated by time and tradition.

Wandering

Of course, in this period, Abraham continued to perform his
duties in Ur society. But, writes Maimonides, his heart wandered.
(Abraham was a wanderer before he left Ur and long before he
left Haran.) The novelist James Joyce captured something of
the quality of this type of wandering. It was not an indolent passivity. Nor was there any quality of despair or boredom, though
there was a certain irresolution. Abraham would hear voices
summoning him to acknowledged duties—the constant voices
of his father and of his colleagues and then a further voice and
yet another voice and then a worldly voice, all urging him to
persist in tasks not of his own choosing.[55]

This wandering, barely a stance and then only of the most
provisional kind, has always had its critics, including philosophical critics. It can look feckless. So blind is the curiosity by which
human beings are possessed, one might think, that they often
conduct their minds along unexplored routes, having no reason
to hope for success but merely willing to risk the experiment of
finding whether the truth they seek lies there. As well might a
man, burning with the desire to discover treasure, continuously
roam the streets, seeking to find something that a passerby might
have chanced to drop.[56]

Criticisms of this order were made of Abraham by the few
(colleagues, mostly) who noticed his abstractedness, a certain remoteness in manner. If called upon by these men to defend him-

self, he might have responded, "A philosophical problem has the form: 'I don't know my way around.'"[57] Until, that is, you find that you do.

Reorienting

To orient oneself is to find one's bearings. For a person to be without orientation toward the world is a desperate thing. The world then presents itself as unknown and hostile, a chaos of impressions and occurrences without order.[58] But to have lost one's orientation, to become disoriented, is especially bewildering, unnerving. It can then be the most difficult thing in the world to reorient, to find some new way of making oneself at home in the world. This is the place, the "no-place," that Abraham reached. Untethered, drifting, an aimlessness, but heavy with anxiety, one language lost, no new language found, one set of positions disavowed, no new set on the horizon.

To *re*orient himself, he had to find a new project, one that in its pursuit (and not just its outcome) would stabilize his relation to his environment. Given his intellectual disposition, the project itself had to be an intellectual one. Time passed, the alienated condition deepened, and then he surprised himself. "I will make myself the primary point of reference, and I will make the object of my inquiry the cosmos," Abraham resolved. "I will stand alone, unencumbered by inherited beliefs, and ask fundamental questions." "I have detached myself from Chaldean thinking," Abraham reflected with satisfaction. He had wandered, freely, glancing at this and that, picking up, putting down, thoughts, possibilities. At last, he had settled on a reorientation. And at last he was ready to declare, "I am free." Philosophical reflection, he concluded, is an act of absolute freedom; it lifts itself out of the sphere of givenness by a free choice.[59] It begins as cosmology; it ends when it has established our place in the cosmos.[60]

Reasoning

Abraham began to experience a joy of reasoning, a pleasure in the free use of his mind, a new reflective activity. He had freed himself from the corruptions of prejudice; his mind was not obscured by passions. Or so he believed. He was at last in possession of his own intellectual faculties, for so long formerly occupied by bogus divinities, imposter priests.[61]

His reasoning was experimental in its essential character: a constructive skepticism, in which acting rationally meant viewing his conclusions as provisional only, regardless of how successfully they had allowed him to navigate the world. Tradition would for sure be allowed no veto; he would advance under the flag of the antitraditionalist.

He had dispatched the gods; patently, they were mere inventions. But what now? Was the universe eternal and without ruler? This was the question that preoccupied him. His hypothesis? That he would find the answer by the application of principles of structure and creativity. Together, they guided his inquiries, allowing him to make sense of what he observed around him and in the skies above him.

- *Structure*: He was impressed by the splendid order and beauty in Nature. The world disclosed to him an immeasurable showplace of manifoldness, order, purposiveness, and beauty. Everywhere he found clear signs of an order according to determinate aim, carried out with great wisdom, and in a whole of indescribable manifoldness in content and magnitude in scope. He was astonished and awestruck,[62] which stimulated him to further thought and the devising of theories to account for these qualities.
- *Creativity*: The newly emerging sense he had of his own selfhood, as a work of self-creation, encouraged him to think in similar terms about an active creator of the universe. An

analogy between the products of human ingenuity and the products of the natural world also impressed itself upon him. What exists must be so in consequence of an act of creation, he speculated. Everywhere he looked he found confirmation of this thought.

The world, Abraham reasoned, was created by an entity, one whom he was ready to designate with the name "God." More than one god could not have been involved in creating the world, he reasoned. The gods, as the Chaldeans understood them, were not capable of coordinated action. And anyway, entities are not needlessly to be multiplied: if positing one designer makes sense, why add a second or third?

Further, the regularities of the natural world, its seasons and cycles, its complex orderedness, encouraged Abraham toward the conclusion that, having been created, the world was self-maintaining. The laws of nature are absolutely unchangeable, he decided. Abraham began to think of himself as a "one-godist." He had reached a conception of one God; he had pulled God out of his mind.

He had a sense of advance. He had moved beyond childish, merely traditional understandings of the cosmos, reaching a more pondered, more reflective understanding of it. This, certainly. But there was more. He had not just made an advance in comprehension; he had also, and thereby, made an advance in intellectuality itself.[63] *This* thought was prompted by his apprehension that the God toward whom he had reasoned was utterly unpicturable. This God could not, by His very nature, be rendered in material form. The very attempt would not just be an act of shocking disrespect; it would also be an exercise in futility. "Ur's myriad gods and goddesses, demons and spirits are only vivid in the versions of them imagined by artists and sculptors," Abraham mused. "Not so with my God. Knowledge of Him can be gained only by thought processes; His existence cannot be grasped by mere sense perception."

And then he took a further step, which for him was a step too far. Can the world continuously be in motion, he wondered, without God causing it to revolve? Surely not. The world must require God's constant engagement. If He withdraws from it for even a moment, chaos will break out. And if this is so, as it seems to be (contrary to his earlier thought), Abraham went on, why not infer a God who also concerns Himself in the everyday life of the world's inhabitants?

He felt the ground under his feet give way. What do I know of this divine concern? Has my reasoning so far outstripped my experience that I am myself a designer, but of only imaginary constructions? He intuited too that reasoning is not just building but also demolishing—indeed, demolishing what one has oneself built. So he began to pick apart his conclusions.

He pondered, How precisely *does* one get from the "last" in the series of empirical powers to a transcendental power, from the conditioned to the unconditioned? Where is the bridge? How does one by reasoning get to a necessary, all-sufficient original being, so overwhelmingly great, so sublimely high, that He is fully external to the world that He has created? If every single thing has a cause, then nothing can be the first cause, that is, a cause that has no cause. And where, then, does this leave the conception of God?[64]

His self-questioning took on a somewhat rhetorical edge. "What is the mandate for inferring that the 'something' I call 'God' has entered by itself into the state in which it finds itself, the state of being self-originating and self-subsisting?

"The world may instead be without beginning and without author; there may be no original Being different from the world. Why not an endless series, a chain of ruler and ruled, cause and effect, a never-ending coming into being and then perishing, a blindly working eternal nature, an abyss of infinite contingency?[65]

"Why must the laws of nature have an author? Why are they not just the brute facts of the universe? And if that is so, then the laws have no explanation at all. Perhaps *they* are the 'unexplained explainers,' not God."[66] He wondered, "Why would that not be fine?" He had no answer, so he moved on.

"Say there is a God. Say further that He is the designer of the world. Further questions arise.

"First, does that make Him the creator too? Perhaps He gave order to available matter?" (Call this the "creator *ex nihilo* question.")

"Second, it is unfathomable why a God who has the power to create anything He wants would create the world as it is given to us. Were His design decisions determined by His benevolence? Does He *want* his creations to flourish?" (Call these the "actual design" and the "purpose of the design" questions.)

"Third, if God is indeed to be compared to an architect, His perfection must be proportional to the harmony of the structure He has designed. Now, while the organisms around me seem quite well adapted to their surroundings, the adaptation is certainly not perfect. Does this mean that the designer is imperfect too?"[67] (Call this the "imperfect design question.")

These were not happy thoughts for Abraham. There was a compensation, however. He had discovered the pleasure of attacking one's own conceptions. If criticism is prose, self-criticism is poetry. Abraham was invigorated; he marched forward to the next question.

"So, fourth, is God also the world's *ruler*?" This seemed an unpromising line of inquiry, given the world's disorders: triumphant evil and humiliated virtue, natural disasters, and our diseased, finite lives. (Call this the "world's ruler question.")

Still further questions bred in his mind, all prompted by the thought that there should be more to say about God than that He was the mere designer of the universe.

"Am I a mere trifle, of no consequence to Him, this inaccessible highest cause? Is He interested in *me*? If God *is* interested, is His interest benevolent? And if it is, is it conditional on my behavior? If conditional, what behavior will please Him? Are there rules to follow, or do I just wait to be told what to do? How will He communicate His wishes to me? Can I influence His judgments?" Abraham doubted that God can be won over by flattery and bribes or even by prayer. (Call these questions the "character of the world's ruler" set of questions.)

The strength of Abraham's conviction faded.

"It may be," he thought, "that I can go no further than the most limited conception of God. An original intelligence established a certain type of causality once and for all—I can say *this*. Metaphysics is never anything other than an introduction to physics, and Providence is a mechanics—so it seems. God has left the world He created; He does not accompany His creation.[68] He does not reveal Himself in the world.[69] He is unchanging, above time, motion, alteration. He does not hear prayer, does not pay attention to individual human needs, does not redeem history."[70]

"It may also be," he further thought, "that I can only hold this conception as a plausible hypothesis. It is a little shaky, after all. There is *some* God. That's it. I must live in the realm of likelihoods; certainties are beyond my reach."

Abraham could not get to any more determinate concept of the supreme cause of the world,[71] still less to its engagement with the world following the moment of creation, *still less* to its interest in Abraham himself. The cosmos presented as a mysterious, alienating place to him.

He was aware that he had stopped short. The light of his reason had brought him to a qualified affirmation of God's existence and to the remote possibility that God is concerned with the world He has created. The creator *ex nihilo* question, the actual design question, the purpose of design question, the imperfect design question, the world's ruler question, the character of the world's ruler set of questions? This was not a new religion; it was a research agenda. His new positions were as a result different in kind to those he started out from. He had ceased to be a person of faith.

Acquiring a Character

When Immanuel Kant (1724–1804) pondered how we become our own person, he could have had Abraham in mind. Our character is not given by nature, Kant wrote. It has to be acquired, and rare is the person who has acquired it by his fortieth year. The moment of acquiring character is a kind of rebirth; it remains unforgettable. It is not achieved by education or by examples or by instruction. It can only be effected by an explosion, prompted by disgust at the unsteady condition of instinct. Mere gradual self-improvement in a fragmentary manner is no alternative at all. It is a vain endeavor, one impression fading away as we labor on another.[72]

The path to being distinctively one's own self is itself personal to each one of us. The endpoint, however, is the same in every case, the ability to answer to our own satisfaction the question, "Who am I?" Abraham, posing the question to himself, answered, "I am a person who has both committed himself to the free use of his reason and, in the exercise of that commitment, arrived at an understanding of God's existence." Had he the language, he would have said, "I am a rational deist." He privileged the adjective over the noun, "rational" over "deist," since "rational" was a free-standing attribute, not a mere qualifier of "deist."

His first and overriding commitment was to an uninhibited internal truthfulness, both toward himself and toward others.[73] This became the ground of his existence, the "One True Method," the foundation for everything else. He recognized the element of dogmatism, or at least intransigeance, about the commitment. He understood that it had its limits. He could not, that is, be open-minded about his open-mindedness, provisional about his embracing of the virtue of provisionality. What was vital to him was the conviction that while this or that reason for some position might fail (convincing at first and then collapsing), reasoning itself would never fail him. Abraham recognized in reasoning a free and universal theoretical disposition, liberating to all who would embrace it. In its pursuit of truth, it refuses to stop short;[74] it is an enterprise without end. Its business must always remain incomplete because the questions never cease.[75] That this was so gave Abraham joy. He found the essential tendency of his own mind in reasoning's operations.

So much for the "rational." What then of the "deist"? "Reasoning has led me to a determinate conclusion," Abraham reflected. "There is a force behind matter. This force is God. There is only one God. I have reasoned my way to Him. All that belongs to nature is uniform, immutable, the immediate performance of the Master. It is He who created the laws by which the moon contributes to the ebb and flow of the ocean.[76] At the very least, God's existence is reasonably possible." The conclusion presented itself to Abraham as one of those newly self-evident things that only original minds discover. This idea of God was the product of the newly autonomous, self-governing Abraham, reached in the exercise of his faculties of judgment and reason. Will he discard this idea? No, but he sensed that it would be open to him to do so.

This second commitment was not a settling place or not for sure. It might turn out to be a stop along the way to another place. He did not know. This will leave him exposed when he advocates for his new views. It sat in his mind, an anxiety, an insecurity, not a goad to further thought. It didn't stimulate him. When he came to impart his discovery, what was it that he had discovered? Not a new deduction but rather a new procedure. Abraham could not be certain that he knew everything about God; but he did know that by his use of reason, he had given up erroneous beliefs. He knew what was false, even if he did not know very much of what was true. This reflected something of reasoning's character, the strength of its negative, subtractive energies. As directed by Abraham, it achieved the depopulating and depersonalizing of the heavens.

He experienced the coexistence of "rational" and "deist" as a tension; he felt the tension inside himself. He wanted *both* the continued free use of reason *and* deism. He did not want free reason just as a procedure to get to his deism and discarded thereafter. But he *also* did not want to think that there was any alternative available conclusion. He wanted to think, "There is nothing else to think but that there is one God."

And certainly, he wanted to be able to rule out of consideration some possibilities. He couldn't even identify them. He just had a sense of possibilities that would be distasteful to him and in respect of which, were he to entertain them, would not count as thinking. In sum, he wanted to affirm, "Thought has its own normativity. When I choose not to think this or that, it is in fidelity to thinking. It is because I do not want my thinking to miscarry, to go off the rails. Holding that the world has no meaning or that it is ruled by malign forces would be instances of such miscarriages. Thought is vulnerable to going wrong." Abraham wanted to hold, and hoped that it was so, that moving away from a neutral one-godism would be a failure of thought.[77]

And yet, no doubt, there was a certain fragility about him, a sensation of dividedness. It bothered him to be a free reasoner and a confirmed monotheist. Yet how can one be a provisional monotheist? Surely, that would be an absurdity, as absurd as being a provisional father. One can be a *bad* father, of course.

Pausing

Did Abraham consider that he had arrived at a complete account of God? Or a partial one, in consequence of reason's limits? He could not say for certain. Under one aspect, of course, the uncertainty was a gift, because it generated his most valuable insight, that philosophy is not a body of doctrine but an activity.[78] Abraham imagined how he might explain to others his new position: "I champion critical thinking, not my own tentative views—the direction of travel, not the view from my window. On your own journey, you will see other landscapes. And that's as it should be." And here he paused. Even if, as a principle, the thinking was without end, with him it had for the moment stalled.

Of course, Abraham had not become a mere thinking machine. He had not grown and withered at one and the same time; he had not become his own person in order to become less than a person. He had found himself in finding a vocation. He was a creator and a discoverer; he was a scientist and a conquistador. He was enraptured, exultant. He had discovered a new human capacity, the capacity to think without armatures. How to do justice to this new joy? We might borrow the language of a great poet, witness to a great revolution. For Abraham, Earth lived in one great presence of the spring; it was as if he had heard a voice that cried, "Sleep no more!" His soul was in triumph; great was his glee of spirit.[79]

And yet there was also an undertow of some distress. He could not eliminate earlier emotions of distress, of panic, of gloom. They had pressed upon him at precisely the moment he had seen through his ancestral faith's false claims. He had seen the sun setting, and he had concluded, "That is no god." He had seen the moon and stars retreat before the dawn, and he had concluded, "These are no gods." But who is then in charge?[80] Is there no one in charge, no god at all? He had since then answered this question to his satisfaction, it is true. But what if he were wrong?

So, thinking was stalled in his own mind. Yet the immediate, practical political implications of his thinking were active, even if beyond his control. The first implication, that there is no divine underwriting of political rulership, meant that rulers could not look to the gods (or to God) for their mandate to rule.

The second implication was that internal to critical reason is a drive toward gestures of impiety toward *all* conventions, *all* settled practices, *all* established faiths. The third implication was that this impiety was liable to foster politically disruptive behavior in the city, because treason tends to follow blasphemy.[81] Last, and in consequence of these other implications, was that Abraham had put himself at risk of sanction, indeed persecution, by the authorities of his city, who would regard him as a threat to their standing and security. How could they not?

Abraham

At last, Abraham began life in possession of a self, self-begotten.

He led the life of a philosopher, as this life would come to be understood in later ancient times. Though he continued to live in Ur, he did not live like everyone else. He was marked out by his moral conduct, his frank speech, his attitude toward the gods, toward wealth, and toward conventional values. He understood philosophy itself to be above all a form of life and not just a discourse.[82] He was not led to this condition of life by either revelation or instruction (that is, not by God or by priests) but by the solitary exercise of his own superb, elevated powers of reasoning.

There is a type of philosopher who is best understood as a "terrible explosive," a "danger to everyone."[83] We must imagine Abraham to be of this type. The rabbis wrote of his "*open* opposition to paganism."[84] "Judaism in its very essence came into being as an act of dissent," one rabbi wrote, with Abraham in view. "Dissent, that is, from paganism, as an act of non-conformity with the surrounding culture."[85]

Philosophy's essential characteristic, which makes its study distinct from science and all dogmatisms, is criticism. It examines critically the principles employed in science and in daily life;

it searches out any inconsistencies there may be in these principles, and it only accepts them when, as the result of a critical inquiry, no reason for rejecting them has appeared. Philosophy is a criticism of knowledge.[86] It is a protest against the finitude of existence and its restrictedness and external necessity. It seeks to overcome the deficiencies of immediate reality.[87]

In philosophy, nothing is a given. For a philosopher, nothing should be taken for granted. Preconceived and established meanings must be constantly reevaluated and new possibilities opened. Of the philosophical life, wrote one philosopher, "Most people inside are filled with *unexamined junk*—only (perhaps) philosophers and (?) saints ever get rid of it. (Sorry, delete saints)."[88] As for the rest of us, well, we tend to be "content to live lazily on scraps of begged opinions."[89]

In consequence, philosophy done well *always* provokes. It exposes confusions to interrogation, and who would not resent being characterized as confused (especially if the confusion is not apparent)? The philosophical life is one of creativity, commitment, and independence of spirit. There is something radical about true philosophizing—audacious, potent, fundamental. It commits itself to the constructing of a life lived according to the dictates of rationality and not blindly following tradition, no matter how deeply entrenched.[90] How could one possibly avoid getting into difficulties, if one led that life?

Still, the kind and intensity of the hostility that the philosopher risks is determined by the choice to be made between remaining in the study or going out into the public square. Each option has certain risks. The risks associated with study harm no one but philosophers themselves: their ideas will lack impact and will probably suffer from the absence of critical attention. The risks associated with the marketplace are greater: the wrong kind of impact, in the attracting both of disciples and persecution; the congealing of arguments into vulgarized, simplified versions of themselves; a betrayal of vocation, as the philosopher turns into a mere preacher; distractions from work, from writing.

So the case for remaining in one's study is strong. There, the philosopher can be as daring as he or she pleases and can entertain outlandish possibilities; his or her mind will be an impassable barrier to hostile vested interests. Publication is a peril avoided. "Anyone who is studying high matters will be the last to write about them and thus expose his thought to the envy and criticism of men," wrote an ancient philosopher. "Whenever we see a book, we can be sure that if the author is really serious, it does not contain his best thoughts; they are stored away with the fairest of his possessions. And if he has committed these serious thoughts to writing, it is because [he has been robbed of his wits]."[91]

Notwithstanding its attractions, Abraham did not make this choice. He could not dissemble, teaching one thing, believing another. Nor even could he teach two versions of what he now believed, one for the general public and one for a smaller, philosophically minded audience. Moreover, he was pulsing with a pedagogic energy: he wanted to share his discoveries. He imagined a certain position of leadership, one that would be central to his vocation.[92] He imagined that it would be offered to him upon request. He had confronted some obvious difficulties in Chaldean religion: the gods are incapable of creating order, and yet the universe is an ordered one. His alternative thesis was derived from observation, an engagement with the natural world available to all. His advocacy of reasoning justified itself, he believed.

Abraham reflected, "What is difficult about any of this? My arguments will only flatter audiences. They point to a human capacity, underused but accessible to each one of us, the free use of our reason. What limitless possibilities this opens up! And what current, humiliating subserviences they expose. We no longer need to worship those imaginary entities to which we give form as idols! Are these not liberating thoughts?"

That the very fact of his independent reasoning struck a blow at the Chaldean way of life was not obvious to him. He did not think of himself as a warring philosopher, one who needs opponents of comparable strength to his own, who has an instinct for attack, who seeks out resistance, who shuns allies.[93] That type held no appeal for him. Indeed, reflectiveness, a turning inward, had become his default. He understood, however, that while each man decides on the place he will occupy in the world, he must occupy one. He cannot withdraw from it. The wise man is a man among men.[94] He will go to the marketplace, he resolved, but with a glance back to the study. He did not anticipate that the marketplace would become a place of vexation and threat to him, provoking him to make his own displays of truculence and violence.

But we run ahead of ourselves. For now, full of goodwill and enthusiasm, inflamed with hope,[95] this zealous devotee of the contemplative life now committed to a relentlessly active life,[96] Abraham was resolved that he would not keep to himself his discoveries and would launch himself on Ur. His first audience would be his family, but before he addressed them, he would speak with Sarah.

2

Abraham 1's Crisis

Family

Abraham's family sensed that something was up.

Sarah

Abraham began with Sarah—but not because he thought she would be the most responsive. She would give him the chance to rehearse his arguments in safety. She would not understand; still less would she object. He told her first, because he wanted to think aloud. Astonished, he heard her responding warmly, with an immediate grasp of his thinking. And yet more—she told him, "You have caught up with me!"

She was exultant. They had arrived by different routes at the same destination, a passionate commitment to the unfettered use of one's reason and the rational confidence in the existence of one ungendered god, the creator of a self-regulating universe. They found, with the force of revelation, that they had been perplexed by related problems. Sarah had the edge. She already knew what Abraham had to reason toward, that "the gods" were a fiction. How otherwise could one make sense of the changes in ranking over the past decades? To historicize the gods was to expose them as human constructions. Their shared positions were free of any implication of male authority. Sarah was not tempted to give way before the brilliance of the "male master."[1]

So she responded to Abraham, "Let us now reason together. Our common isolation is at an end. You have done well alone—and so have I. But the very faculty of thinking, in the end, depends on its public use. You will not be able to hold to that standard of critical thinking by yourself. Reason is not made to be practiced in solitude." Her flushed, shining eyes were fixed on him. "Autonomy is achieved in solidarity. We must do this together. We will not impede each other. We can find a way of living together that does not require my subordination to you. Let us build the community of tomorrow. Let us make judgments together. Let us hold our society to account."

She looked at him with love. She heard his passionate account of new convictions as his own declaration of love—which it was, but not for her. She imagined a life lived together. She anticipated further growth, further realizations of self, in partnership with Abraham. What she had at first taken to be creative solitude had already, some time before this conversation, dwindled to loneliness for her. She craved partnership.

It was too much for Abraham, this love. He was happy that Sarah had responded with such warmth—more than this he could not take in.

For both Sarah and Abraham, their new concepts were rooted in the circumstances of their life.[2] Both had inherited positions from which they reasoned. They did so out of a sense of alienation from Ur's beliefs. That she reasoned at all was her transgression; that he reasoned *away* from those beliefs, instead of with them, was *his* transgression.

They were both autodidacts: Sarah because she did not have access to official knowledge, Abraham because he had to reject it. But they were autodidacts in a more fundamental sense. Learning is always autodidactic: one is not knowledge's mere receptacle; one works it up oneself in the acquiring of it.[3] In the matter of gaining knowledge, then, we are all in the end left to our own devices.

Their reasoning was both free and urgent. Free because it was not demanded, it was not a duty, they were accountable to no one in its exercise, they could pause whenever they wished. Urgent because the reasoning derived from needs that could not be disregarded.

But their circumstances were not altogether the same. For Sarah, the thinking came from grief, from fear, from the tenuousness of her status. Her new ideas germinated out of intolerable material conditions, from the grim, and getting grimmer, facts of her existence. For Abraham, the thinking came from thinking, from the desire to make his thoughts his own. He was driven by the felt necessities of thinking itself.

Sarah gave Abraham the courage to speak to his father.

Terah

The old man listened in silence. At first, what Abraham said made no sense. "Critical reason?" "One God?" Terah looked at his son. He saw an intoxicated person, talking nonsense. Something to do, perhaps, with abandoning following customary ways. Something that the younger man thought up himself. What even does it mean, "thought up himself"? Terah had no desire to argue with his son, nor even to disagree with him. What he must do, he thought, is spell out as if to an imbecile the consequences for the whole family if Abraham does not just *stop*.

"You were our way forward. Through you, we would live among the elite of Ur. We would no longer be middling; we

of the world imposed mechanically by our environment? That is to say, by one of the many social groups, in which everyone is automatically involved from the time we enter the conscious world. Or is it better to work out our own conceptions, consciously and critically, and out of this work of our own brain choose our own sphere of activity and participate actively in making the history of the world?

"The latter, surely!

"When one's conception of the world is not critical, it lacks coherence; it is haphazard and disconnected; one belongs simultaneously to a multiplicity of groups; one's personality is put together in a miscellaneous and disjointed way. It contains elements of both the most primitive men *and* the most modern, of the shabbiest, most local prejudices *and* intuitions of a future philosophy of the whole world. Criticizing one's own conceptions means making them coherent and unified.

"What is more, religion and common sense can only constitute an intellectual order, can only be reduced to unity and coherence, by force: authoritatively, never freely. And the authorities will only ever educate us into stances of resignation and patience, never to thoughtful action, still less to protest.

"In addition, the second option answers to the imperative 'Know thyself!' We should not be strangers to ourselves. We should understand not just the contents of our mind but the way it works. Since we travel in it, we should grasp its principles of construction.

"We do not want to be anachronisms in our own times, fossils, rather than modern men and women. Our language must become adequate to our new understanding. We must liberate ourselves from the clichéd, the stereotypical.

"And then, at last, we will gain a sense of our own creativity, our own strength. We will realize that what we took to be the work of the gods was our own work, the work of humankind. Vistas will open. We will dare, routinely. We will have the sense that we have spiritually caught up with our organic adulthood. We will have become fully mature. We will have shrugged off our guardians.

"We will then be philosophers in the better sense, not possessed *by* a philosophy of which we are mostly unaware but in possession *of* a philosophy, one that is an object for us, open to scrutiny, to revision.

"What then will be our standing in society?

"Perhaps we will reconstitute ourselves as a cadre, renewed in spirit but essentially unchanged. Every view of the world has its scholars and authorities. We would become a new community of the faithful. We would have our own orthodoxy to defend. Were this to happen, it would be a matter of regret, a misfiring. Cadres petrify. Whole herds of studious men share in the world's blindness.[11]

"But perhaps instead we will find allies among the generality of our citizens, those who, by our example, have embraced self-government as a new way of living. We will enjoy with them, and among ourselves, relations of friendship and common interest, with no boundaries to association and no barriers to exit. Each of us will be free to analyze and cast doubt on what others are saying. Self-emancipation is best achieved as a collective endeavor; there is more chance of an entire public enlightening itself than a few isolated individuals managing it. I was fortunate; but I am not a model.

"We will thereby effect a great transformation. We will replace that chaotic amalgam of guesswork, tradition, superstition, prejudice, dogma, fantasy, and self-interested error that up to now has done service as human knowledge and human wisdom, the chief protectors and instigators of which are our dear priests, with a new, sane, rational, happy, just, and equally self-perpetuating human society, which will be able to preserve itself against all hostile influences, even, to an extent, the forces of nature.[12]

"I acknowledge that we will need experts. Self-mastery does not require mastery of every field of study. But our reliance upon others will be defined, conditional, provisional, and without servility."

Abraham would speak thus—adjusting his presentation to the size and responsiveness of the audience.

Sarah waited in their home for the after-event reports. She was eager to hear how he had been received, what challenges had been made to him, and how he had dealt with them. And later, she would ponder how *she* would have dealt with them.

He would be questioned: "You say that the gods do not exist, gods with whom we have daily, intimate contact. You insist that that there is only one god, with whom you have no contact whatsoever. How did you get to that conclusion?" So he would take them through his design argument and conclude with the stirring appeal, "Let us celebrate the fact that a distant god, creator of the world but not interfering in its affairs, leaves us free to act as we choose!"

It was no good. By this point, he had lost most of his audience. Those who still had been paying attention were left uneasy, wondering about his ambitions and how they would be received by the city's ruler. At one gathering, a priest of considerable insight and sophistication offered this challenge: "You say you want to help us free our minds and to understand the critical approach. But that is not true. You do not want to teach us. You want to impress us, even captivate us. You present yourself as a leader, a prophet—a proclaimer of the dark secrets of life and of the world. But if you are right, we are grown men who do not need leaders, and we must keep at arm's length men with this ambition—men like you!

"If you were truly what you say you are, you would not want to talk us into anything. You would not even want to convince: all the time you would be aware that you might be wrong. You would value our intellectual independence too highly to want to convince us in important matters. You would limit yourself to challenging us to form free opinions.[13] You would say nothing about 'God.'

"'God' is your misstep, the way you betray yourself, how you show your hand. If you succeed with us, your new 'one-godism' will itself become what you call a prejudice, defended by its own guardians, its propositions reduced to formulae and rules, its speculative conclusions reduced to dogmas, defenders persecuted by a new order of priests and mystagogues—just as you represent our present 'polytheism' to be!"

"No," he insisted—but too quickly. "I am not contending for 'Y beliefs' in substitution for 'X beliefs.' Nothing could be more unphilosophical than to be dogmatic on *any* subject.[14] Besides, my theory is incomplete, as I most readily acknowledge. It is not *capable* of laying the foundations of a sect, still less an ecclesiastical establishment. Its very incompleteness and provisionality inoculate it against such risks.

"I will always put method above substantive positions, critical reasoning before the truth as I presently understand it.

"If you press me to elaborate my purpose, I would say this: I want the freedom to propose lines of reasoning, to suggest standards and rules for argument, to pose questions, to make comparisons, and to open up possibilities. I want to be an example for you of a new way of being—dare I admit, a new kind of person.[15] My intention is not to teach even a method of reasoning that everyone must follow but only to demonstrate how I myself have resolved to reason. I do so in the hope that it be useful to some among you and that my openness will be well received by you all.[16]

"As for God, He is infinitely beyond our comprehension, since being indivisible and without limits, He bears no relation to us. We are therefore incapable of knowing either what He is or indeed (I will allow) *whether* He is. That being so, who would dare to attempt a certain answer to the question? Certainly not

Belligerencies

And Ur? It grew hostile. Abraham had alarmed his culture.[27] Of course, the display of intelligence was itself a provocation, experienced by his enemies as self-display, as showing off. He made them blush at the solemnity with which they performed sacred rites. He did not recall them to their best selves; he shamed them. Pieties violated, the city found its voice.

"We are not so stupid as to believe that mere stone and wooden objects become gods when we fashion them so. Some of us worship them as symbolic of the gods, and some of us believe that they acquire a quality of indwelling, a presence of the god in the object, when fashioned to replicate him. They are not just things—they are temporary seats of indwelling presences, centers of extraordinary powers and virtues.[28]

"You ask us to exercise our judgment? Very well. We exercise it against you. Of course, we have always been thinking, judging. How could we otherwise live? Maybe you have been too self-involved, too sunk in yourself, to see this. You have some ideas, which we don't embrace, and straight away you conclude that we are stupid. Your intelligence exhausts itself in demonstrations of contempt for us. You do not get to scorn us; we scorn you.

"You wound us. You insult us. You would destroy our temples, dispossess our gods. When you urge us to think for ourselves, you are demanding that we reject the teaching of our parents, and you are inciting our children to reject *our* teaching. You are not our benefactor; you are our enemy. You do not bring us gifts; you would poison us."

In this way, the educated people of Ur pushed away the humiliation of their encounter with him, the unanswerable objections to their faith, the childishness of their imaginings, the triviality of what they took seriously.

The priests were outraged. Their reputed sagacity had been characterized as simple credulity, their esoteric instructions obscurantism, when not fraud. What would be left of their role as mediators to the gods, interpreters of the gods, if the gods themselves were mere figments?

The poets were outraged. What would be left of their role as celebrators of traditional wisdom and narratives of the gods, if the wisdom was phony and the narratives were lies?

Ur's parents were outraged. Their role was to teach deference to the gods and to themselves, but how could deference survive independent, critical thinking? Abraham made them look fools in front of their children, just as he made his own father feel a fool.

These remonstrances did not impress Abraham. So then they all tried to ignore him. Since ignoring him was a strategy, however, and not an instinct, they could not quite adhere to it. Indeed, they began to undermine it with mockery and name-calling—mostly, abusive versions of "intellectual!" Their performance of indifference did not reflect the reality of their continuing, involuntary engagement with him. His contempt mattered too much to them.

His very existence had become an affront. At the very beginning of philosophy, persecution asserts itself, a philosopher once wrote.[29]

Yet he was as impervious to threat as to any appeal. All his insecurities were gone. He rejoiced in a new vulgarity of thinking, armor-plated against attack. He failed to seek out the necessary periods of solitude, inquest, and self-recovery,[30] during which time one can reflect on what one has said and retire it if found inadequate or wrong. His thinking began to lose its elasticity, its provisionality. He was unyielding; he was both courageous and complacent. "Of course they rail against me. These are the accusations that the intellect draws to itself," he thought.[31] "Common sense cannot understand speculation; and what is more, it must come to hate speculation when it has experience of it; and, unless it is in the state of perfect indifference that security confers, it is bound to detest and persecute it."[32]

He took more extreme positions, declaring absolutely worthless all the idols in the marketplace, indeed in the world.[33] His "reason" had become a war machine.[34] To priests: "Your 'thinking' is the thinking of people who do not think—who are *resolved* not to think." To buyers at his father's shop: "At your age, don't you know any better than to worship this thing that my father's household manufactured today?" He was not above mere insults. To an elderly Chaldean: "You are a complete fool!" It was as if he put the entire population of the city under indictment.[35] He acted as if he just *knew* that the whole world was in error.

He was like a man who had awoken too early in the darkness, while everyone else was still asleep.[36] He inaugurated philosophy in his society. He relied solely on observation and his own judgment. He taught that authority should be looked down on and that imitation of ancestors should be repudiated.

Of course he met resistance. In most human beings, the need for support from an authority of some sort is so compelling that their world begins to totter if that authority is threatened. Only an Abraham could dispense with that support; and even *he* would have been unable to do so, if he had not learned in the first years of his life to be independent of his father (see Freud, 11:122–123).

Betrayals

And then, his final blow. In the full tumult of Abraham's exchanges with the city, Terah resolved on a plan. He would invent an appointment that would take him away from the shop for an afternoon, and he would ask Abraham to mind it in his absence. It would recall Abraham to his filial duties.

Working in his father's shop had made Abraham happy as a boy. Terah, too. The father, confident as teacher and mentor, secure in his own space; the son, transported with admiration for his father's instinctive sense of command, his ready, bantering way with customers, his astute bargaining with suppliers, intimating a certain sovereignty of presence. Was this not the best time in the lives of them both? Would Abraham not want, as Terah dearly wanted, to re-create, if not to return to, that time, if the chance of such a return were to be contrived? And would not Abraham then give up his current folly and return to Terah's side, beloved and loving son of a loving and beloved father?

But things did not go as Terah intended.

Abraham accommodated his father's wish and came to the shop just as Terah was ready to leave. A formal handshake, and his father was gone. Abraham surveyed the smaller figurines on the shelves of the shop's walls and the larger figurines on the floor. Dead-eyed, expressionless, poor replicas of human form, mere things.

A man came into the shop. "I'll have two of those," a gesture in the direction of a shelf, "and that one, that big fellow, over there," another gesture, to Abraham's right. Abraham stared at the customer. "How old are you?" "What do you mean?" "It's a simple enough question for a buyer of gods, isn't it? How many years have you spent among the living?" The man, indignant but not knowing what to do with the indignation and thinking that giving his age would compel greater courtesy, replies, "I am sixty years old, old enough to require some respect from you, young man!" "What a disaster!" responded Abraham. "A sixty-year-old worshiping a day-old object!" The elderly customer, confounded, stormed out.

He could have challenged Abraham, "What has the age of the statue to do with its function? You are mistaking a contingent feature of the idol, its age, for a refutation of idol-worshiping. You are the fool, not me!" Precisely this thought occurred to Abraham himself, and he knew that he did not have an answer to it. How stupid he was! This unforced error, this misfired piece of mockery, would get back to smarter heads than this customer possessed, and they would laugh at him—at the very least, for misunderstanding his own position. It wasn't enough to rely on argument, Abraham decided. After all, he couldn't win every encounter. The city had put itself beyond reach of his reasoning. His missteps in debate were caused by their hostility, their refusal to hear him. No surprise that his shouts were becoming incoherent as they contracted to jibes.

He had to act. He took the axe lying on the floor by the shop's rear exit and swung it at the figurines, left and right, chopping and cutting, with a wild energy of rage and frustration and self-pity. And Abraham then stood triumphant, axe still in hand, choking on the wood dust and the clay dust, surveying the fragments and shards, the fragments of limb and torso—everything that was of value to his father in the shop. He gloried in his impiety, wild and dangerous, this apostate from an ancient faith.[37]

There was a momentary commotion at the door. Abraham twisted around toward the sound. Terah had returned. He looked, bewildered and frightened, at the scene of destruction. "What have you done?" Abraham stared at Terah for several seconds. Then, as if providing a report but in an affected, trance-like tone, he said, "The biggest one started a fight with the others, and as you see, they didn't stop smashing each other up until . . . Well, see for yourself." And then, with exaggerated, theatrical gestures, Abraham pointed toward the floor and at the shelves.

Terah turned away, staggered out of the shop, and stumbled down the street. He was a broken man. Abraham had taken an axe to their bond. He had to be stopped. Terah's pace quickened and became purposeful. He didn't stop until he reached the palace of the king, the ruler of Ur, the great Nimrod.

Ruler

Nimrod

Nimrod enjoyed absolute power. He was in charge of the religious practices of his society, as well as the object of much religious devotion. He was a hunter, because hunting was akin to war: face down a lion, face down one's enemies. Ur's poets typically wrote of the city's kings with admiration and reverence, with faith and trust in their deeds and achievements. The king was the perfect human being, intellectually acute, a fearsome warrior, a just ruler, and so on. When he died, his retainers would be killed, so that they could serve him in the afterlife.[38] The kings wanted glory; they required glorification. If the glorification wasn't supplied in satisfactory quantities, there was always the consolation of *self*-glorification. One king hymned himself: "In my reign, the father is respected, the mother is feared, the older sister is not contradicted."[39]

Nimrod was an unusual king, not least because of the exceptional intensity he invested in fulfilling his role. He was a ruler to whom myths attached themselves. Associated with his name was the great project known as the Tower of Babel. It was said of him that he conceived it, and then directed its execution, the storming of the heavens. When that failed, conquest of land became the next available work of mastery. He first rebelled against God; then he sought to tyrannize over humankind. He was a hunter not just of animals but of humans, regarding them as creatures to be tamed and mastered. He considered himself to be an intellectual. He was alive to the implications of his challenge of all divine authority, and his self-belief knew no limit.

His orientation toward the world was as an appropriator, a consumer of its riches, its resources. He destroyed others to enlarge himself. He wished to make a name for himself; the name was to be more widely celebrated than any other. The logic of this vocation led to a challenge to every power greater than his own. The space between his own authority and divine authority was never small enough; the very *fact* of a space became unbearable. When he used the first-person plural, the *pluralis majestatis*, it was a divine voice he desired his subjects to recognize.

There had been great men in the past, but he was the first

person to pursue greatness as a vocation. Nimrod centered his whole character, his livelihood, and his view of life on the concept of greatness. What became known as his "Nimrodian schemes," ziggurats and pyramids, were monuments of glorification and self-glorification, works of anti-art, built at the price of immeasurable suffering and deprivation.[40] They were monuments that would outlive the ruler who built them, while perpetuating his rule. Their purpose? To intimidate onlookers; to overawe; to project power and enhance standing; to support further schemes of conquest and subjugation.

Nimrod thought of his authority as aligned with the deities and other supernatural forces that ruled the world. He was not their representative; he was to be counted among their number. However, in what became Abraham's understanding, and in turn the Jewish understanding, Nimrod took his place not among the great rulers but among the rebels against rule, against God's rule.

The Jews demonstrate an admirable realism here. A psychoanalyst writes that no concrete person (parent, teacher, president, etc.) is truly an instance of the "Big Other"—because one is always only human, inconsistent, if not altogether weak and pathetic.[41] Jews, in their disciplined refusal to divide the world melodramatically into the wholly good and the wholly evil, suppose "Nimrod" to be as close to the Other, the Big Other, as a human can be, which is not very close at all. In Abraham's contest with Nimrod, he exposed the farcical aspect of claims to absolute authority.

Arrest

So, Terah informed on his son to a court official. "My son has lost his mind and is attacking our gods. He must be stopped." He was given a detachment of soldiers and returned to the shop. Abraham was still there. He allowed himself to be arrested and marched back to the palace. Terah trailed after the soldiers. He took Haran with him, in part to warn his son off from following Abraham's example and in part to identify him to Nimrod as a respectful, useful member of the family. The tacit declaration was to the effect, "See, I have a good son, as well as a bad son. It's not my parenting but his own perversity that has led Abraham to this moment."

Terah's betrayal of Abraham was a complex thing. He wanted to punish Abraham and needed Nimrod's power to do so. But he also wanted to save Abraham and trusted that Nimrod would allow Abraham a second chance by not punishing him too severely. Terah was sure that he could manage the situation. It was a terrible thing he did, prompted by the terrible thing that Abraham did, which was to destroy Terah's fantasy of their loving bond, leaving it in pieces, as if among the waste of idols strewn on his shop floor.

But Terah was also invested in Nimrod's regime. He responded with alacrity to the opportunity to demonstrate his loyalty. And he was circumspect, prudent. Informing made sense; it was in everyone's interests (including Abraham's). "Nimrod is already aware of Abraham's activities," Terah reasoned to himself. "It is only a matter of time before the king will summon him. *This* way, with me as informant, I can engineer both the sanction and the release. I will come to Nimrod's aid—Abraham's threatens the city's peace. I will then come to Abraham's aid—Nimrod will menace Abraham. I will win favor with Nimrod; I will reclaim my authority over my son."

At no point, however, did Terah acknowledge to himself that he was offering up his son as a sacrifice.

Abraham, for his part, was glad to go. "I am now paying the price of my own rebellion," he thought. "Nimrod's rebellion was a phony one. In me, he will see the genuine article. In him, I will find a worthy adversary. We will debate, and I will defeat him."

Debate

Abraham came into Nimrod's presence. He was forced onto his face. Nimrod had great power; his look drew audience and attention.[42] It was death for subjects to address him or even to find his eyes with their own. There was presumption in Abraham daring to raise his head from the floor, holding the ruler's gaze. Nimrod preserved his authority by giving him permission to look and then to stand. Nimrod remained seated.

Abraham had his first lines prepared: "Authority can humble, but it cannot instruct; it can suppress reason but not put it in fetters! Laws do not alter convictions; arbitrary punishments and rewards produce no principles. Fear and hope are no criteria of truth. You lay hold of the wrong means when you seek to induce me through fear and hope to live under your rule and the rule of the 'gods.' Disputes must not be decided in any manner other than by rational arguments. There is nothing that should be fenced off from investigation." Another Jewish intellectual, millennia later, will utter the same words.[43]

And so they began. It was a disputation. Nimrod assumed the role of adversary. He affected equality of arms. His courtiers were impressed. Like all Sumerian kings, he did not shun battle with the enemy. He always placed himself in the heaviest, most dangerous, parts of the battlefield. He was superb, unafraid. He was always on the attack. Even when defending, he attacked.

It was no one-sided affair. Abraham had his own force, while Nimrod was not without arguments. Each spoke only for himself. Abraham did not represent an enslaved people; Nimrod did not speak for a civilization; *that* exchange, between later avatars of the two men, would come many generations later. Versions of their exchanges recur through history, and the speeches and writings of those later participants can be heard in what follows; their arguments have standing in major works of political theory.

Nimrod made the first move.

"Your arguments are bad. They make an arbitrary halt. They tend toward atheism, of course. But the depopulation of the heavens that you initiate remains incomplete. What you set out to prove you in fact undermine. I am quite sure no one doubted the existence of divinities until you set out to prove the existence of your one god.

"What is more, your double position is itself unstable; it cannot be maintained. The two are only connected in your own head: 'Think for yourself,' 'God exists.' The free use of reasoning and the conviction that God exists—one will have to go. Either you will sink into a god-stupor all of your own, disconnected from all reasoning and inquiry, submissive to 'visions,' anxious for commands, a stranger to self-reliance, let alone moral autonomy, or you will reach that unforsakeable point in your critical career where 'God' reveals itself to be a ridiculously crude answer, an indelicacy—in effect, a ban on thought. And your curiosity, your high spirits, will revolt against this 'answer,' and you will respond to that mind-denying 'Thou shalt not think!' with a great defiance.[44] You will be forced to choose: God as God or Reason as God? Either way, you will be lost.[45]

"You cannot even maintain a consistent view of your audiences. I have had reports of your verbal assaults on them. You praise them as fellow philosophers, heavy with as yet unrealized free thinking. But you also satirize them as beasts in want of discourse of reason.[46] You want to educate them, and yet you attack them, you encourage them and you despise them.

"Allow me to continue. What anyway is this God of yours about? You say that He is supreme. But He is no more than the idle spectator of the great moving drama of our mortal lives. You have banished the other gods and drained the one remaining of all active energy. You assert that nothing can be known of Him. You don't have a conception of god. You just have a conception of 'not-god.' For you, while the gods are not gods,

once hidden and palpable, has appointed a certain number of species to devour the others. Humans themselves kill to obtain food and drink, to clothe themselves, to defend themselves, to amuse themselves. The whole Earth, perpetually steeped in blood, is nothing but a vast altar on which all that is living must be sacrificed without end, without measure, without pause. Your optimism is banal, jejune. There is nothing but violence in the universe.[56]

"My subjects are more than mere city dwellers. They have their place in a containing, intelligible structure. It is one consecrated by my own history, rebel and ruler, blasphemer and priest. I encompass the world's possibilities. In contemplating my career, Ur's inhabitants are able to mark out the boundaries in which they themselves live. They do not dare to transgress them; they do not need to. I have done that—and they can witness it, with awe and gratitude, in the life that I lead and in the poetry and the art that I commission in my own honor. While I fulfill their most fundamental needs, you propose to them nothing more than a method of thinking.

"I am a hero to the Chaldeans. They experience the gap between my existence and theirs with awe. It is the most immediate instance of the distances that constitute the order of the universe—gods and humankind, within the order of the gods. It is in hierarchy that we find the meaning of our lives, to whom, to what, we relate."

Abraham brushed all this aside.

"My own mind is my church![57] The religion you champion prohibits thought itself—of course, in the interests of its own preservation.[58] As for Chaldean knowledge of the heavens, can you not recognize that your astrology's relation to astronomy is as nothing more than the very foolish daughter of a wise mother?[59]

"The 'given' is not consecrated; it is just *given*. Things are what they are and come down to us with thick encrustations of error and malevolence. Your arbitrary usurpation, in its unjustified force, is the best example of how even the most egregious crimes over time are viewed as authorized and 'natural.' Your self-interested arguments do not impress me. You only value what keeps you on top, though you dress it up as something more general. It is all just so much opportunism, self-deceiving opportunism at that.

"You glory in the verses your hired poets write to celebrate your iniquities, and you forget that they would execrate you just as readily, if paid to do so and safely beyond your reach. The existence of art can never justify tyranny, what is more.

"My critical reasoning will keep in check my one-godism, whenever it is tempted to intolerance. But what keeps *you* in check? *You* are the tyrant. Your rebellion was mere power-craving vanity, your rule more of the same, to set yourself in glory above your peers.[60] *This* tyranny is real and immediate and unchecked. It is visible in the very dynamic of this engagement. You stand over me, free to do with me what your fickle, vain heart wishes. I am fully in your power. There is no tolerance in your polytheism."

Nimrod had identified critical reasoning, rather than God, as the greater threat to him, and so he focused his firepower on that target. But he opened with a jibe.

"You think you have depopulated our heavens. All you have done—and indeed, I salute you for it—is add another god to the company. The heavens throng with gods—your impersonal, abstract, etcetera, etcetera, deity is no more than a fresh entry to the group. That is—for people like you and me, anyway—the great thing about what you call 'polytheism.' It allows us to posit our own ideal and derive from it our own laws, joys, and rights. 'Not I but a god through me,' we shout! I see in you a practitioner of this wonderful art and power of creating gods. You affirm the free-spiritedness and many-spiritedness of humanity in your god-devising[61]—you are just not aware of it and deny your own creativity.

"So much for your 'one-godism'—in reality, merely 'another godism.' As for your 'critical reasoning,' it would *destroy* everything that makes life beautiful. You are oblivious to everything that eludes reason: the unconscious, the mystical, the demonic, the dark reaches and mysterious depths. And so you dismiss art, poetry, myth. You think everything that deserves to exist must have its existence justified before the tribunal of your reason. How absurd! No less absurd than requiring speech itself to be justified or art or love or the plants and animals of the world. Belief is no more the product of the intellect than taste, the capacity to experience art.[62]

"Concede that poets require as a stimulus to their imagination the illusions and myths of the religion in which they have been brought up. Allow further that some honorable rationalist like you refutes their beliefs, shatters their illusions, dissipates the myths; this clear gain in knowledge and rationality will be paid for by the diminution or destruction of their powers as poets. They will be less free to write the kind of poetry they used to write. Your 'knowledge' cripples—even kills.[63]

"Poetry is the mother tongue of the human race, as the garden is older than the ploughed field, painting than writing, song than declamation, parables than logical deduction. A deeper sleep was the repose of our most distant ancestors, and their movement was a frenzied dance. Seven days they would sit in the silence of thought or wonder—and when they opened their mouths, it was to winged sentences.[64]

"What is more, poets work best with restraints—when they are limited, say, to conventional wisdom or myth. Dancing in chains, making things difficult for oneself, and then spreading over it the illusion of ease and facility—that is the artifice they want to demonstrate to us. Indeed, the most adventurous among them devise new constraints, which they then conquer with charm and grace: so that both the constraints and their conquest are noticed and admired.[65]

"The very existence of art affirms the plurality of ultimates. Every great work of art is a source of ideals, a distinct source, and each work has its own integrity, its own value—no one work is subordinate to any others. There is no art-God—no God—to stand above them. The very practice of art affirms the truth of our 'polytheism.'"[66]

Abraham began to take pleasure in these exchanges. At last—someone to make him think, to take him outside the precincts of his own mind.

"I acknowledge that the language of poetry naturally falls in with the language of power. It is antileveling in its nature. It aims at effect; it exists by contrast. It is everything by excess. It rises above the ordinary standard of sufferings and crimes. It presents a dazzling appearance. It has its altars and its sacrifices. Kings, priests, aristocrats are its train bearers; tyrants and slaves are its executioners. It puts the individual before the species, the one above the infinite many, might before right. A lion hunting a flock of sheep is a more poetical object than they; and we even take the part of the lordly beast, because our vanity makes us disposed to place ourselves in the situation of the strongest party.

"The insolence of power is stronger than the plea of necessity. The tame submission to usurped authority, or even the natural resistance to it, has nothing to excite or flatter the imagination: it is the assumption of a right to insult or oppress others that carries an imposing air of superiority with it. We had rather be the oppressor than the oppressed. The love of power in ourselves and the admiration of it in others are both natural to humankind: the one makes us tyrants, the other slaves. Wrong dressed out in pride, pomp, and circumstance has more attraction than abstract right.[67]

"We have no need of heroes. I do not want to be a hero—"

Nimrod interrupted him: "You say this, yet if you persist in your activities, you will be a hero to your few followers. I think

68

you nurse that ambition. You are proud—how could you *not* have that ambition? You destroy to build up, to build yourself up. Everyone knows that in order for a shrine to be set up, another shrine must be broken into pieces.[68] As for shrines, so for leaders."

This was the first intimation of threat. While Abraham did not notice it, Terah caught his breath. Father began to worry for son. Abraham concluded his thought, with insouciance: "Anyway, I do not care for art."

Nimrod persisted with his thrusts against critical reasoning.

"There is nothing original or impressive about mocking vulgar superstitions from a lofty perch. It's very easy to poke fun at ordinary people. You are not challenging; you are merely insufferable. You elevate yourself to a superior position over us, the detached, uncommitted judge of Ur.[69] You embrace a hyperindividualism that counts for nothing the weight of tradition and the binding force of civic loyalties.

"Though you fancy yourself a philosopher, your arguments are vulnerable to a schoolchild's objection. For example, your insistence that 'no statement is immune from revision' is clearly false. Would it be rational to reject, say, the statement 'Not every statement is true'?[70] Patently not. And through this gaping hole in your case, tradition may drive its carriage, fully upholstered with its many time-honored practices and beliefs! Your rationality covers a multitude of irrationalities.

"Do you *truly* want your fellow Chaldeans to give up their ancestral practices? For what? A life lived rigorously under the conditions of constant self-examination would be intolerable—and intolerable to others too. You cannot cut reason off from tradition and custom and faith. You cannot cut people off from their own experiences, from their loyalties and their pieties, without alienating them from themselves. This painful act of self-discipline you have undertaken for yourself will have no appeal to anyone else. They live their lives. They understand that no one can invent their own content; at best, they became aware of what is given in them by their family, their national community, the religion into which they are born.[71]

"Religion is a sufficient satisfaction for their metaphysical necessities. It is easily understood, while also possessing the right measure of obscurity. It has the support of an authority impressive in age and universally recognized. (I refer here to myself.) It gives them something tangible that they can grip, on the slippery and thorny pathways of their life, a beautiful fable by means of which life lessons can be imparted to them. It is their most sacred treasure.[72]

"And who is to say what is superstitious and what not? Let me assert: belief in causality, in the causal nexus, is *itself* superstition,[73] while ancient and jealously held popular beliefs are nearer the truth than the judgment of what you are pleased to refer to as 'philosophy.'

"Let this philosophizing go; it is no more than perverse submissiveness. It has its own quality of servility. Critical reason has become your idol—slay it! Content yourself with living. Accept what is in the world, what comforts and sustains you.[74]

"Servile to your god, you will seek compensation in the devotion of followers. You will solicit disciples; even if you do not, they will force themselves on you. When you address crowds, you hear yourself arguing for independence of judgment, critical reason, and the like; what they hear are variations on 'Follow me.' You will not be able to make men and women; you will only make sons and daughters. Geniuses beget idiots—you are not exempt from this dismal rule.[75]

Abraham became indignant, still unaware of the danger of his position, unaware too that the exchanges were drawing to an end.

"I will no more encumber myself with son surrogates than with sons.

"You dare to speak the language of compassion! You pass

off cruelty and oppression as 'traditional'! Everything you say is self-interested. You defend traditional society because you are in charge. You exercise critical reasoning yourself, but you deny it to everyone else. Your positions are incoherent, inflated by arrogance and immoderate self-belief. Let the air out—you are just a person making distracting noises, clinging to titles and possessions. You know that subordination is impossible unless reason is denied—so you deny it. You do not value intellectual curiosity. In any event, you cannot stop the natural progress of the human mind.

"You elide the real and the ideal. You defend the one by identifying it with the other. Who doubts that there may be great goodness, great happiness, great affection even, under the absolute government of a good man? Meanwhile, laws and institutions require to be adapted, not to good men but to bad men.[76] You are a bad man, the worst man, I think!"

Nimrod was not offended. He heard only childishness in Abraham's language. And so he changed tack, pointing to Terah, as he addressed Abraham: "You do not respect your father." This was a promising theme.

"You attack his livelihood; you undermine his standing—and with cheap stunts. You know perfectly well that we do not believe that the small statues are animate. They are figures by which we show our respect and reverence for the gods. We worship them as proxies.

"Must I remind you of your duties? A debtor should discharge his first and greatest obligation and pay the debt that comes before all of us; he must consider that all that he has and holds belongs to those who bore and bred him, and he is meant to use it in their service to the limits of his powers. He must serve them first with his property, then with hand and brain, and so give to the old people what they need in view of their age: repayment of all that anxious care and attention lavished on him, the long-standing loan they made him as a child. Throughout his life, a son must be very careful to watch his tongue in addressing his parents, because there is a very heavy penalty for careless and ill-considered language; I am the appointed overseer of these things. If a person's parents get angry, he must submit to them, and whether they satisfy their anger in speech or an action, he must forgive them; after all, he must reflect, it is natural enough for a father to get very angry if he thinks he is being harmed by his own son.[77]

"And yet, you do *not* defer to your father's authority. You live in a city in which, as our poet sings, the word of the father is heeded, bringing well-being to oneself, and where eldership endures.[78] A father is the oldest, first, and for children the only authority, and from his autocratic power, the other, more impersonal, collective authorities have developed.[79] In your disrespect for him, you disrespect me; in your disrespect for me, you disrespect the very foundations of our order. Your actions against your father are an offense against the gods.[80]

"The authority of a father over his son requires no negotiation. It is subject neither to agreement nor to review. A father's authority derives from the fact of his paternity. Your imagined relationships of equality, of freely contacting individuals, will all break on the rock of a father's natural authority.

"How dare you deny your entire formation? What you first learned as a baby from your mother and your nurse—the charming stories they told you, partly for amusement, partly in earnest! What you learned in school—the prayers that were chanted, the stories of the gods that were acted out, the ceremonies and rituals you followed! What you learned from your parents—their prayers and supplications addressed to the gods, offered with the utmost seriousness for themselves and their families in the firm belief that they were addressed to gods who really did exist. You contemptuously brush all this aside. It is impossible to stay calm at such crass arrogance![81]

"Your arguments are the protests of the adolescent. We all

know that a young man must pass through a period of rebellion if he is to reach maturity. Your thinking is no more than speculative gluttony.[82] Plainly, you did not rebel against your father at the appointed time and within the normal limits. And so now, with grotesque and comical belatedness and an utter immoderation of degree, you rebel against *everything*—him, me, the gods!

"You are not a free thinker, you are a neurotic.[83] You want to turn the world adolescent, to make the ultimate value alienation from family rather than family itself.

"Your contempt for your father has an edge of vulnerability. You say you want to liberate him; in truth, you want to liberate yourself from him. Are you strong enough to withstand his force, his power? Scorn in your hand is a weapon of the weak. 'If I imagine him as contemptible,' you doubtless calculate, 'my father will be robbed of the power to crush me.'"

Abraham was not stung by any of this and responded without heat. "I love my father according to my bond, no more. Parents should educate their children to make rational decisions for themselves, gradually allowing them, as their reason grows stronger, to make free and independent use of their powers."[84]

"What are the contents of this 'bond'?" interrupted Nimrod.

Abraham carried on, as if he had not heard the question.

"If I am a teenage rebel, clothing my wishes in reasons, so be it. Adolescence is an underrated period in a person's life! You by contrast are nothing more than a geriatric dictator. Indeed, you are immobilized in that role, without creativity or prospects for growth or change.

"What is more, your claim to be an intellectual is hollow, a mere pose. All your arguments are self-defeating arguments against the merit of argument. And on the subject of defeat, let us not forget your absurd ambition to challenge the heavens! As if your imagined gods had an address! Such *stupid* literal-mindedness! You are jealous of my success. I have depopulated the heavens with my mind—not with footling bricks and arrows."

Nimrod flushed. Could this be tolerated, when others were present? He changed tack again, turning away from argument to make a direct appeal to Abraham. He spoke quietly, so that only Abraham could hear him. He attempted a silky tone.

"We are alike—serve me! You are alienated from your family, while I have no family. If I die, no soul will pity me. You assault the gods; I assaulted God. You put man above all; I put myself, a proud man, in that place. You wish to scale the heavens, if only to contemplate its Ruler; I wished to scale the heavens to displace Him. But humankind's distance from the divine is a standing provocation to us both.

"Let the population of Ur continue to follow their ancestral beliefs. I will be your conversation partner. We will discourse together, leaving undisturbed the frightened minds beyond my palace precincts. What is fit for us to debate is not fit for others to hear. You will not find a more resourceful interlocutor than me. I will make you my chief minister and adviser, and you will be my most valued confidante. Your family will be elevated above all the other families of the city and will want for nothing. We will be friends."

Abraham laughed and turned his back on Nimrod. He made a dismissive, careless gesture with his hand. A heavy silence immobilized the chamber. Nimrod's face prickled red. He could not find his voice. He sensed his courtiers' eyes on him. He too turned his back and walked some steps away from Abraham. Seconds elapsed. Staring at a wall, Nimrod rehearsed his words, first in his mind and then under his breath. Further moments passed. And then, with recovered strength, he too laughed.

"You are a very disrespectful little man.

"If the assertions of bold thinkers would cause the people to lose respect for their gods and prefer finite knowledge to an infinite faith, they would grow accustomed to despising everything great and miraculous and regard it as the dead effect of natural laws. Once your followers submit their religious sentiments to the examination of reason, they will turn to their political sentiments. The exercise of private judgment in the religious sphere is bound to lead to its exercise in the political sphere.[85] Your critique of religion is the premise of all critique. You attack the gods today; tomorrow, you will attack me. And if you do not, it will just be because you have arrested the logic of your position. Such others as you recruit will not be so shy.

"Your Reason is murderous. You deny all Fathers; I think you want to be the new Father. But either way, you work toward my death. I will frustrate you in this intention; it is you who will die. I sentence you to death."

Abraham's eyes widened; he couldn't breathe. Nimrod was delighted.

"Did you not realize you were on trial? Oh dear.

"I will survive you, just as my arguments—they *are* arguments, and good ones at that—will survive yours, forever associated with your failure. People will say, 'It required such very little effort to dispose of a human being. Of what value, then, were the arguments that placed such a creature at their center?'

"Appreciate the irony. You die as a martyr to critical reason, and your death will only have meaning in the very language you reject."

Abraham recovered himself. "You signal your defeat. A death sentence cannot triumph over reason—even if it silences the reasoner. A king is not greater than the laws of the universe. My discoveries can never be forgotten."

Crisis

Nimrod sought to tempt Abraham, as if to say, "I can be a better father to you than Terah." But if he began the conversation with condescension, he ended it in frustration.

He ordered Abraham to the chamber containing the furnace. Terah and Haran followed. Nimrod joined them. Palace guards stood at attention. The furnace was a narrow, high-walled stone structure, standing on stone legs about a shallow pit. Flammable wood chips and rags were piled high against the walls of the furnace and around the rim of the floor, which had small holes to let in flames and smoke from the pit. At Nimrod's signal, the pit would be filled with wood and set alight. The flames would reach up through the holes, and the materials inside the furnace would then catch fire. Abraham would burn to death.

Until that moment, Abraham was best described as a critical monotheist, a depopulator of the heavens, engaged adversarially with his own polytheistic society. He was reliant throughout on his own mental resources; no revelation led him to God. He was not in communication with God; his faith was purely intellectual. Nimrod's arguments were cogent, and Abraham was intrigued by them.

He did not know how his negative stance, his privileging of critique, could sustain him in the furnace—of course, it could not. He did not know whether the God whose existence he had inferred was a God to whom he could appeal. And even if He was, would He answer Abraham? All this made him afraid. He feared Nimrod, who was beyond appeal. He feared that God might not hear his appeal. Abraham thought, "Should I pray? And if so, to whom or what? To the gods who would answer, if only they existed, or to God, who might not answer, even though He *does* exist?" He knew that he must prepare himself for either destruction or a miracle.[86]

We would not condemn him were he to pray to the old gods. A man who has grown rational and skeptical, Freud wrote, may be ashamed to discover how easily he may return to a belief in spirits under the combined impact of strong emotion and perplexity (11:71).

Nimrod gave the signal for the pit to be filled. Abraham stood in the furnace. He addressed God, "Please save me." This was his crisis. Nimrod gave the signal to set the wood alight. As Abraham prayed to God, Terah pleaded with Nimrod. We must

Nimrod waved them off with a final taunt: "Abraham, your household gods came to your aid!" Terah grieved for his son Haran—he did not think it was *that* son who was in peril, and now he had lost him. And Abraham's understanding of his father? As a murderer, a man ready to sacrifice his own son.

3

Abraham 2's Life

The first part of Abraham's life, related in chapters 1 and 2, has a simplicity lacking in the second part of his life, related in this chapter and the next. Though these two parts have the same structure, in each instance a "life" (chapters 1 and 3) followed by a "crisis" (chapters 2 and 4), the iterations are very different in content and outcome. The first life, the life of Abraham 1, was transacted in one place, Ur; the second life is transacted in many places. The first life had a clear dynamic: immersion, confrontation, expulsion. The second life is without comparable dynamic: a series of self-contained episodes that could be reordered without loss of coherence. Or so it seems.

This sense of radical difference holds good for the crises too. In the first crisis, Abraham is in peril and contends openly and forcefully with the person who threatens his life. In the second crisis, it is not Abraham but Isaac who is in peril, and Abraham cooperates with the divinity that threatens his son's life. There is a resolution to the first crisis: stepping out of the furnace, Abraham has a new understanding of the universe and its ruler's interest in him. The second crisis, by contrast, has no such resolution: Abraham leaves Mt. Moriah in a state of perplexity, from which he does not emerge.

This, then, is the story now to be related: a heterogeneity of incident (chapter 3) followed by a crisis without resolution (chapter 4).

Haran

During the rushed, uncomfortable journey from Ur, Abraham pondered his exchanges with Nimrod. He was pleased with his performance. He knew that he had been resourceful, coherent, courageous, unintimidated. But he also knew that he no longer had any commitment to the content of what he had said. These were arguments in a dispute to which he was no longer a party. To rehearse any of them now would be like making a rugby tackle in a game of soccer.

Journeying

He had been a critical monotheist, engaged adversarially with his own polytheistic society. He had been in these respects reliant on his own intellectual resources. And then—crisis. He had found that his resources were not enough. He needed a miracle. He couldn't reason his way out of the furnace. Abraham became God's man at the moment when he prayed. The price of life was determined to be subordination to God's will. God's protection preceded God's direction—through miracle, rebirth.

Abraham understood that he could no longer claim the title of a self-governing, autonomous person. For sure, he would continue to hold himself to account, but by reference to God, not his own understandings. This was not Abraham completing his thought about God's nature. It was not even his "second thoughts" about God. It was an abandonment of his first conception. Indeed, it was an abandonment of thought itself—or at the very least, a radical reduction of its scope and status. The miracle of the furnace introduced to Abraham a new understanding of God. This was a personal God, who rewards the virtuous and punishes the wicked; a God who has shown Himself, whose existence and character can be preached by Abraham, about whom Abraham can speak, as witness to His presence and purposes; a solicitous worker of miracles; a ready respondent to prayer.

He then thought about his minutes in the furnace. It was not the peril he brooded on. The furnace presented itself as a figure of Ur. Abraham reflected that he could no more make for himself a home in the city as in the furnace. The rags and scraps that he had stood among were as Ur's religious, cultural garbage. This would become standard for him. His experiences in the world would be meaningful to him only in relation to his sense of a divine presence. He had become a person of faith.

He looked across at his family. For how long, he wondered, would he be able to remain in their company? If Nimrod had not exiled him, he would have had to leave anyway. That he left with his wife, his father, his surviving brother, and the rest of the household, was a contingency. In the end, the person of faith cannot survive, even in an adversarial relation, in such a society as Ur. God took him out of the furnace, in order to take him out of that society. And perhaps, he pondered, included in this society is the family formed by it, his own family.

As for Sarah, the exceptional Sarah, they would work together to teach his new doctrine. He had found a new commitment, to work with others under God's direction to create a new society, not work alone, standing against his given society. "I will form a countercommunity, not endeavor to change the community in which I was born," he resolved.[1] The departure also marked a move from a focus on the solitary intellectual to a focus on nation-building. For the moment, it was a collectivity of two,

Abraham and Sarah. But there would be more over time, Abraham was certain. He was certain of everything now.

Preaching

They reached Haran, the first city beyond Nimrod's reach. Terah announced to the family that they would settle there. "We don't need to go any further. I have business here, and we will be safe." The commitment he had made to Nimrod, the commitment to go to Canaan? It was dismissed. What will Nimrod care? "Anyway," Terah thought, "he cannot harm us here."

Abraham's arrival in Haran was accompanied by accounts of the great miracle. Rumors circulated, tall stories growing taller in the retelling. Some heard (and repeated) that it took Nimrod's men ten years to assemble the wood, yet God rescued Abraham at once.[2] Others heard (and repeated) that God stirred up a great earthquake, and burning fire leaped forth out of the furnace into flames and sparks of flame, and it burned up all those who were standing around in front of the furnace—83,500 people in all. But there was not even the slightest injury to Abraham from the burning of the fire.[3] Still others heard (and repeated) that Nimrod's servants bound Abraham hand and foot, piling up wood on all sides of him, his father urging them on as they set it alight.[4]

Abraham allowed these accounts to circulate. They provided the starting point for his preaching. The miracle, a public confirmation of God's power,[5] encouraged an openness to Abraham's message. What a privileged place he must occupy in God's dealings with the world! Abraham would tell his audiences, "The wicked Nimrod cast me into the fiery furnace. I said to God, 'Sovereign of the Universe! I stand as firm as a wall.'"

In his recounting of the event, he was all heroic resolve. "I entered the fiery furnace in peace and left it unscathed."[6] He would warm to his theme. "All power is from God. All things and creatures are always and utterly dependent on Him, for their beginning and preservation, their activities and their limitations. God is the author of all things, the lord of the universe. Nothing but by God," Abraham would declare, in the extravagance of his joy at his liberation and new insight.[7] "My relationship with God began in the furnace of Ur."

He criticized his earlier position and the critical reasoning that led to it, his "Ur monotheism." He described himself as a convert, inviting his listeners to follow his example and become converts like him.

"It is strange that I said God created the world. What I should have said is that God is *continuously* creating the world. Why should it be a greater miracle that it began to exist than that it continues to exist? I was perhaps led astray by the simile of a craftsperson. That someone makes a shoe is an accomplishment, yet once made, it endures on its own for a while. But if one thinks of God as a creator, the conservation of the universe is a miracle as great as its creation. Indeed, creation and conservation are one and the same, a continuous creating.[8] I am myself proof of this continuous creation, this conservation of His creation. I live, notwithstanding that I once stood in Nimrod's furnace.

"That God is capable of performing miracles teaches us that He can break the rules that He instituted. The world and its inhabitants are dependent on him. These miracles help us to understand the special nature of God's providential rule of the world, which is both universal and specific.[9]

"It is universal—the world is governed by certain laws, laws that make for order and stability, for permanence and preservation. These laws of nature are the work of God. The implanting of laws of nature in the universe is a token of God's universal providence, for these laws of nature have the purpose of the preservation of the world and of all the kinds of genera and species within it.

"It is specific—God is willing to intervene, in the execution of judgments about human beings, in the operating of the design. Laws of nature are interrupted, suspended, and contravened, to do justice. And so, one form of providence makes way for another. God has reserved to Himself the rights of a free agent to change the laws of his own making. The possibility of a miracle must be for us a fundamental belief. The upsetting of these laws of nature through the working of miracles is a token of God's individual providence, for these miracles have for the purpose of preservation (or destruction) of individuals or groups of individuals—as reward or punishment.

"What does it mean to convert?

"You will no longer think as you once did. You will no longer have opinions. You will rejoice in certainties. These certainties will be shared with your fellow believers. There will be no differences among you, among *us*. 'Thinking'—that is to say, speculating, puzzling things out—will cease to concern you. It will no longer exercise its hold on you; you will be freed from thought's burdens. You will be transformed: a wholly new person, tranquil, clean, and sure of purpose, born again as I was born again when I emerged from the furnace-womb.

"You will no longer associate with family, with friends, with fellow city dwellers—unless you find them among us, new joiners too. As you will break with present thinking, so you will break with present attachments. You will stand in the warmth of your new community, and you will regard your former friends and family as no more than strangers. Their very existence will fade in your memory. God saved me from my father; I have come to preach to you liberation from all fathers. You must not worship the dead or the living. Ancestors are paltry things. Only the Eternal One is worthy of your praise, your service."

Abraham related to Sarah each evening his successes and failures in his quest for converts. Early on, she had asked, "What do you say to persuade them to follow you?"

"I tell them my own story. I do not shy away from the personal. God is a personal God; my story is a personal one. I no longer try to reach the truth of God's existence through a dispassionate application of mind. When I was in Ur, I excluded all nontheoretical interest from my study. I was moved to seek knowledge of God from the same curiosity that moved me to inquire into any truth. Knowing God was on a par with knowing the place of the Earth in the planetary economy. Knowledge of God was not momentous or dramatic. It was cold, safe knowledge, for which a person would not risk one's life.[10]

"After the miracle of the furnace I gave up my philosophizing. I strive now only to gain God's favor. And people hear me."

Sarah asked him, "Why did you fail in Ur and yet you succeed here in Haran?"

Abraham smiled. "I am myself a convert. I speak as one convert to other converts, or candidates for conversion.

"In Ur, I was not able to make converts because, for all my activity, I could not reach people. My God was passive. There was no favor or dislike in Him; He was above desire and intention. He did not know humankind, much less the thoughts and actions of individual people, even less listen to their prayers. He was the Prime Cause, that is all. He was not a Will. He did not create people; He neither rewarded nor punished; He knew nothing of our prayers, offerings, obedience, or disobedience.[11]

"Perhaps I failed for other reasons too. My stance in Ur was one of attack. If it was pedagogic, it was also polemical. What I had to say was unwelcome. My conception of God, and even more, my advocacy of critical reason, could not sustain a community. My thinking, a process of abstraction, of celestial depopulation, had no popular appeal."

Sarah gently probed. "Are you saying that Nimrod was right? I did not think you were seeking converts in Ur."

"*You* are right, Sarah. I was not. My object was to challenge listeners to think for themselves, not to degrade themselves by bowing down to idols of their own creation. I did not so much

86

want to bring them around to my own way of thinking as help them find their own way of thinking. I only ever wanted interlocutors, never disciples and, still less, converts."

"So what now, Abraham?" Sarah asked. "You are gathering converts. What will you do with them?"

"First of all," Abraham replied, "it is not just me who is making converts. You are too. I hear reports of your successes with the women of Haran. You too have followers. You too have converts."

"My followers are your followers, Abraham," Sarah interjected. "They listen to me because they are captivated by my stories of your life in Ur, what you suffered and what you learned through that suffering. I am witness to your witness."

Sarah paused, to acknowledge and dismiss the thought that what she had said was not quite correct. She had *not* been with Abraham in Nimrod's palace. On the way to Haran, he had told her, "It was a miracle." She believed him. But a question niggled at her. Did his witnessing count as evidence that would satisfy a person exercising the free use of one's reason? There is no doubt a valid place for visionary experience—but is it to be relied on as evidence for belief, either as to God's existence or His powers over, or intentions toward, us?[12] She pondered, "Have I slid backward? Do I once again accept authority as a ground for knowledge—even if it is Abraham's authority, the person whom I most trust? Was it that, the authority of his person, that gave compelling weight to the report of the miracle?" She retreated from active address of this thought, but it lodged in her mind.

(Later on, in the full consciousness of the collapse of her marriage, she returned to the thought. She understood then that Haran marked the first moment in that collapse. The contrast with those last months in Ur was decisive, amounting to a rupture. In Ur, the marriage had been a good one, characterized by a strong and loving mutuality of understanding and purpose—

mutuality, not identity. Sarah had been fully Abraham's equal then—precisely because they had each taken their own path, arriving by happy coincidence at a point of substantial convergence. In Haran, however, even at the very highest, when they were fully partners in their conversionary activity, she had already made herself his subordinate. She was the hearsay witness to the miracle of the furnace; she did not experience the miracle herself. It was not Sarah's appeal that was answered. When she made converts, she presented herself as Abraham's first convert, already behind him, rather than alongside him.)

She continued, "Abraham, you are creating a new family, a family of converts. I correct myself. We are creating this family, if not together, then in cooperation with each other. Have you thought how this alternative family might complement your father's household?"

Abraham had *not* thought about it, but a vision came to him that resolved the question, decisively.

Leaving

Abraham experienced a vision of God, who spoke to him in the language of command, promise, and blessing.

The command was peremptory: "Go!" He knew at once that he must leave Haran and go to another, as yet unidentified land. It was a command that operated on two levels, the geographical and the spiritual. Abraham must leave the land of his birth, his kinship community, and his father's household. He must leave without knowing where he is going; he must swap a settled life for a nomadic one. But he must also orient himself anew toward the world, isolating himself from others in a fundamental way. In combination, the demand was that Abraham free himself of all rootedness in place and all obligation to persons. It allowed him to leave Haran in the company of some family members and his and Sarah's converts, while at the same time separating himself from every human being. The command had the character of an unrefusable gift: Abraham must travel to a land that his descendants will make their own.

The promises were of future consequence and blessings. He will be made into a great nation; his own name will be great. He will be blessed, and he will himself be a blessing; those who bless him will themselves be blessed (and those who curse him will themselves be cursed); through him, all the families of the Earth will be blessed—that is, Abraham will be the conduit through whom God will channel His blessings of the world, and the nation that he will found will change the world for the better.

That God had spoken to him moved Abraham beyond measure. "God has taken the initiative! He has not intervened in my life as a rescuer, because summoned; He has instead engaged with me for His own purposes. God has a plan for the world, and I am central to it." The execution of the plan would involve sacrifices on his part, of that Abraham was sure. He had made his first sacrifice already, in leaving Haran. The prospect of greatness, and of many blessings, however, was compelling. Abraham had no cause to doubt God. It was true that the command was in the present tense, while the blessings were only in the future tense, but God had *already* acted, in delivering Abraham from the furnace. "Plainly, there is nothing of which He is incapable," Abraham thought. "Whatever He says He will do, He will indeed do."

Still, and reflecting further, to better understand what precisely was in store for him, Abraham noted that God did not say, "I will give you the land to which I will shortly be directing you."[13] Still less did He say, "This will be the land of your promised nationhood." That was yet to come. For the moment, God had held out to Abraham the promise of a nationhood defined in indeterminately territorial and/or diasporic terms.

This first vision was a momentous event in Abraham's life. He no longer talked *of* God; he talked *to* God. Over the years that followed, he found that his communications with God were not of a uniform type. Some occurred in his waking hours, others when he was asleep; some had the quality of prophecy, others the lower status of intimations. God never made a direct appearance; there was always the intermediary of the imaginative faculty (Guide, II.41, III.24).

He readied himself to leave. There was no question of his resisting the command, but he went further. He didn't just comply; he *enthusiastically* complied. When you are the beneficiary of a miracle, he thought, you place yourself under the direction of the miracle maker. You respond with alacrity to His commands. Of his family, he took his wife and his nephew.

Sarah left behind her grandfather and father-in-law, Terah. This was an excruciating parting, which she was ready to effect even though she herself had not received any command. She loved the old man. Lot, however, left without a backward glance. Orphaned in Ur, he looked only to Abraham for support. He did not leave because he was moved by God's command to his uncle but because he did not want to be separated from Abraham.

Nahor was not invited to go but would not have gone anyway. His duty was to his elderly father. Abraham's own duty to Terah was a matter of indifference to him. God had relieved him of that duty, and in any event, as far as Abraham was concerned, Terah had forfeited the right to any filial concern when he had run off to Nimrod. Abraham found some indignation to supplement the somewhat abstract, divine waiving of his duty to Terah. Later on, when news reached him of Terah's death, Abraham did not mourn.

And the vision? Abraham reflected on it as they journeyed from Haran. It was not one mind, self-interrogating. Nor was it one mind encountering another, each sealed off from the other. For the duration of the vision, God had inhabited Abraham's mind; the effect was a vertiginous expansion of consciousness, a terrifying loss of sense of self. Abraham did not "have" visions;

visions took hold of him, hurling him into a fearful, awed state. These thoughts were only a beginning. Abraham would continue to reflect on the nature of these visions. He would also ask himself, "What is it to be a person who has such visions?"

Episode 1: Altars

They traveled to Canaan, passing across plains and over mountains. In the course of the journeying, Abraham had a further vision. God told him, "To your descendants, I will give this land." Just this, a communication of an instant's duration. Abraham did not share it with his family, but he halted the company on a plain in order to build an altar. He made no sacrifice, however. He called out God's name over Canaan. They traveled on a while and reached a mountain. Abraham halted the company again and built another altar. Again, he called out God's name. Again, he gave no explanation to his family, and again, there was no sacrifice.

Communications with God, silence toward family—a theme was emerging. Abraham placed himself outside human society in his search for God. He excluded himself from the Chaldeans; the journey to the mountain was a further instance of that same journey of self-exclusion. The first time in the period that he addressed his family was when he had built the second altar. He turned in their direction and proclaimed God's name, speaking at them, not to them.

Altars with no sacrifice, promises with no performance—a further theme had emerged, a certain complexity in Abraham's understanding of what he could expect from God, a groping for a response that was proportionate to what God demanded and what God promised. In this respect, the demands were easier to address than the promises. The demands could be met with simple assent, but promises that were yet to be fulfilled? Here the proper response was less obvious. Abraham grew a little wary.

Why had God not given the land to him, why only to his descendants? And *which* descendants? There were no children of the family and no prospect of children.

He had a sense, however, of a lesson being taught.

He had already abandoned ancestor worship in Ur, as part of his break with Chaldean religion. No more would he defer to his father and the line of fathers behind that father; he would be his own person, accountable to no one but himself. Self-authored, self-legislating, his objects of concern chosen *by* him, not given *to* him, he gloried in his autonomy.

That was then. And now? God's promise had demanded a commitment from him. It was not one that he himself had chosen, though. And so, to the renouncing of ancestor worship, Abraham had to add renunciation of independence of judgment. This was the sacrifice that readied him for all other sacrifices—indeed, that was the precondition for all other sacrifices.

Abraham had been content in Haran, busy with his preaching, making converts, secure in the household provided by his father. That God had the power to command his departure from the city was clear, of course. But for what purpose was the command given? Not any evident one, though there was an aspect of this obscurity of purpose that gratified the new Abraham. "I do not know; I do not need to know; submission is what is required; this is the lesson; I should be grateful to receive it."

Yet it still troubled him, just a little. "Do I really need to go to a land I will not myself be given? Why could I not be told while still living in the security of Haran about God's plans for my descendants?"

Episode 2: Descent

When some time later famine struck Canaan, Abraham made no request of God for assistance. "The famine is not the furnace," he thought. He could not walk out of the furnace, but he could ride out of Canaan. This he could do something about. He did not need a miracle. Indeed, he did not even pray to God for one. He just went down to Egypt; return to Haran was out of the question. He seized the opportunity to act on his own account, to act independently. It was as if the events of Ur, the prayer and the rescue, constituted an obscure humiliation for him. And this was aggravated by his sense of the promise to him weakening, if not being broken. God promised the land, an altar was built, and so on. But then, in place of fulfillment, there was a famine. The land could not even support him, let alone submit to his rule. "What is going on?" Abraham wondered.

Abraham found that the instinct of self-reliance, developed in Ur, was not so easily surrendered. It equipped him in situations of threat to take the necessary measures of self-protection. "I will not be put in a position again when my only recourse is to prayer," he resolved. Abraham anticipated that Sarah would be thought desirable by the Egyptians, the object of solicitous and more than solicitous attention. And so he made a request of her. "Announce yourself as my sister, rather than as my wife. This way, it will go well for me. I will not be killed as a barrier to you but rewarded as the person with the right to make decisions on your behalf." Sarah looked askance. Abraham spoke with greater urgency and a certain rising sense of shame. "The Egyptians are abductors and rapists—we do what we must, what is necessary, to stay alive—you, Sarah, by submitting, and me, by prospering."

The request to Sarah, in its resourcefulness, its inventiveness, its improvised quality, recalled his mode of operation when in Ur. He had to think quickly and without reliance on any other person. It was a corrective to the feeling he had had since leaving Haran of a certain loss of agency. He had been told to leave Haran, and he did so, against what would otherwise have been his wish and in full view of family and converts. He was in consequence forced to endure the ignominy of being a parent-abandoner. This time, however, when he moved on—not well fed in Haran but hungry in Canaan—it was his decision alone.

There was a quality of sacrifice intimated. Sarah was being sacrificed as the price of refuge in Egypt and the price of Abraham's own safety. They could have stayed in Canaan. Or they could have gone to Egypt, and Abraham could then have assumed the risk of harm by insisting that Sarah stay with him as his wife. He did neither. Here "sacrifice" meant, "Sarah's interests are to be sacrificed in favor of my own," or words to that effect.

As Abraham anticipated, Sarah was soon noticed by court officials. They invited her to Pharaoh's palace, where she was quickly installed. As he further anticipated, he himself was treated very well, both for her sake and for his own. Gifts flowed toward him: sheep, oxen, donkeys, male and female slaves, asses, and camels. Sarah's beauty was a marvel to the Egyptians, as was Abraham's learning.

Sarah was both fearful and dismayed. She found herself the object of an intense libidinal attention, an unrefusable desire to gaze at her, smell her, touch her, pet her, penetrate her. Her sense of self was barely equal to the force of this attention; she was alarmed to feel herself sinking toward a merely creaturely state. She did not exist for her jailer-hosts as a thinking, reasoning person; she feared that soon she would no longer be such a person. Her beauty was her peril.[14] "Where is Abraham?" This was her most insistent thought; it would also, she knew, be her last, desperate cry, before she altogether lost the capacity for reflection.

Where, indeed, was Abraham? He too was the object of an intense attention, though of a quite different character. It was respectful, solicitous, deferential, extravagantly flattering. Egypt's intellectuals ran to meet him. His reputation, both as Chaldean astronomer and disputant with Nimrod, had already reached them. He represented for them a horizon of achievement: the master of academic disciplines, the subjugator of political rulers. By the welcome he gave to them, an intellectual in communion with other intellectuals, he elevated them in the eyes of Egyptians at large. He taught them, initiating them into mysteries, instructing them in sciences. He introduced them to arithmetic and taught them the laws of astronomy.[15] The Egyptians were mute before him, and Abraham was intoxicated by their regard. *Of course* they pressed gifts on him: he not only was brother to the most gloriously beautiful woman but was also a renowned astronomer and a fearless controversialist.

Pharaoh, exultant in possessing what every one of his subjects most passionately craved, was suddenly incapacitated by a mysterious illness. Unable to take his pleasures with Sarah, barely able to rise from his bed, he sought an explanation from his doctors, who were of no use, save to urge him to call for Abraham.

He was very ready to oblige, telling Pharaoh, "Return Sarah to me, and you will recover your good health. It is my God who has caused this affliction. He has struck you down in order to protect Sarah. She is not my sister; she is my wife."

"But why didn't you tell me? I understand that any ordinary person, married to such a beauty as Sarah, might have feared for his life," Pharaoh replied. "But you have on your side a god of immense power, capable of injuring anyone who threatens those who are under his care. Did you not trust that he would come to your aid, even if we were as wickedly predatory as you thought *and* we knew she was your wife?"

It was a fair question, one that Abraham could not answer. So instead he blushed.

Pharaoh pressed on him further gifts, of livestock, silver, and gold, and told him, "Go!" Abraham set off back to Canaan, Pharaoh escorting him and his household and retinue across the border. By happy coincidence, the famine had come to an end.

Abraham pondered, "I did not ask for God's help, and yet

He helped me. I did not trust God in Canaan and went to Egypt. But there, I needed Him, and He did not fail me. He is all I need; He is everything to me." Abraham returned to the altar he had made and, standing before it, called out God's name in gratitude, his faith reaffirmed and strengthened.

At the same time, Sarah pondered, "And whom can *I* trust?"

Episode 3: Quarrel

Abraham's wealth was by now very great. Lot's was too, as a result of his association with his uncle. The size of Lot's wealth made him independent; the source of his wealth, and his ability to keep it secure, depended on Abraham. Their livestock grazed on the same land, but the sheep and cattle were so numerous that the land could not support them all.

This was a problem for Lot, then: dependence and independence in unhappy conjunction. And there was a further problem, one for both Lot and Abraham: scarcity amid plenty. Actually, the first of Lot's problems was also a problem for Abraham too, though it was as imperceptible to him as it was burdensome for his nephew. And this in turn only added to Lot's sense of oppression. Though in his appearance he was a copy of his uncle, he had none of Abraham's qualities; he encouraged others to treat him as if he *were* his uncle and resented them when they did not.

News reached Abraham of a quarrel between Lot's men and his own. The proximate cause of the quarrel was access to pasture. The fighting among them was itself the consequence of striving between the livestock. Abraham's men championed his sheep and cattle; Lot's men, Lot's sheep and cattle. The animals' contest was pure physical collision, noisy mooing and baaing—cacophonous thumping and thrashing about. The herdsmen's contest was physical menace and angry words—no blows landed, but there was much shouting and abuse. Abraham's herdsmen insisted on their precedence over Lot's men and the precedence of their animals over Lot's animals. They asserted their claims with many disparagements of Lot: he poses as his uncle, he is nothing more than a fraudulent impersonator of his uncle, a masquerader, and so on. It was true, essentially. He was a derivative figure, altogether without originality.

Abraham and Lot heard the commotion. Lot was humiliated and angry. He was mocked by Abraham's men, his own men were demoralized, and his livestock were weakening for want of adequate food. Abraham was alive both to the technical problem (access to resources) and to the psychological problem (Lot's subordination to him). The solution to both problems was obvious, it seemed to him. Let them separate. Lot should establish his own household, of which he would then be the incontestable head. In addition to Lot thereby becoming visibly independent of his uncle, his men would be free of the overbearing presence of Abraham's men, and his livestock would no longer go hungry.

Abraham made his proposal to Lot. He began with some mild words, avuncular in tone. "Come, let there be no strife between us. Let us not allow our men to quarrel." Lot thought, "Abraham is intimating that the fighting between the men is proxy combat and that he and I are the undeclared principals in the quarrel. He is also intimating that, by acknowledging the fact, he is unbothered by it. He will be the victor if the quarrel plays out to a conclusion."

Abraham continued, "We are brothers." Lot thought, "And who is Abraham to preach family? He did not mourn the death of my father, Haran; he abandoned his father, Terah; he gave up his wife, Sarah, to the Egyptians. Or perhaps, by saying 'brothers' rather than 'uncle and nephew,' he wants me to suppose that we have a more equal relation than in fact we do. But this must be flattery for a purpose. What is it?"

But Lot *said* nothing. He saw that Abraham had more to say, and he did not speak, out of respect for his uncle and out of curiosity for what Abraham would say next. Abraham continued, "Look at all this land. There is more than enough for each of us. We should separate. You choose where you want to go. If you go left, I will go right; if you go right, I will go left."

Lot was stung. He did not want to separate; he experienced the proposal as a rejection. And yet, he also understood that the proposal had to be accepted precisely because so much of himself was bound up in his uncle. His only chance of independence, of gaining some fully formed and independent self, was to put physical distance between himself and his uncle. So, caught between the appeal of a gamble (attempt to be my own person!) and his instinctive submissiveness (do what I am told!), he contemplated the choice he had been given. In one direction was the fertile Jordan Plain, with its many cities; in the other direction was Canaan's open lands. He raised his eyes, gave them each an appraising stare, and then made his choice. He would go to a city—indeed the one notorious for its vicious ways, Sodom, a city about to destroy itself. Abraham pitched his tents nearby, in the plains of Mamre.

Abraham was taken aback. Why did Lot choose Sodom? It was situated in fertile, well-watered land, certainly. But that was not the reason. It had something to do with Sodom itself. It was a city in which no one was burdened by family obligations, just the place to which a person exasperated by his subordinate position in a family would go. To live there would be an active repudiation of family ties.

Lot, for his part, experienced Sodom as freedom. And after he had lived there for a while, for the clarity of his embrace of the city, the citizens chose him as a judge—indeed, the senior judge of the city's court. He started to boss them about, trading on his relationship with Abraham.

When the split between the two had been accomplished, Abraham had another vision. God told him to raise his eyes and regard the land. "Everything that you see," God says, "I will give to you and to your descendants, forever. They will be as numerous as the dust of the Earth." In celebration of this almost-news (much of it he had heard before) but also alive to the use of the future tense, Abraham built his third altar.

Episode 4: War

Famine, quarrel—and now war. Abraham believed that *this* disruption, at least, he would be able to sit out. In the part of Canaan where he was then residing, four superior kings waged a war against five vassal kings. It was the action of a collective security pact. They treated a rebellion against one of their number as a rebellion against them all. They quickly defeated the lesser kings. One among them crossed the valley of Siddim, while two of the lesser kings, the kings of Sodom and Gomorrah, rode into mortar pits. Of these two, Sodom's king managed to scramble free.

The superior kings then turned their attention to Abraham. Having seen off a rebellion, they sought to subjugate him, correctly regarding him as a strong, independent presence in the region. They set out to kidnap him, but in error seized Lot instead, mistaking him for his uncle. They made off with him, grabbing what they could of his wealth and everything else in Sodom that was within their reach.

On this occasion, Abraham did not ponder, as he was prompted to ponder on leaving Egypt, "When should I act, and when should I await a miracle? When will the laws of the universe take their course, and when will God disrupt them?" He had no time for reflection: he must act, or Lot would be lost. And he must project his own power, so that the kings did not seek him out, when they discovered their mistake. So Abraham gave chase, supported by a small force made up of members of his household. He tracked them down, surrounded them, and compelled them to give up Lot and all the slaves and treasures they had stolen when they abducted him.

Abraham was a reluctant but effective warrior; though not a king himself, he was a vanquisher of kings. He returned the hapless Lot to Sodom (so much for separation) and restored to its king everything that the superior kings had taken as spoils from the city. The king, in an extravagant show of gratitude, said to Abraham, "Return to me the stolen slaves and keep the stolen goods for yourself."

Abraham had done the king many favors. He had returned what was stolen; he had enhanced the prestige of the lesser kings by siding with them against their overlords. The king's escape from the mortar pit had come to be celebrated as miraculous, a demonstration of the favor of Abraham's god. But Abraham refused the king's generous proposal, responding rather loftily, "Neither a thread nor a shoelace will I take from you. You will not be able to say, 'I have made Abraham wealthy.'" The lesser kings made much of him, nonetheless, offering him leadership positions among their number. These too he refused. It was not that he had an objection to receiving gifts; it was that he did not want any relationship with Sodom. We tend to overlook this episode in Abraham's life.[16]

He came to be referred to in the region as the "Ivri," the "Hebrew," which means "from the other side." It was an epithet that he welcomed. He had been in versions of an adversarial relation with his milieu ever since Ur days. To be an "Ivri," to have one's identity forged in opposition, in confrontation with hostile powers, is exactly what he was. But was it fully Abraham standing *contra mundum*, against the world? It had sometimes *felt* like that to him, but so far it had not fully *been* that. He had always had allies—partners, even. And he had always had the ambition to bring others over to his side, to inspire critical thinkers (Ur), to make converts (Haran), to acquire slaves (Egypt). And of course, he now had God on his side.

Sarah watched all this, fearing for Abraham, and then taking pleasure in his triumph. Yet she wondered, "Why would my husband be brave for Lot but not for me?"

Episode 5: Challenge

The quarrel with Lot, the war of the kings, the rescue of Lot, the importunities of the king of Sodom . . . The world invaded him, crowding his mind with its tumult and wild demands. It was all too much for him. He withdrew into himself and was rewarded with a further vision.

In this vision, God told him, "Do not fear, Abraham. I am your protector, and your reward will be very great." The statement settled into Abraham's mind. Its unconditional, unspecific character made it hard to grasp. It had a certain immensity of implication for him, but what, in its practical implications, did it mean? What fear? What protection? What reward?

"Do not fear"—against what fears was God warning Abraham? Fear of harm? The rational fear, the kind that makes us proportionately, rationally cautious? The more indeterminate fears generated by anxiety? The fear that opportunities will be lost if one does not take a risk? He did not know. He sensed, however, that the statement had an admonitory edge. "You should not have feared the famine," say. Perhaps also, "Do not fear false gods." And, as silent companion to the injunction against fearing, Abraham intuited the injunctions, "Fear My commands; fear My power; fear My judgment. Fear Me!" He wondered, "What does it mean to be 'God-fearing'? To proclaim openly one's faith and live by its principles? Or to surrender all decision-making to Him, even if on occasion contrary to those principles?" He knew that he feared God in the first sense; he did not quite know whether he feared Him in the second sense.

"Protector"—that is, "as I have already demonstrated to you, Abraham." But what was the extent of that protection?

Did it include protecting Abraham from, say, being required to make a tragic choice—that is, being put in the position where whatever he did would be wrong, whatever decision he made would be the wrong decision? This was worse than moral *jeopardy*: not the risk of doing something wrong but the certainty of it. Perhaps God meant, "I will protect you from everyone *except Me*."

"Reward"—that is, something other than the riches he had already piled up and something other than the riches he had refused. But what then? A reward that he would himself live to enjoy? In his trance state, Abraham sounded out in his head these words, "What *exactly* will You give me, my Master, since I am still childless?" As if to say, "Enough of generalities. Let's get down to details." Abraham recalled the promise made in his previous vision, the one following his separation from Lot. To have countless descendants, one has to start with at least one, surely? And so far there was none. His servant Eliezer performed a son's duties in Abraham's household.

Was Eliezer to be his heir? In this internal dialogue, Abraham intuited the response, "No." Further words followed in elaboration of the response. "Only he that will come from your own loins will be your heir." It was not a complete answer to Abraham's question. A narrow, abstract definition of "heir" excluded Eliezer, certainly. But had a child been promised to Abraham? The question formed itself in his mind: "And *will* You *give* me an heir of my loins?" But he did not sound it. Instead, sinking back into that deeper level of trance, where he felt most open to God yet was least able to reflect on what He had said, Abraham looked toward the starry sky. "My descendants will be as numerous as the innumerable stars." For the moment, this satisfied him.

He then intuited the further declaration, "I am God who brought you out of Ur to give you this land as an inheritance." Why did God persist thus? He had already said as much to

Abraham. Why say it again? It made Abraham anxious, so he posed the question, "How will I *know* that I will inherit it?"

And then, the most extraordinary thing. By way of a response, Abraham understood that he had to perform a complex, never-to-be-repeated sequence of steps, killing several kinds of animal (heifers, goats, rams, a dove, and a pigeon), the carcasses to be split and arranged in a pattern. There was no apparent sense to it, and no explanation was given.

Abraham experienced it, first, as an assertion of God's authority, arbitrary in content to serve precisely that purpose. As if God were saying, "I instruct you to do something that will make no sense to you, and you will do it, without question or even investigation. You will do it because I ask it of you." Abraham had offered a bold challenge: "You tell me I will inherit, but how do I know that what You say is true?" It was, he realized, an extraordinary affront. And so of course God had responded by making His incomprehensible demand.

Then, a further thought came to him, in opposition to the first one. "Perhaps I am still a little stuck in my Ur way of thinking, all unforgiving striving for mental autonomy, heroically resisting the pressure of other minds. Perhaps a *third* orientation, neither adversarial nor submissive, is disclosing itself to me, one that follows God's showing of Himself to me. An orientation of radical receptiveness? Absurd to acknowledge, I have not yet accommodated God in my thinking. There must be traces of Nimrod in my understanding of Him. I am still cautious, even wary. I must guard against all mistrustfulness."

Birds of prey settled on the pieces of animal flesh. Abraham drove them away. He saw himself doing all this, in his wakeful trance. He fell from the trance into a deeper sleep; a sense of dread gripped him. God repeated the assurance of inheritance but also gave him less welcome intelligence. "Your descendants will be slaves in a land not their own for four hundred years, though they will then leave with great wealth and return here, to Canaan." And then God gave him some intelligence regarding his own life. "You will die at a good old age and will join your fathers in peace." Did this promise reveal a wish on Abraham's part for reconciliation with his father? The thought of it floated into his mind and was not rejected.

A smoking furnace became visible, and a torch passed between the pieces. Abraham dreamt on. God made a covenant with him. "To your descendants, I have given this land, from the river of Egypt as far as the great river, the Euphrates." So many peoples would be dispossessed! The Kenites, the Kadmonites, the Chittites, the Perizites, the Refa'im, the Emorites, the Canaanites, the Girgashites, and the Yevusites.

There were mysteries within the mystery of the vision, the sacrifice, and the sleep, opacities of meaning impossible to penetrate, an atmosphere of inscrutable, portentous solemnity. Promises and warnings, warnings inside promises, dispossession of other peoples, enslavement of his own descendants. Such torments awaited, and for what offenses? Abraham grieved. "If through me, all the families of the Earth will be blessed, what of these dispossessed families? If I am to be rewarded, what of my own enslaved descendants, generations of whom will live and die in bondage?"

Two God-related experiences had become available to Abraham in this episode, which he named "the covenant of the pieces." Call them the experience of the sublime and the experience of dread. The one is awe in the register of elevation, the other awe in the register of terror. The one offers an experience of expansion, the other a sense of paralysis; the one a merging of self with the sublime spectacle, the other an extinguishing of self by the object of dread. These encounters with God, in their vertiginous intensity, acquired for him a momentousness and an intimacy of contact wholly lacking in his everyday existence, which even more than before seemed to him both inconsequential and remote.

And then events in that household drew him back, with an unignorable insistence, into the world.

Episode 6: Ishmael

Time passed, and there was still no son. So Sarah proposed a solution to Abraham. She wanted to be practical and to align herself with Abraham's new purpose. She could help. She was fitting in with him, though with a certain reluctance. "Wait no longer. God has kept me from bearing children, so why don't you approach my maid? Perhaps I can have a child through her. What do I care if Hagar conceives? Childbirth is not my purpose. Let her do it—for me. As I might have her perform other services for me. She will save me from labor here, as she does in other respects."

This far, she spoke to Abraham. Beyond this, she spoke only to herself: "I will arrange myself what God has kept from me. I won't wait for a miracle; I certainly won't submit to the implications of God's decision for me. I'll take it into my own hands."

Abraham complied, readily. When Hagar first conceived, she miscarried. Abraham was not sorry; he went to her again, and again she conceived. By then, she had spent some time with Abraham. She had ceased to be (if indeed she ever was) that instrument for his use that her mistress imagined. She began to think better of herself. Sarah sensed this and imagined Hagar reflecting, "I no longer belong to Sarah; I now belong to Abraham. I have conceived, while she has not; I have succeeded where she has failed. I must be more righteous than she is." It was impossible that Abraham's wife and the mother of his child could remain a maidservant. His proximity to her, and his great spirit, shattered Hagar's own spirit of servitude, awakening in her a sentiment of dignity and the aspiration for freedom.[17]

This is the very opposite of what Sarah had sought. Her plan was for her own status to rise, the proud mother of a surrogate child. She had made a serious mistake. It was not Hagar's superciliousness but the presentation of a free person that Sarah could not bear—not when she herself was falling into a condition of servitude. She felt defenseless before the scorn she attributed to Hagar. How could she avoid that judgment, given her misery, her frustration at the uselessness forced on her? That she should be picking quarrels with servants in abject quest for the return of some measure of independence! Indeed, how could she not add to Hagar's scorn her own self-scorn?

So Sarah recoiled from her earlier proposal. What an act of self-sabotage! She should never have suggested Hagar as carrier of Abraham's child. She berated Abraham. "The insult to me is your fault. I gave my maid to you, and when she saw that she had conceived, she slighted me. I am diminished." She concluded, "May God decide between you and me!"

But she did not wait for God's decision. Her statement had the character of a flourish rather than an actual appeal to God. Abraham retreated immediately and gave Hagar up to Sarah. "Do with her what you will." Though she was pregnant with his child, he stood by while Sarah beat her. (If he could surrender up Sarah to Pharaoh, it was no struggle for him to surrender up Hagar to Sarah.) The treatment was so harsh that Hagar ran away. Sarah did not try to get her back. She was content to let Hagar die in the wilderness—and the unborn child too, for that matter.

Sarah's plan had failed. It had always only been about Abraham. And this is why she was angry with him about Hagar's new manner. "It's your fault!" But what precisely was the fault? She was angry that her proposal had not brought them closer together. She had instead made herself fully redundant.

Later on, reflecting on what had happened, on what she had done, she reproached herself. She knew that she had been cruel. Abraham would have helped her if he had reproached her too. But he did not. He created no opportunity for open exchanges with her. His silence was more oppressive than any criticism.

Hagar walked and walked, the sun high in the sky. Heavy with her unborn child, she collapsed and prayed for relief. Rewarded with a vision, she understood that she must return to Abraham and be delivered of her child under his protection. In due course, her son, named Ishmael ("God will hear your prayer"), was born.

Episode 7: Circumcision

After a further passage of time, a further vision came to Abraham. God intimated a new demand and made an already-given promise, but in slightly different language. "Walk before me and be perfect. I will establish my covenant with you and make you exceedingly numerous." In the thrall of his vision, Abraham knelt and then, one hand at a time, lowered his upper body onto the ground, pressing his face down into the soft sand. The gesture expressed total submission to God. This is *not*, let us affirm, the most congenial posture for a speculative thinker. The thinking part of the body, the head, is level with the ground; the face, what is most distinctive about a person, is not visible at all.

Abraham understood that he had a fresh act to perform, this time not to part with his homeland but to part with something of himself—to *sacrifice* something of himself.[18] He was commanded to circumcise himself and to circumcise all the males of his household. These circumcisions would be the sign of the covenant that God had made with these circumcised men. Every male child eight days of age, either born of Abraham's house or bought from a stranger, was thereafter to be circumcised. The nation promised to Abraham would be defined by this mark on the bodies of its men. No male who refused circumcision could join the nation; any male born into it who refused circumcision would be cut off from it.

It was another terrifying command. Why this further imposition on him? Had he not already demonstrated his readiness, his responsiveness to God's demands? He had left his home, abandoned his father, exposed himself to peril and uncertainty, all on God's peremptory instruction. Yet he was being tested again, Abraham thought. His assent was immediate.

The command formed in his mind at the same time as the commitment to honor it. Blood had to be drawn. It had a certain quality of sacrifice. Abraham offered himself as a sacrifice; he then offered his son Ishmael as a sacrifice.[19] Still, he wondered, "What does the command *mean*? Is it the marker *of* the covenant, confirmation of its existence? Or is it another of my obligations *under* the covenant, just as leaving Haran was?"

The circumcisions were done in public in the daytime, light flooding the scene of cuttings. A small assembly had gathered, in anticipation of a spectacle. The circumcisions were a bloody and at first somewhat experimental and haphazard affair. The spectators looked on, both bemused and repelled by what they were witnessing. Among their number, one addressed Abraham. "You have submitted yourself to a painful and ignominious practice that is as senseless as the practices you mocked when in Ur and does not even have the merit of being sanctioned by tradition. You have exposed your hypocrisy. It was vanity, not principle, that led you to reject Ur's gods and jeer at its forms and rituals of worship. You have unmanned yourself—and why? To confirm the abandonment of your vaunted independence of thought!"

Abraham had not been afraid of the idolaters; he was similarly unafraid of the scoffers. This was a distinct independence, quite different from the autonomy he enjoyed in Ur. The negative act of destroying idols was to be set against the positive act of *brit*, the idol-destroying, an act of radical scoffing, *brit*, an act of radical severance from the world of scoffers. It marked Abraham's passage from destructive critique to creative affirmation, from critical engagement with his society to rejection of it, in

was all criticism; Ur was all custom. Sodom was cynicism; Ur was ancestral wisdom. Sodom was bereft of religion; Ur was rotten with idolatry. Somewhat embarrassed, Abraham told the men that his nephew Lot lived there.

The cry from Sodom of the people tortured, maimed, and killed there had reached God, Abraham was told. The judges were in the pay of the richer litigants; the city's populace preyed on each other. It was only a matter of time before the city would destroy itself. The men told Abraham of one of the more recent outrages. "There was a young woman who would take bread out to the poor people in a pitcher, so the people of Sodom would not see it. The matter was revealed, and they smeared her with honey and positioned her on the wall of the city, so that the hornets would come and consume her." "God will hear her cry, and the cries of all the others who suffer in that terrible place," Abraham said.

The men receded from his attention. He had a powerful sense that Sodom was in terminal peril. It had only escaped catastrophe thus far because God had not noticed it. The question flitted through his mind, "How can that be? But wait. What if there are decent people living there? Will they be lost too? If the city is wicked, God will destroy it, entirely. All will perish." Abraham worked through the problem and, in doing so, imagined himself in debate with God. And yes, he thought, "Though I am but dust and ashes, I have a mind that is my own, to ponder, to question, to challenge."

"Suppose there are fifty righteous people in the city's midst. Why would You not suffer the city for their sake?" Abraham went on: "It would be sacrilege to attribute to You such an act, to kill the righteous and the wicked alike. Shall the judge of all the Earth not do justice?" Lower and then still lower numbers were urged—fifty, forty-five, forty, thirty, twenty, ten.

Abraham was daunted, resolute, impatient in argument. The annihilating flame of divine ire burned before his eyes every time he spoke, it is said.[22] Yes, true enough. But he was also absorbed in the back-and-forth. And he recalled his exchanges with Nimrod, and the marvelous dwindling of power's majesty under the force of argument, the quailing of authority before reason.

Abraham rested at the number ten. He was clear: if less than ten, then there would be none. There was no smaller number to fight for. It would be to the credit of the city if virtuous people were able to live in it. But if not even ten such people could do so, because it was so wicked that it destroyed everything good that made the mistake of coming into contact with it, then *no* virtuous person could live there.

There is a political theory implicit here. What is the significance of ten? It is the smallest number for a self-sustaining group. It is therefore also the smallest number of virtuous people who could survive in a wicked city. Were there ten such people in Sodom, they could look out for each other; they could support each other. Fewer than ten could not survive. They would be overrun: killed, expelled, or corrupted. It is not possible to be virtuous unless one is in the company of at least nine other virtuous people.

Insofar as the exchanges between God and Abraham could be characterized as a contest, Abraham was the winner. He had held God to His own standards.[23] It was quite the outcome. It is not surprising, then, and hardly to Abraham's discredit, that it encouraged in him a certain complacency with regard both to his relation with God and to his grasp of God's character. These complacencies became doctrines to his descendants.

First, Abraham considered, and his descendants believed, that a distinctive relation with God had been established, one characterized by moments of challenge, even protest. Though we Jews are but dust and ashes, we are also the God-arguers, it came to be said.[24] When He acts against our understanding of what is just, we will protest. We are His interlocutors, His partners, His beloved. He will listen to us. The listening is an aspect of our covenantal relation with Him. Abraham himself will return in moments of catastrophe, to plead our case to God.[25]

Second, Abraham further considered, and his descendants believed, that the episode demonstrated God's essential justice. Granted, He should have come to the aid of the persecuted of Sodom, rather than merely intervening afterward to punish their tormenters. But insofar as His timing raised a question, it was a simple one. Is the freedom of the wicked to do ill worth the pain suffered by their victims? The question became a familiar one, part of the Jewish people's dialogue with Him. In their religious imagination, it had the stability of a topic; in their liturgy, it contributed a type of prayer, the "argument-prayer."[26]

In consequence of these complacencies, which combined to form the conviction, "I will never have cause to fear God," Abraham was left unprepared for the moment when God would play the part of perpetrator, rather than tardy bystander, and no challenge to His plan would be possible.

Episode 10: Destruction

It had become clear that the collapse of Sodom was only a matter of time. Two of Abraham's three visitors, moved by his hospitality, sensitive to his embarrassment, went to the city to warn Lot. They intended to deliver the message, "Go!" They came across him at the city gates, where he was presiding over a case. He stood up in their presence and bowed worshipfully, with his face toward the ground. He invited them to his home. They said, "Don't trouble yourself. We will find somewhere to sleep." As with Abraham and the king of Sodom, they did not want to put themselves under an obligation to him. But he persisted, and so they relented. Later in the evening, once they had rested, they dined with him. They were struck by how alike he was to his uncle and yet how much not like him. "He is a *version* of Abraham," they reflected.

They had not yet retired for the evening when the men of the city surrounded Lot's house. "Bring out the visitors. We want to use them." It was not a mob, with mob passion, free of the usual moral restraints. There *were* no restraints in Sodom, other than bargained ones. The citizens had no obligations to the visitors; they could be used as ownerless animals that had strayed into inhabited spaces. Private law governed relations between parties; those without the protection of a contract comprised mere resource material. Sodom did not recognize the family as an institution with its own boundaries and privileges; it did not acknowledge family ties as creating obligations that might rival, or even trump, contractual ones. So it was less a mob than a deputation that assembled outside Lot's house, a Sodom-specific combination of the decorous and the vicious.

The demand made on Lot was not intended as any offense to him. But he took it badly, because he was alive to those duties of hospitality honored by Abraham, duties of proximity that gave practical effect to his refusal to distinguish between family and strangers. The citizens regarded him as one of them, however. In a mode of address that affirmed this Sodomite identity while also denying it, Lot called out to them, through the closed door, "My brothers!"

And then, out of the chaos of his thinking, duties acknowledged and denied, tangled ties of paternity, of hospitality, of citizenship, he made a grotesque proposal: "I have two daughters who are virgins. Take them instead and do with them what you please. Leave the men alone; they are my guests." To be a protector, he must become a procurer.[27] If the offer was made nonchalantly,[28] the nonchalance was not of the moment; it came out of a certain moral insensibility. Without capacity for growth, and incapable of independent action or reflection, Lot was lost the moment he was unanchored from Haran.

The citizens refused Lot's counteroffer and pushed harder

against the door. He panicked, thinking only, "Am I to be man-handled in Sodom a second time? Must I await my uncle's rescue once again?" His daughters cowered. Only the guests stayed cool. Within minutes, the pressure on the door weakened, the commotion subsided, the assembly thinned out. And then—silence. The frantic Lot, the terrified young women, all looked with gratitude to these two strangers in their midst, who told them, "The city is doomed. Escape now or perish."

Early the next morning, with wife and unmarried daughters waiting on his direction, packed and ready to leave, Lot hesitated. He went to his married daughters and their husbands, divided between warning them and seeking their counsel. "Run for your lives!" Pause. "Do you think it's real?" Contemptuous of his indecision—only Lot could be insecure about his own panic—they laughed in his face. Lot, who never rose to the occasion, returned home. He was disconsolate, immobilized by the scornful reception he had met. The two visitors urged him to get out of the city straightaway. Still no movement. Exasperated, they took hold of Lot by his arms and marched him toward the city gates, wife and daughters trailing behind, belongings in tow, fully alive to the ignominious manner of their exit.

The party first made for a nearby city but quickly retreated further, to the mountains, convinced in their simplicity that the world itself was coming to an end. Lot's wife was by then dead, and Lot himself was drunk, having knocked back spirits continuously as they made their upward ascent. His mind returned to the events of the previous night: "I knew that my offer would be refused; my daughters were never at risk.[29] I was confident that all would be well—and I was right." In a mood of some self-congratulation, induced by these thoughts, he collapsed in a heap. His daughters carried his lifeless body into a cave. Night fell. The young women, contemplating the great responsibility that had fallen on them alone, to repopulate the world, made use of the only inseminating agent available, their father. Each conceived a child with him across the period of their stay in the cave, Lot himself reduced by his life experiences to a cipher.

This is the last time we will encounter Lot, the unaware accomplice to his daughters' mad, transgressive undertaking. What to make of him? As both the mirror version and the low version, both photographic negative and base copy, of his uncle Abraham. And as the Jewish people's first schlemiel. Hapless and dependent, he kept getting into trouble, and Abraham had to keep saving him. He made his own misfortune by moving away from Abraham. He was accident-prone, putting himself in harm's way. No hero, no stalwart, he relied on help from any quarter whenever in a jam. He exacted no deference; he won no admiration. He was the object of a general contempt, misperceived as affection because it was so unthreatened. There was a quality of the ludicrous about him.

To make the case for Lot as Abraham's mirror version, we need only list his humiliations: to depend on Abraham's generosity; to be captured and require rescuing; to offer his daughters in Sodom; then to have sex with them in a mountain cave. It is a life of ignominy. He is the family nudnik, his career a failure in every register. He always makes the wrong choices, and he has the worst luck. He wants respect, but he can't earn it. He is in a state of constant, permanent exasperation, with himself and with the world. In his vulnerability, he makes impotent assertions of independence. He can't quarrel himself; his herdsmen do the quarrelling for him. He's saved by the person he's trying to run away from. He offers up his daughters for abuse and is then in turn abused by them. His character has a comic aspect; he is the family member who does embarrassing stuff. Against Abraham, who is exemplary of the elevated life, Lot is everyday man, the person no better than he should be.

But Lot is also a poor copy, a low version, of his uncle Abraham, just as his father Haran the scientist was a low version of his brother Abraham. In Ur, Abraham became his own person in the boldness of his own reasoning; by going to Sodom, Lot attempted but failed to affirm *his* autonomy. While Lot negotiated with rapists, Abraham negotiated with God. While Lot ignominiously offered his daughters, Abraham submitted to the command to give up his son. Lot's daughters conceived by incestuous manipulation; Abraham's wife conceived by (what is understood to be) a miracle. The citizens of Sodom referred to Lot as a foreigner (*ger*); Abraham described himself to the Hittite tribe of Hebron as a foreigner-resident (*ger v'toshav*). Abraham went down to Egypt and then came up from it to Canaan, the land he will inherit; Lot went down to Sodom and likewise then ascended, but only literally, to a mountain cave, whereupon he disappeared from history.

Abraham went down to the ruins of Sodom, not to look for his nephew, or for his nephew's family, but to contemplate what he took to be God's work of destruction. The smoking city reminded him of a fired-up furnace. He thought back on his own escape from a furnace.

Episode 11: Abimelech

Leaving the desolate plains, Abraham traveled from Mamre to Gerar, a royal city on the southern border of Canaan.[30] The local king was Abimelech. He was both the last and the least of the kings with whom Abraham had dealings. First, there was Nimrod, God's challenger; next, there was Pharaoh, the ruler of an entire civilization, the second of the two limit-powers between which the Israelites will assert their own sovereignty claims; then, the warring four kings and five kings, not in themselves significant but, as a group, dominating the region to be secured by the Israelites and standing for the tribes thereby to be dispossessed. And then there is Abimelech, just one king, fully local to one city only and utterly insignificant in the larger scheme of things, the meaning of his name, "father of kings," in satiric contrast to the triviality of his status.

Abimelech was reputed to be sexually predatory, and Abraham was therefore once again afraid for his life. And once again, he protected himself by an act of deception, introducing Sarah as his sister. But the king learned of Sarah's status and told Abraham that God had revealed it to him in a dream. "Do not go near Sarah," Abimelech related Him saying. "She is married to Abraham. He is a prophet. Stand back, and all will be well with you. Pursue her, and you will die."

Abimelech asked Abraham, "Why did you say she is your sister?" Abraham replied, "I was afraid. I thought there was no fear of God here." He told Abimelech that Sarah was indeed his sister. "She is the daughter of my father." (Not true—she was Terah's *grand*daughter.) He then told Abimelech that he had asked Sarah to say in "every place" they came to, "He is my brother." (Also not true—it was only in Egypt where he made this request.)

Abimelech loaded Abraham up with sheep and cattle and male and female slaves; he gave to him a thousand pieces of silver. He said to Abraham, "Stay here as long as you like."

What did Abraham mean, "No fear of God here"?

It was, first of all, a manner of speaking. There is no proper behavior; standards of civility are not met; people act without a sense of accountability; shame and guilt are not known. To live in a place conditioned by fear of God is something everyone would want. It has little to do with a relationship with God; it has everything to do with relationships among humankind. Abraham did not know whether Gerar was a God-fearing society.

It was also a thought that followed upon Sodom. Both then and now, behind the exchanges with God and with Abimelech, lay the question, What is a decent society? Answering this question matters, not least because only decent societies may demand toleration.[31] By "no fear of God," Abraham gestured toward an answer. It is a society in which murder cannot be committed with impunity, a society in which people do not live in fear of their lives. The price they pay, if it is a price, is that they must live instead in fear of God. "Fear" then takes on the quality of a political emotion, one that drives the formation of societies and then sustains them, for either good or ill.

God had said to Abraham, "Do not fear." But Abraham was afraid. God had said to him, "I am your protector." But Abraham believed that he had to take steps to protect himself. Whence this persistent skepticism about God's promises and assurances?

The external circumstances of the episode, in their similarity to the Egypt episode, impressed on Sarah the extent of the deterioration in her relations with her husband. It was as if "Egypt" had been restaged to teach her how bad things were now between them. The contrasts presented themselves to Sarah as very striking indeed.

The Egypt story began with a famine. Abraham and Sarah traveled south out of a shared sense of need, even though she was not consulted before the decision to leave was made. The decision to risk harm by going to Egypt was justified because of the certainty of greater harm were they to remain in Canaan. Still, they went there with great trepidation: the Egyptians were said to be steeped in lechery and murderousness, depraved beyond measure.[32] Abraham made the request to Sarah, "Please say you are my sister." She was content, if only because it was a gesture toward their equality—she was not his possession; she stood independent of him. She understood that it was not proposed for that reason, but still: let this be a public, if partial, even uncomprehending, affirmation of that relationship.

By contrast, the Gerar story began with an unmotivated decision to travel to the city. Abraham did not need thereby to expose either himself or Sarah to harm. Once in Gerar, he announced that Sarah was his sister without first consulting her. (The moment had passed when Abraham could secure that assent.) When he was challenged by Abimelech with his deception, Abraham gave answers that made Sarah the spectator to his dishonesties. What was dismaying for her was not just the spectacle itself but the fact that Abraham didn't care that she witnessed it. His statements were experienced by her as a further repudiation of their marriage bond, the most recent in a series of repudiations that she traced back to the very moment of their departure from Haran.

They had reached the lowest point in their relationship. Sarah contemplated the decline with horror.

Episode 12: Isaac

This is a complex episode, made up of two parts. In the first part, God keeps His word, and a son, Isaac, is born to Sarah and Abraham. In the second part, Isaac is weaned, and Ishmael is expelled at Sarah's demand. This episode has more of Sarah speaking than any other episode. Her speech is addressed both to herself and to the world at large; it is introspection and it is command. She has much to say here, but then she falls silent, never to speak again.

Sarah conceived a child. Abraham was moved at the prospect of its birth, notwithstanding his age and Sarah's age and notwithstanding that they had both believed that she couldn't conceive. God had kept His word, Abraham concluded. He had remembered His promise.

When the child was born, malicious gossip circulated that Abraham was not the father and that Sarah had rescued an abandoned baby.[33] Abraham circumcised the baby at eight days. Though he witnessed his son's blood flowing from the cutting, he welcomed it joyfully, in fulfillment of God's will.[34] The child was named "Isaac." Abraham gave him this name, he explained to Sarah, in compliance with God's instruction. The name "Isaac" means "one who laughs" or "one who will laugh."

Sarah invested it with her own meaning. "There is something absurd about me being a mother at my age, and people will laugh," she said. "And yet, let me celebrate with laughter the miracle that is my son." That is to say, she feared that people would laugh at her, and she hoped that people would laugh with her, at her good fortune. This ability to elicit the ambiguity of a position had always been typical of Sarah, a gift of her clarity of mind. She never let down her guard. She was detached, even here. She had strong analytical capabilities. She always saw what was happening; she could read a situation. Her slight emphasis on the mockery, as against the rejoicing, reflected her sense of where she was now.

Two years passed. Abraham held a party to celebrate Isaac's weaning. The boy had detached himself from his mother and was now of his father. Isaac had joined the paternal order. He had become his father in appearance and demeanor. His face, his father's face; his gait, his father's gait—fully a "little Abraham," said the household servants.

Sarah's experience was one of loss and separation. She retreated into her own body. She knew that the baby was never her possession and that though so small and utterly dependent on her help, he was a separate entity and ought to be treated as an individual human being. She knew that she must not tie him too much to herself but assist him to grow up to independence. And she knew that the earlier she acted on what she knew, the better.[35] Yet it was bitterness to her, all of it.

At precisely this moment of mourning, Sarah seized on Ishmael. She believed that she had witnessed him mocking Isaac, just as Hagar had once mocked her. A sudden spurt of hatred toward Ishmael made her dizzy. She was already sensitive to any claim that the rivalrous Ishmael might want to make, by virtue of being the older son. For her, the mere fact of his existence was a threat to her own son. In Sarah's imagination, whenever Ishmael laughed, he was "Isaac-ing."[36] For him to laugh was to play the imposter son, just as Hagar continued to play the imposter wife.

So Sarah told Abraham, "Throw them out! This son of a slave woman will not inherit with my son, my Isaac." This was her last speech. Abraham recoiled from her demand. It was wrong in his eyes. It was excessive. Not just disinherit him but kill him. Or if not kill him, discard him, without concern for his welfare, not caring whether he lived or died. The instinct to comply, the counterinstinct to refuse, paralyzed Abraham. He couldn't breathe, he couldn't think. His face grew hot; his vision blurred. He turned from Sarah and walked away. Soon he had left their encampment and was trudging in open fields. He walked for two, perhaps three hours, before he was able to stop trembling. And then stillness came over him, and he sat in a field, the sun low in the skies. Alone and at peace, he sank into a trance.

He heard God tell him, "Regarding all that Sarah tells you, listen to her." He must trust her judgment; her insights were deeper than his; she was the superior prophet. God continued, "Only through Isaac will seed be considered yours." Ishmael would not inherit, and there was no need for Abraham to keep him close by; better to let him go and make his own fortune. But God then added, "I will also make Ishmael into a nation, because he too is of your seed." Abraham had to substitute his wife's wishes for his own. But he had everything he needed. His line would *only* pass through Isaac; his line would *also* go through Ishmael. In visions, as in dreams, there is no principle of contradiction.

Abraham got up, returned to Sarah, and told her that he would do as she requested. The following morning, he drove out Hagar and their son, Ishmael, placing some bread and water on Hagar's shoulders, supplies enough for a day or two at most. They did not want to go, but they were not given the choice to stay. The parting was harsh and summary. Hagar was greatly distressed, and Ishmael was torn between grieving for his mother and fearing for his own life. Abraham stood motionless, watching them as they walked away, getting smaller and smaller in the distance, until they disappeared into the far fields. He mourned Hagar, and his sadness for Ishmael was heavy with self-disgust. He did not think he had it in him to act with such cruelty toward one of his own children.

Thus ended the series of Abraham-Sarah-Hagar-Ishmael-Isaac episodes, which had their own continuities of person and theme and which contained all the materials for a full typology of laughter, a four-part classification:

- *Delight*: Abraham's laughter on hearing that he will have a son is an instance of delight in existence itself. It is pleasure in the essential hospitality of the world, the security of one's place in it—a sense that all is essentially well. It is also Sarah's *second* laugh. This second laugh has a quality of amends-making, as if to say, "I once laughed in disbelief; my former disbelief is now itself the object of laughter." Nothing is safe from being made ridiculous, not even oneself, to oneself.[37]

- *Contention*: Sarah's laughter on hearing that she will have a son, the first laughter, has an adversarial quality. It is an engagement with a proposition, after a preliminary judgment of it has been made. It is thoughtful; it is companion to other, temperate registers of expression; it is impersonal; it is not self-important, self-aggrandizing. Sarah's laugh, writes Jeremy Dauber, is a laugh of irony. She "knows the way the world works, and she's mocking her foolish husband for his fantastic beliefs."[38] This is a little unnuanced and overlooks the laugh's self-critical aspect, but still, Dauber is essentially correct. The laughter of contention makes use of many of humor's modalities: the skeptical,[39] the ironic, the mocking, the satiric.

- *Disrespect*: It is a disrespect toward truth-tellers; it is *also* a disrespect toward folly. It is a leveler, the instrument of the resentful, the envious, *and* of the egalitarian, the democrat. It is a neutralizer, blunting the challenge of everything that is new, unusual, unconventional; it is *also* a provocation, a dismissal of everything that is stale, standard, conventional. It is a defense against truth *and* error. It is Hagar's laughter, the laughter at Abraham's and Sarah's expense; it is Abraham's own mockery of idolaters, which makes of idolatry itself nothing but an affair of foolishness.[40]

• *Hatred*: Ishmael's laughter is informed by a deep animus, driven by envy. It expresses a defensive, reactive contempt, one that reveals vulnerability, insecurity. It is bad laughter, aggressive, sour, malicious, cruel.

There are complications, of course. Instances of these complications are strong in Jewish history.

There is the humor of contention, turned inward. Return to Sarah's laughter in the tent. She laughs at the memory of menstruation: a womanly chuckle, the bodily knowledge that only a woman can have. She laughs too at a time of hope, not for children but for her marriage. It is sad laughter, the news of a child confirming that she has forever lost her vocation as Abraham's partner. And last, it is a self-reproaching laughter. Sarah laughs at herself for once taking on trust everything that her husband had told her and had asked of her.

There are humorous responses to hatred, an asymmetrical laughter of disrespect. We are an object of disdain, of mockery and scorn, of derision to our neighbors, laments the Psalmist (44:14).[41] They taunt and insult us. To this cruel sport,[41] this "Jew-baiting" (as it was once termed), Jews often respond with jokes at the expense of their tormentors. The jokes display a mirthless delight in human stupidity; the humor has a serrated edge.[42] "Did you hear? The Jews sank the *Titanic*." "The Jews? I thought it was an iceberg." "Iceberg, Goldberg, Rosenberg, they're all the same."[43] This is not Abraham's instinct, of course. The humorous response to persecution is a phenomenon of modern times. Hillel Halkin dates its arrival to Yiddish literature in the second half of the nineteenth century.[44]

It is here, with this complication, that we touch a counter-response, the very opposite of anti-antisemitic humor. Instead, there are sentiments of self-reproach, even self-condemnation, the locating of the cause of Jewish suffering in Jewish actions. Not humor directed against our enemies, then, but blame directed against ourselves. What they do to us is in consequence of what we did to them. Call this the "Esau's tears" theory of antisemitism.[45] (Esau weeps bitter tears when deprived of his father's blessing by his deceitful brother, Jacob.) It is always available to Jews as an explanation of their suffering, but it is especially favored in times heavy with persecution and oppression.

A story about Abraham inaugurated this thinking. It is obscure and unverified. I imagine it to be spoken of by later generations of Abraham's family and then adopted as part of the ancestral knowledge of the Jewish nation. Like so much else in Abraham's life, it is not incorporated in the authoritative Torah, save for a small bit of genealogy: "Timna was a concubine to Eliphaz, son of Esau, and she bore Amalek to Eliphaz" (Gen. 36:12).

Timna was the sister of Lotan, one of Esau's chiefs, and therefore the daughter of royalty. She sought to convert and join Abraham's household. She declared, "Better for me to be a handmaiden to this nation [Israel] and not a noblewoman of that nation [the chiefs of Esau]." Abraham, Isaac, and Jacob would not accept her. So she became instead the concubine of Eliphaz, one of Esau's sons. This union produced Amalek, who would cause Israel to suffer.[46]

The rabbis assert that Timna's willingness to surrender her status of noblewoman attests to her pure intent to convert (Sanhedrin 99b). The patriarchs should have welcomed her; instead, they rejected her. Why were the Jewish people punished by suffering at the hand of Amalek? The offense to Timna was avenged by Amalek and continues to be avenged by Amalekites.

The Timna story is the binary opposite of the laughter stories. It is a moral fantasy of responsibility and is at the opposite end of the spectrum of explanations for Jewish suffering, a conspiracist fantasy of culpability. At one end, the dark humor, which sees clearly the depravity and stupidity of antisemitism; at the other end, the hand-wringing assumption that Jewish suffering is self-authored.

Episode 13: Well

Abraham was still living in the vicinity of Gerar, in Beersheba. One day, Abimelech said to him, "You have God on your side. He is with you in all you do." He then made a demand of Abraham. "Swear to me, by God, that you will not deal falsely with me or with my son or grandson." And he added, "Show me and the land where you have lived as a stranger the same kindness I have shown you." He had Pikhol, the commander of his troops, with him. There was more than a hint that if Abraham did not swear as demanded, he would be handled roughly.

Abraham was taken aback by the demand's incivility. How, he puzzled, could Abimelech think to make such a demand, given his acknowledgment of Abraham's standing with God? And *such* a demand! It was insulting: it assumed that, absent the promise, false dealing was likely. It was pointless too: a person ready to deal falsely would also be a person who would lie about his intentions. A false-dealer would readily take an oath in vain; indeed, he would find an advantage in it. Still, Abraham confirmed, "I will swear." He acknowledged to himself that he had *already* dealt deceitfully with Abimelech. So perhaps the demand was indeed a fair one.

Abimelech made no further demands, and now it was Abraham's turn. He raised a grievance. "Your servants have taken a well that I dug." Abraham was glad to be able to offer this re-proach, given the oath just extracted from him. Abimelech re-sponded, "I do not know who has done this. Besides, this is the first I have heard of it." In response, Abraham brought gifts of cattle and sheep for Abimelech, and the two of them made a bargain. Abraham set aside seven ewes from the flock and said, "Accept these as my testimony that I dug the well." Abimelech and Pikhol left Abraham, who planted a tree and declared God's name.

It was not a happy episode. Abraham was put on the defen-sive, attempted a recovery, failed, and was returned to his de-fensive posture. He was left in a somewhat squashed, humbled state. He was reminded that he lived at the pleasure of another. In this context, calling out to God is to be understood as a ges-ture of self-consolation. "Whenever I am bullied, it is good for me to remember that God is with me, my benefactor, my pro-tector. He is on my side; he is with me in all that I do."

Wandering

What would Abraham make of these episodes, lived in twenty-five years of wandering? In a sentence, perhaps he would have concluded thus: "I have been delivered into my new life by a miracle, and I live it in the consciousness of God's promises, managing as best I can until their fulfillment." The implication is of a diversity of incident, the contingencies of a long life lived under conditions not of his own choosing and yet with a stabil-ity of essential purpose, a fixedness of stance.

And what sense can *we* make of the episodes? At first glance, perhaps nothing more than a "dizzying sequence of hopes and frustrations, blessings and curses, fulfillments and setbacks,"[47] although with Isaac's birth, there is some sense of newly stabi-lized momentum, of an upward direction of travel.

If we then analyze this trajectory, in its distinct moments

or episodes, two projects come into view. In their most realized respective forms, they are, first, the creation of the Jewish nation and, second, the perfection of the Jewish soul. All the episodes relate to one or both of these projects, each making an important, unduplicated contribution to them. The two converge on the perfecting of the Jewish people, *its* "soul." Neither project is free of difficulty; the prospects of reaching that point of ideal convergence are remote indeed.

The nation-formation drive, which operates with a certain intensity among Jews whatever the given circumstances of Jewish collective life, must contend with the enmities, alienations, divisions, and self-exclusions adumbrated in various episodes in Abraham's post-Haran life, the life related in this chapter.

By "enmities," I mean all those external forces engaged with the Jewish people in hostility, the category derived from the episodes concerning Egypt, the war of the kings, Sodom, Abimelech, and the Canaanites. These enmities were not of the same character, of course; and "enmity" is not to be muddled with "enemy."[48]

By "alienations," I mean all those rejections or subordinations of elements in the life of the people, the consequence of the continuing work of self-formation, the category derived from the episodes concerning Terah and Ishmael. Family members may be extruded; converts may not be eligible for certain positions; pretenders to inheritance may be disappointed.

By "divisions," I mean all those fissures in the integrity of the nation that lead to a weakening of it, the category derived from the quarrel with Lot. (It raises the question of coexistence between groups that constitute the people.) The episodes tend toward the defining of a specific collective, neither wholly an ethnic community nor wholly a community of faith. It has both genetic and ideological aspects, each existing in complex and diverse versions. "Family" and "converts" are the two building blocks of the nation. The formation of each, and the combining of the two, is the subject of several episodes. Generally, while "family" is subject to disintegrative, expelling pressure, "converts" accumulate, in an active movement of incorporation.

By "repudiations," I mean those members of the national community who leave it, in anger or other active repudiation of its practices, values, or beliefs, the category derived from the person who refuses circumcision, whose soul is thereby (we are told) cut off from his people.

We can identify across the episodes a certain weakening of given family ties and an accompanying emergence, or the promise of emergence, of a different kind of collective, character yet to be defined but in size and internal organization, in governance and connection with land, tending toward national expression, a mix of the genealogical and the covenantal. Abraham's descendants will say, "We are Hebrews" and "We belong to the Hebrew people," instead of, "We are of the family of Abraham the Hebrew."

The soul-perfection drive, as well as addressing all the usual distractions (so to speak), must negotiate relations both with the world and with God. The challenge in the first case is fear; the challenge in the second case is critical reason.

By "fear," I mean all those defensive orientations that are prompted by a sense of separateness, actively engaging with the world without reference to God and taking precautions on the assumption that we are alone, the category derived from all those episodes in which Abraham acts without reference to God, in order to protect himself against the risk of harm.

By "critical reason," I mean all those interrogative engagements prompted by a sense of the sovereignty of intellect (or prompted by either the memory of when it was affirmed or its practice by others), the category derived from all those episodes in which Abraham questions, expressly or by implication, God's actions.

And against these challenges, there is the bond between

God and Abraham, which is the destination of this soul-forming. Thomas Mann gave it a matchless description. It combines openness *to* God and absorption *in* God. There is Abraham's full openness to God's mighty qualities, and to God Himself, experienced in His objectivity, His exteriority to Abraham. And at the same time, these qualities are in him and of him as well. The power of Abraham's soul is at moments scarcely to be distinguished from God's own powers; it consciously interpenetrates and fuses with them.[49]

We can venture this thesis: Jewish existence in its negative mode, that is, in the forces it engenders or attracts that are precisely *destructive* of its existence, was given its first expression in episodes in Abraham's life and thereafter has been conditioned by just those episodes. There has been nothing radically *new* since then—only variations and versions. Jewish life continues to be lived in the face of enmity, of alienation, of division, of repudiation. And Abraham himself?

In the perspective of nation-formation, Abraham is subordinate to God but governs His community. He has the burden of subservience but the consolation of mastery.

Abraham inherits the three categories: (a) family members; (b) friends, colleagues, and so on; (c) fellow citizens, members of Ur. He creates a fourth category, a composite of (a)–(c), the "elective national family." The object of the Hebrew Scriptures supports choosing life in a collective that it names Israel.[50] It is a countercommunity, because it undoes, stands against, all notions of community constituted by blood. It is thus particularist but nonexclusivist and inaugurated by the covenant of circumcision.

(In the Jewish tradition, circumcision is the eighth of God's commands and the first limited to one group alone. The seven commands given to Noah, "the Noahide laws," are universally binding. They include laws against bloodshed, theft, and blasphemy.)

In the perspective of soul-perfection, though instructed by

God, Abraham continues to exercise his critical reason and thus has the unrelieved burden of reconciling the one with the other. ("Instruction" by God comprises *both* commands *and* promises; the "exercise" of critical reason comprises *both* hypothesizing *and* questioning.) He has to negotiate in his own person precisely those two challenges, fear and critical reasoning.

This soul-perfecting is an even more arduous undertaking than nation-formation—except nation-formation cannot be realized without soul-perfection. In contrast to Plato's *Republic*, where the construction of a polity is but an extended metaphor for the perfecting of the soul (369a), in the Jewish understanding, each has its own integrity, its own autonomy, its own grounding.

Soul-perfecting and nation-forming meet in the figure of the convert. Abraham is himself a convert; he converts from Ur's conformity of spirit, a slavishness.[51] His first activity, his most purposive activity, is conversion. Converts are to be esteemed. They follow in the path of Abraham, "who also left his father and kindred and inclined Godward."[52] Israel comprises those born to a Jewish mother and converts—that is, those who inherit their membership and those who acquire it, those who inherit their faith and those who find it through inquiry and reflection.

There is no essential difference between Jews and Gentiles; biological factors are insignificant. God's providence is not limited to Jews. To a convert, Maimonides wrote, "Abraham our Father taught the people, opened their minds, and revealed to them the true faith and unity of God; he brought many children under the wings of the Divine Presence. Ever since then whoever adopts Judaism is counted among the disciples of Abraham our Father. Abraham is *your* father."[53]

Abraham has made good progress in each of his two projects. The thirteen episodes confirm Abimelech's judgment: God is on Abraham's side. His story could end here; Isaac's story could begin.[54] Instead, something happens that takes Abraham by surprise and throws everything into doubt.

4

Abraham 2's Crisis

Time has passed without further event. Abraham reflects on his journeys, from Ur to Haran, and then from Haran to Canaan; from Chaldean sage to dissenting, critical thinker, and then man of God; from a culturally consecrated, thronged heaven to an abstract conception of a possible God and then to a powerful, personal God, heavy in Abraham's life. He considers himself blessed and thinks hardly at all of the price it has exacted in family disintegration (father, wife, brother, nephew, elder son). Were he now to compose a spiritual autobiography, it would be all upward ascent, from darkness to light, from ignorance to knowledge, from a loneliness endured in every register to a life saturated in divine presence, an experience of continuous elevation and joy.

Crisis

Abraham is exultant. He has a sense of trials undertaken and passed—not just passed but *dispatched*. He has been tested in battle. He has been tested in dispute. He has secured great wealth. He has every reason to think well of himself. God is of the greatest moment to Abraham. He lives for his visions; they affirm him to be God's friend. Their openness to each other is a constant, flowing channel. He wants no one but God; he needs no one but God. And yet, two anxieties twist in his mind, insinuating themselves, disturbing the lofty equilibrium of his spirit. One is an anxiety about God; the other, an anxiety about Sarah. The two anxieties are not of the same order.

As to God, the anxiety is that his faith may not be perfect, not perfect to his standard of perfection. It is not that he doubts: "doubt" is the name for the torment of those later generations who do not know God as Abraham does. Quite the reverse— his anxiety is that he finds his complete certainty of God's continuous presence a little suffocating. It permits no room to any play of intelligence, to any freedom of inquiry, to the joy of questioning, of experimenting, of daydreaming. He finds that his thoughts are no longer his own, and his actions, subject to a meticulous supervision. He catches himself wistful about that free creativity of intellectual enterprise in Ur, a form of life pulsing with such happy intensity. And then he recalls that unearthly moment when he was required to slaughter animals, following a sequence that had the form of a ritual but that was never to be repeated. It followed his challenge to God. Would another challenge encourage God to command the performance of some further puzzling act?

As to Sarah, the anxiety is that the woman with whom he was once so closely aligned, and from whom he is now so utterly alienated, is still his wife, with a wife's claims on him. How to meet those claims, when Sarah has lost all distinctness for him? He oscillates between placating her and disregarding her. She exists mostly as the representative of that problematical collectivity in his life, "my family," which makes its own claims on him (care for me, rescue me, don't drive me away, etc.). Do they not understand that for Abraham, "family," both as a given group of persons (wife, sons, nephew, etc.) and a set of values (ties of affection, duties to protect and nurture), has been demoted—indeed, twice over—and now barely figures in the ordering of what matters? The first demotion, in God's favor, subordinates them to divine demands; the second demotion, in the nation's favor, subordinates them to divine promises. He has little by little been detaching himself from human fellowship.[1]

Call

And then one evening, keeping his own company, a vision comes to Abraham. God calls him, making an irresistible demand for his attention. "Abraham!" A peremptory mode of address. He responds, speaking aloud, alone in his tent, "Here I am." It is a strong statement of preparedness, not "Over here!" but "Ready!"[2] Taut, motionless, waiting. A demand is coming, not a promise. But what, precisely? He has an instinct that it will be related to that first command, that he should leave his father. What now?

The command is a straightforward one, to be performed straightaway. There is no room for doubt. Abraham must take his son, his only son, the one whom he loves, the one with whom Abraham's own life is bound,[3] Isaac, and travel to the land of Moriah. There, on a mountain that God will tell him, Abraham must sacrifice Isaac as a burnt offering. God says, "Take him, I beg of you." Is Abraham thunderstruck, astonished, by this command? Does it paralyze him? No. He gives it an immediate, wholehearted assent.

Abraham does not consider, "Should I comply with the command?" It would be intolerable, indeed, were he to pause to think and only *then* assent, in the exercise of his autonomy, his judgment, his independent power of reasoning. He must foreswear thinking in this strong sense, in the extremity of his subordination to God—a foreswearing that, he grasps, is part of the point of the command. Of course he will do as God directs. The entreaty, "I beg of you," is a mere civility, Abraham judges. He no more hesitates here than he did in Haran, when commanded to leave the city, in violation of his filial duties. Just as he did not then *choose* between deserting his father and delaying his departure, so he does not *choose* between killing his son and refusing God's command. He recalls Abimelech's aggrieved "You have God on your side. He is with you in all you do," hearing it now as reassurance.

And thus settled, undisturbed by resistances or doubts, Abraham can relax into an exploration of the demand's principal terms. *Which* son, *what* love, *how* sacrifice?

Which son? He ponders his relations with his two sons. A privileging of the younger son is affirmed in the formulation of the command. Reading backward, Isaac is the son Abraham loves, his only son. Ishmael is unloved and not a son—not in the sense that *Isaac* is a son. "Is this what I believe?" Abraham asks himself. "Is the destructive character of my favoritism revealed? Destructive not only of the less favored but of the favored one too? And what drives this favoritism? I did not want a child until I was told I would have one; I did not petition God for a child, as I petitioned Him in the furnace for my life. Isaac came into the world not for his own sake but to contribute to the national project, itself an enterprise I did not myself conceive."

What love? "Love" puzzles Abraham. It is on the wrong side of many loyalties. It is particular, not universal; it is affective, not intellectual, an affair of the heart, not the head. (Oh these binarisms, beloved of philosophers for millennia!) Abraham understands loving-kindness, of course. It is bestowed on all with whom one comes into contact; it is a general orienta-

tion, a standard benevolence, one that leaves its bestower undisturbed. Loving-kindness is detachment in its most benign
aspect. It does not mark out any one person as more deserving
of it than any other; the world teems with candidates for Abraham's loving-kindness. So, that is difficult enough. But it gets
worse. "Love" means too many things; it governs too many
orders of attachment. What does love of God have to do with
love of wife, love of children, love of nation? It is *so* particular
that it lacks determinate meaning; it is not a fit subject for
thought.[4] If the experience of love distracts from thinking, the
concept of it bewilders thought. Its meanings are too elusive,
its singularities too diverse, its status too obscure, its claims to
priority too insistent.

   How sacrifice? Abraham has an idea of what sacrifice as a
practice might look like. The victim would be a member of his
community, its representative, though not essential to its functioning; the killing would assure the community's continued
well-being; the offering would be to a god or gods and have pro-
pitiatory and amends-making iterations; it would follow a pre-
scribed ritual, one in which the community would participate; it
would be performed at regular intervals.[5] What God has commanded of Abraham has *none* of these features, and so far from
securing a desired object, it *defeats* one—indeed, *the* object, di-
vinely given, of nation-formation. In the most practical of terms,
Abraham does not know what is required of him. What are the
mechanics? He has not performed any sacrifice. Yes—in Ur, servants were killed to accompany just-deceased monarchs in the
underworld. Is Isaac to be drugged and then garroted, as they
were? And yes—traveling through Canaan, he has caught talk of
murderous ceremonies, dark idolatries of regional deities. Utter
horror: officiants besmeared with blood, parents' tears, children's wailings.[6] Is this what God wants? Must he improvise?
The earlier occasion, when he cut up animals and laid them
out—that was *not* a sacrifice, he is sure of it.

And what, then, of God's purpose? It is not the settling of the debt incurred in the furnace; the demand is not that he return to God his future in his other self, his son.[7] Nor is it to introduce the first instance of a ritual, something that the promised nation will have to perform in its practices of worship. Abraham entertains neither one of these possibilities. The purpose is mysterious, then. How could it *not* be, given that the sacrifice of Isaac means not just the loss of his son but also the revocation of God's promises to him?

The thought occurs to him, however: "Did I press God too hard on Sodom? Though I spoke humbly, styling myself a creature no more than dust and ashes, my challenge to Him was unmistakable: 'Shall not the Judge of all the Earth do right?' Perhaps God tests me now, as I then tested Him. I put Him on the defensive, and He now attacks back, very hard indeed." Is this not the subtext of God's command?

The thought develops. "Was my challenge proof that I have not fully, unconditionally, given up my Ur-existence? Did that first version of me truly die in the furnace, as it should have? Did my independence of mind stage a return? It is true, those exchanges with God were intoxicating to me. They brought to my mind—dare I acknowledge this?—my exchanges with Nimrod. I was as fearless before the Lord of the Universe as I was before the ruler of Ur." The thought completes itself. "I have brought this test on my own head; indeed it is a test that I myself should have set for myself; by sacrificing my son, I sacrifice myself or that earlier, self-aggrandizing, fearless version of myself. My surrender to God, my openness to Him, has not been complete. More is demanded of me; I will prove that I am equal to the demand."

It is a momentary illumination. And then his mind darkens again. "I fool myself. Reason cannot undo itself. I cannot argue myself out of argument. I am affirming my Ur-self in the very attempt to extinguish it. I am at an impasse. I know what I must

ABRAHAM

do. I do not know why I must do it. I know that this must not weaken my resolve. This is as far as I can think."

Preparation

In Ur, Abraham reached his provisional conclusions about God by the application of his new method of critical reason. Decades later, Abraham recast this moment as a divine revelation. He didn't discover God; God disclosed Himself to Abraham. God was not some loiterer at the end of a sequence of reasoning. *He* was the active one, illuminating Abraham's mind with divine light. Or so Abraham told himself, in a characterization indispensable to his new conception of himself, repressing what he once was.

He never denied to himself, however, that it was to Sarah that he then went. She was his first interlocutor, the first audience to his witnessing. For sure, he did not go to her as a partner might, with eagerness, in the certain knowledge that his joy would be hers. His purpose was a lesser one, to test out the reception he might receive. Her excitement was gratifying, though. And surprising. That it did not give him the reassurance he sought then became of no consequence. True, thinking as he did, she could not demonstrate how people who did *not* think as he did might respond to his ideas. No matter! Her response introduced the possibility of something joint between them, some common cause that might unite them.

But here, with *this* revelation, God has not just given a command; he has thereby disclosed a further aspect of Himself, something that Sarah will receive as bewilderingly, incomprehensibly cruel. This is something that Abraham therefore cannot share with her. She would forbid it. If he persisted, she would raise the alarm. He could not rely on the members of his household taking his side. Eliezer, perhaps. But the others? They had seen him defer to Sarah in the matter of Hagar and Ishmael. Why should they cross her now, even were Abraham to demand their support? And if they *did* side with him, at the extreme, would she not kill Abraham sooner than let him kill Isaac? And would she, Abraham wonders, be wrong to do so?

So how to get Isaac away from the encampment without raising her suspicion? Abraham considers various possibilities. He could lie to Sarah, of course. At breakfast, he could say to her, "Isaac has grown up without instruction. There is a place far from here where teachers may be found. I will take him there."[8] He rehearses his words to himself. But no—he could not maintain the pretense. There would be questions; he would have to improvise. Sarah would sense it; she would see through him. So what else could he say? He is taking Isaac on a stroll, "back soon"? They are going on a longer journey, one without purpose? Absurd ruses. How could he explain the urgency? How could he explain the need for altar wood?

It is clear to him that he must leave without offering any explanation. And that means without Sarah's knowledge. He reasons with himself, taking both sides. "I must with haste go from hence." "Why then I kill my wife. This unkindness will be deadly to her. If she has to endure my departure, death's the word." "I must be gone. Under a compelling occasion, let women die. It were pity to cast them away for nothing, though between them and a great cause, they should be esteemed nothing."[9] But if he sets her "mother-right" at naught, does he affirm without limitation his "father-right"?[10] No. He is not among those fathers who "keep alive the old red flame of fatherhood, fatherhood that has life-and-death authority over children, a great natural power," to be held until their sons "arrive at manhood and become themselves centres of the same power, continuing the same male mystery as men."[11] No—Abraham is not that kind of father. He will sacrifice Isaac not as a right but as a duty. Submission to God requires Abraham to act in accordance with His will and *therefore* (for Abraham, it is just a matter of logic) to sacrifice Isaac.

All that remains is for him to plan a departure that doesn't risk Sarah's detection and a journey without risk of Sarah catching up with them. It is one and the same plan. They will leave very early, well before she rises, and that will ensure that the distance they cover will put them beyond her reach when she discovers they have gone. He wants to leave very early anyway. He is impatient to fulfill God's will.

Journey

Abraham rises the following morning. He splits the wood for the altar, and he saddles his donkey. Though he is taking two attendants on the journey, Ishmael and Eliezer, he asks neither for any help. He will chop the wood; he will attend to the donkey. The responsibility, all of it, will be his and his alone. He wants no conspirators. The command was to him alone; its performance will be his alone.

The journey is hard. The pace is slow. Abraham sits astride the donkey; the others walk, carrying the wood. Nothing is said between the travelers for three days, not even a word. The silence is not companionable. No thought passes through Abraham's mind. The young men take his lead, wait for his direction. Ishmael ponders, "What is my purpose on this journey?" Isaac avoids him. If he walks on one side of the donkey, Isaac ensures that he walks on the other side. The simple Eliezer, who exists to serve, is simply happy to be in his master's presence.

Arrival

They reach the foot of the mountain—more a steep, craggy hill, the summit dimly visible. Abraham tells the attendants that he and Isaac will make their way up to the top and there prostrate themselves in worship. Materials for sacrifice about him, he says nothing about a sacrifice. The men exchange hard glances and turn back to him. Abraham continues, "And then, we will make our descent, returning to the two of you." These are lies, but no matter. Abraham knows the duty of truth-telling is suspended in the execution of God's command. So Eliezer and Ishmael wait, and Abraham and Isaac begin their ascent. They carry a knife, a flaming torch, rope, and plenty of wood and kindling material. Isaac has the wood, rough planks, long and short, heavy in his arms; Abraham holds the knife and the torch together in one hand, the torch level with his head but away from his face.

Trudging up the mountain, which has no path, father and son in heavy silence, in the noonday, airless heat, Abraham's gaze is fixed on the peak. Just before they reach it, Isaac speaks, his voice jarring, unwelcome to Abraham. "Father?" "Here I am, my son"—not breaking his step, treading carefully. "Haven't we forgotten something?" Light, almost glib. Fathers! Abraham doesn't look up. "God will show the lamb for a burnt offering, my son." The answer is equivocal. He means, "You, my son, are the lamb," but he could mean, "My son, we will find our lamb up there, on the mountain top." Abraham's tone is flat, so there's room for interpretation. He is worried that Isaac might bolt if he is told the truth. He was untroubled by his lie to Eliezer and Ishmael, but a scruple holds him back from a full-blown lie to Isaac. While the scruple mitigates nothing and is of no benefit to Isaac, it indicates the smallest of anxieties on Abraham's part, at this eleventh-hour moment.

They reach the summit—a scrubby, flattish surface, stones and pebbles, brambles and weeds, grit underfoot. Abraham begins to erect his makeshift altar, a low, table-like structure made of wood and stones. Isaac looks around him. No lamb. He is puzzled. And then he stops being puzzled. "My father is going to kill me! I am the sacrifice!" He is seized by an overpowering fear and a violent trembling. He asks again, "Where is the sacrifice?" And only then does Abraham respond, "It is you."[12]

The question is, At this moment, expanded to eternity, from when Abraham approaches Isaac to bind him until the moment when he is bound and cannot unbind himself, what does Isaac do? Does he submit, or does he struggle? He does both. He is caught between despair and rage, resignation and resistance. He is silent and he shouts. He weeps and he reasons. "What of your love for me? What of God's promise?" Abandoning hope for himself, he pleads for his mother. "Keep the facts of my death from her. Do not tell her about what you did. The deed will be unbearable to her. She will kill herself."[13]

Isaac goes limp. He is barely standing. Abraham holds him up and ties his arms behind his back. He leads him to the altar and gestures to Isaac to lie across it, left side down. Isaac complies, head flat on the surface, legs bent at the knees, the body the same length as the altar. Abraham then throws more rope, longer this time, across Isaac's chest, drawing a rope end under the altar and tying the ends together, the knot pulled tight, cutting into the body. Isaac cannot move. Abraham stands over him, now improvising. He imagines, "What I do will define the ritual to come." He has no mind to his son. He raises his hand, knife firm in his grip. "I must bring it down on the neck. Don't twist your head, Isaac."

Abraham hears his name, "Abraham!" Who is it? A second call: "Abraham!" The voice unsettles him. It is God's messenger, not God. "Why not God Himself?" he thinks. Panic. "Have I done something wrong? Why a messenger? Was I too slow?" "Here I am," he says, arm still raised, knife still in hand. The messenger continues, speaking in God's name. "Do not touch the young man. Do nothing to harm him. I know now that you fear God. You have not withheld Isaac from *Me*." Ah—it *is* God speaking. Relief but also puzzlement. "Fear"? It is not the obvious word. A thought to postpone.

His arm drops to his side. He lets the knife slip out of his grip and fall to the ground. He sets about untying Isaac, as instructed. He takes care now not to harm him—not scratch him, not bruise him. He throws the ropes off Isaac's chest and loosens the rope fastening his wrists. Isaac, eyes shut tight, twists his body left, drops his right leg onto the ground, and pushes himself off the altar, bringing his left foot down. He takes a few steps and then collapses, dazed. In *such* pain; it cannot be borne.

Abraham looks up from the altar and sees a ram. It is trapped in a thicket, twisting its head in tired frenzy, snorting, panting. Irrelevantly, he decides to offer it to God as a sacrifice, but not because he has been commanded to make the sacrifice—he has not. Instead, he thinks, "I *told* Isaac that God would provide a lamb. Here it is—or close enough, anyway. Better—it is an adult male, probably a father. Let me act on my prediction and thereby make it a truthful one."

He is also troubled that while the command to sacrifice Isaac was given by God Himself, the command to desist was delivered by a mere messenger. An implication in this delegation of God's displeasure? It cannot be. But he cannot push away the fear that it *might* be, or if not that, if not displeasure, then perhaps a certain distancing on God's part from Abraham. The conviction that he *must* sacrifice this animal, straightaway, grips him. It would be a most compelling act of ingratiation toward both Isaac ("I told you the truth") and toward God ("not only do I perform your commands, but I go beyond them").

He binds the ram while it is still trapped, using the same ropes that held down Isaac. Traces of his blood spot its fibers. He first secures the front legs, then the rear legs, and then he ties together the two sets of knotted rope with a further rope, so that the ram is fully trussed. He pushes his hands under the ram's body and heaves the beast upward and forward, stepping-stumbling, knees giving way, toward the altar top. The ram crashes down on it hard. Abraham pulls his arms free, straightens up, and steps away. The sun is high in the sky; the ram is writhing, stinking, moaning. Isaac, a few feet away, is still slumped on the ground, shaking, dazed, rope cuts on arms and ankles, dirty.

Abraham, frantic, deliberate, picks up the knife, gripping it tight, palm and fingers slippery with sweat. He stabs down hard on the ram's neck, too hard. Fountains of blood. The knife is deep in the altar wood. With a trembling, bloody hand, Abraham draws it out. His fingers momentarily sink into the neck wound. Flies buzz in his eyes, settling on the carcass. He makes a flame, setting alight the kindling rags piled under the altar. Soon it is burning. Smoke, crackling flesh, scorching heat.

Minutes elapse. Cinders stirring, blackened bones, scraps of charred flesh. Isaac has stopped shaking. He stares hard at his father; Abraham will not look at him. "Just go! Please go!" Abraham is desperate for Isaac to remove himself from the scene. He moves around the site, busying himself some more, making tasks for himself, barely able to stand. Isaac stays and stays and stays. His presence weighs heavily on Abraham, breathlessly wandering but making sure that he keeps his back to his son. The lightest of footfalls and then silence. Isaac has gone.

"What to do now? What do I do now?" All sense of agency evacuated, a hollowed-out figure, Abraham stands, without the resolve, the self-possession, to take a single step. He wonders, "Who will tell me when to blink? With whose authority am I breathing? I have done everything asked of me. Am I to resume making my own decisions?" Of all improbable things, it comes into his mind, "I will name this place. I will name it 'God has seen.' No. 'God sees.' No. 'God will see.' Yes—'God will see.'" "It is His mountain," he says aloud.

And then, a second messenger of God calls to him, once again speaking in God's name. "I have resolved, because you performed this deed . . ." Abraham thinks, "What deed? *Did* I kill Isaac?" ". . . and did not withhold your only son, I will greatly bless you and make your descendants as numerous as the stars of the sky and like the sand of the seashore. Your descendants will possess the gate of their enemies. Through your children, all the nations of the world will be blessed. All this, because you heeded My voice." It is the last time Abraham will hear God's voice.

Departure

Abraham makes a slow descent. His mind reverts to the word "fear." Other words come to mind: "obey," "love."

"Obey" falls short, however. He thinks, the messenger could have said, "I now know you will *obey* God." Perhaps that would not have been the right word, because while one obeys specific commands, one lives in a state, a condition, of fear. "I live in a state of fear," Abraham says to himself. It is true. A state of constant fear. A fear that kills.

And "love" misstates the relation. The angel could not have said, "I now know you love God." Love can no more coexist with fear than it can be commanded. Abraham recalls the language of God's command, "the one you love." Love of one's child gives way to fear of God.

But if "fear" is indeed the right word, Abraham continues, in what sense of the word, when applied to God? Three possible senses jostle in his mind: "God-fearing," "awed," and "intimidated." Which fits? He reviews each one: "'God-fearing' as in my exchanges with Abimelech? Yet no 'God-fearing' person would kill his own child, just as no God-fearing people would take a man's wife from him and kill the man. 'Awed,' yes. But the God I now fear is not the God I thought I knew, and the fear itself has a different quality to it. 'Intimidated'? Yes, too. In the sense of a frightened, coerced condition of ready compliance with demands, however unconscionable they might be. But how can that be a relation with God?" Yes, he fears God. And he fears that some further demand will be made of him, something even crueler than this one, which he will once again agree to perform. It is enough to make him mad.

Unsettled by this line of thinking, he goes to the promise—in particular, to "enemies." This is a new word. "God has given me better news of my descendants than he gave to me in an earlier vision. Then, I was told that they would be enslaved and oppressed for four hundred years in a land not their own. But now, I am told that they will enjoy great triumphs. I understand the meaning of this, I think. My descendants will have dominion over their enemies because I have placed myself under God's dominion. I have submitted to Him; their enemies will submit to them. Why is God telling me this? Isn't my fear of Him its own reward? An even more radical worry: What is an enemy? A person who causes one to suffer, who robs one of one's possessions, who takes one's life and the life of one's child—" Abraham stops short. He lacks the resources to think further.

At the foot of the mountain now, he sees the dutiful Ishmael and Eliezer and makes his way toward them. He notices that Isaac is not with them. They do not ask him, "Where is your son?" "Perhaps," Abraham thinks, "they saw him when he came down. Perhaps they know what happened up there and know too that he will not be returning with us." He turns away and walks a few paces back toward the mountain, as if in re-enactment of the earlier ascent. But then he gestures to them, and they bring over the donkey to where he is standing. Abraham mounts the animal and, without a word, heads off toward Beersheba, the two men walking by his side.

When they get back, Abraham is told that Sarah has left for Hebron. He makes no attempt to join her. She had left the encampment as soon as she realized that he had taken Isaac. Days later, when she hears rumors of the transactions on Mt. Moriah, grief and rage overwhelm her. She has not protected her son, her only son, the one whom she loved. She faints and dies.[14] Abraham has no further exchanges with Isaac. They avoid contact with each other. When Abraham needs to communicate with him, he uses Eliezer as an intermediary. And God? Friend no more,[15] He withdraws from Abraham and does not appear to him again.

Harm

This episode does irreversible, noncompensable, unmitigated harm to Abraham, Isaac, and Sarah. Irreversible? There is no return to the status quo ante. Noncompensable? There is no substitute available for what has been lost. Unmitigated? For Isaac and Sarah, altogether nothing; for Abraham, promises only.

Begin with the harm to Abraham, harm that was self-authored. Is not this the seed of the harm—that it has a quality of the self-inflicted? Added to that, there are many distinct harms—a bewildering number of harms. We should enumerate them; they are so often disregarded. The harms are distributed across the episode. They can be clustered into three baskets of injury. There are the harms of the command. There are the harms of its execution. And there are the harms of its resolution.

In the first basket, there is the intrinsic violence of the command. There is the appetite for violence that it discloses on God's part, unassimilable to any justice-executing action. There is the violence that it anticipates and thereby evokes in the foretelling. There is the violence to Abraham's sense that the cosmos makes sense: it returns him to his earliest understandings, the inherited sense of the world as a mysterious, dangerous place, thronged with malevolent gods and demons, intent on harm. Abraham reflects with bitterness, "God, my great friend? A delusion."[16]

In the second basket, there is the damage to his expectation of God's promises being fulfilled—not remedied by the averted sacrifice, because what God can do once He can do again. There is the damage to his sense of himself as a person of loving-kindness, a person of moral integrity; it cannot survive the deceptions he practices, not to mention his readiness to kill Isaac. And there is the deranging disorientation he experiences in the actions of almost-sacrifice and sacrifice.

In the third basket, there is the damage to his relationship with his son. Abraham would no longer even know how to answer the question, *Do* you have a relationship with Isaac? There is the death blow to his relationship with his wife—so utterly at an end that even her death did not *further* alienate her from him. And then there is the harm to Abraham of God's withdrawal, of His new unintelligibility, of a new kind of fear of Him, a fear without trust. Abraham no longer understands what he means when he says "God." All he knows now is that his ways are not God's ways, nor are his thoughts God's thoughts.[17]

(The injury to Abraham is passed on to successive generations. After the *Akedah*, God will astonish by His deeds and perplex by His absences. As the generations pass, there is less astonishment but more perplexity. The period of astonishment? Moses's adult life. The period of perplexity? Jewish history thereafter, in its entirety.)

And harm to Isaac? It should not be underestimated, still less dismissed. It was of a radical character and unqualified by any reward. (No placating promises are made to *him* after the event.) We think only of violence averted, of the arm suspended, the clenched knife, the blow averted. We do not, even in that very image, see the young man, delirious with fear, bound with rough ropes, eyes shut tight, despairing. Whatever miracle took place was too late. Isaac was withheld from sacrifice; he was not spared injury.[18]

It was too late to erase the deception. "No one," wrote Lionel Trilling, "sets a higher value on truth than a boy. Truth is the whole of a boy's conscious demand upon the world of adults. He is likely to believe that the adult world is in a conspiracy to lie to him, and it is this belief, by no means unfounded, that arouses boys to their moral sensitivity, their everlasting concern with justice, which they call fairness. At the same time it often makes them skillful and profound liars in their own defense, yet they do not tell the ultimate lie of adults: They do not lie to themselves."[19] Isaac is a "boy" in this sense.

It was too late to erase the jeopardy. Consider this thought experiment: A man is given a pistol and locked in a room with his son. Kill him and walk out free; refuse to kill him, and you yourself will be killed. The man pulls the trigger. Click. The chamber is empty. It was "only" a test. But the relationship with the son is over. The father can never go back to the moment before the decision to pull the trigger. He is a broken man; the son is broken; the relationship is broken. The readiness was all.

It was too late to retrieve the love. Abraham teaches Isaac an unforgettable lesson: "My love is a thing to be surrendered in the face of a fear. I love you, but I fear God more. A second command, to the same effect? Of course—I would submit as before." Who would want to live in a world in which one's father is one's enemy? And so, Isaac has to make an interpretation of what happened on Mt. Moriah. Did it demonstrate the limit of every father's love? Or did it demonstrate the limit of *his* father's love? The more tolerable interpretation has to be the first one. In the order of oppressive burdens, to know that it's *his* father, perhaps *alone* among fathers, who would surrender him up, must flatten a son more quickly, more completely. Isaac takes from Mt. Moriah an impoverished, even crass, understanding of what it is to be a father. He loves Esau because he loves the food Esau brings to him. His second son, Jacob, scorns him for this and deceives him in retaliation. "You do not love the person," Jacob thinks in silent reproach. "You love his utility. You *love* Esau no more than you love me."

It was too late to erase the self-knowledge. He is consumed by the thought that he had cooperated with Abraham in those last minutes, that he was a volunteer to the undertaking. A mortifying thought. "What kind of person does that make me?" The sense that he was a coward, that even in his death moment he ingratiated himself with Abraham ("tie the ropes tighter, father, lest I resist and thereby disobey you"—did he really say that?),[20] floods him with self-contempt. Or if not a coward, deluded. He despises himself. It was as if, confronted by his father's despotic power and the ruthlessness with which he exercised it (Freud, 4:256), unable to defend himself against this murderous attack, he chose to endorse it, with an enthusiasm even greater than his father's, a perversely excessive cooperation in the service of self-annihilation. "I do not have the strength to stand against him as enemy. I will stand alongside him as ally, not victim but coconspirator."

It was too late to erase the hatred. In addition, that is, to those typical motives for hatred inherent in the natural relationship of son to father (Freud, 19:88), he is given a further, personal one. It is not one he can acknowledge. Such is the reverence with which Abraham is regarded by all—that is, by all except his own family—that the smallest intimation of criticism, let alone animus, would expose him to a crushing opprobrium. And so the hatred boils inside him. As does indignation toward his admirers. The man revered for his hospitality, his acts of loving-kindness, was ready to kill his own son! The question will not leave him alone: "Why does nobody but me see the absurdity? And such cruelty, to make me carry the wood that would burn me!"

Forever marked by trauma, Isaac remains bound by Abraham. His behavior is conditioned by the binding; he cannot unbind himself. Hence there is an irreversible depletion of life energy, of vitality. He never finds peace—only its counterfeit, peaceful sloth.[21] His actions are muffled and vague; he attempts no experiments, nor does he create any new forms; he gives the impression of being a nonentity.[22] He repeats his father's dealings with Abimelech, devising the same subterfuge, offering the same excuse when it is discovered. He replicates his father's embrace of the principle of fear but expands it into a general orientation. When he discovers that Jacob has impersonated his brother, Esau, he "trembles violently"; Jacob swears in the name of "the Fear of Isaac." This "fear," writes Adin Steinsaltz, was the mood of Isaac's life. It captured him at the time of the *Akedah*, the sign of his instrumentality. Isaac had to remain forever bound on the altar.[23]

And harm to Sarah? It was many things over a protracted period, and then it was one immense thing. Her state in the moment before the *Akedah* was one of sunken, demoralized misery. She was also in a state of moral collapse. She was burdened by a sense of waste and of the abuse of her energy and courage. She did not want to be excluded from Abraham's own trials of courage. She was not a woman who feared alarming or offending men. Her reliance on Abraham was material; it lacked all morbid dependency. She did not overrate him; she ascribed to him no godlike role in her life. Her center of gravity was in herself, not others; her own wishes counted for her, not just the wishes of others; she did not overvalue love—she did not suppose that it could solve all problems. There was no trace of the neurotic in her makeup.[24]

By now, she has experienced in full the disillusionments of marriage.[25] That tender and mutual attachment, which is marriage's promise,[26] had not been met. It was founded on a misunderstanding. She had taken that turning point in her life, the discovery of the free, critical use of reason, to be of the same character and content as Abraham's. They had "turned," at the same time, together, and toward each other—so she had once thought. But it was not so, and accompanying, as a dismal partner, the deterioration in their married life was this knowledge of that original misunderstanding. She understood now that Abraham could not say to her, without essential dishonesty, that love for her was one of the two decisive elements in the turning point in his own life,[27] even if merely coincident in time with the second element, the discovery of critical reasoning and of God. It was always only these last two, and then in Haran, it was just the last one. Her emotional register passed between love and hate; Abraham's, between preoccupation and indifference. Abraham and Sarah were fully alienated from each other.

She caused herself great distress by proposing to Abraham that he take up with Hagar.[28] It was an act of agency consequent on an absence of agency. In violation of her command of expulsion, Abraham allowed Ishmael back, behind her back. Isolated from Abraham, she also found herself isolated from Isaac. There was the promise, on Isaac's birth, of solace. But it had not been realized. All her speeches are about children. She speaks to make the proposal to Abraham that he take Hagar; she speaks to urge Abraham to throw out Hagar; she speaks to express doubt about her ability to conceive; and she speaks to remark on the reception she anticipates to Isaac's birth and then to urge Abraham to throw out Ishmael.

That equality enjoyed by Abraham and Sarah in Haran, the two engaged together in the making of souls, disappeared on their travels. Her will became weaker; it ceased to act on the world. Her conflict with Hagar was itself indicative of a certain collapse of authority. Her complex, unappealing responses to this collapse, made across the years of her post-Haran life, were driven by envy and paranoia.

The envy? Of so many in her circle. Throughout, envy of Abraham, of course, but with an oppressive regret too. "He has God. He has his projects. I have neither God nor projects." And envy of Hagar. Sarah had once rejoiced in a sense of her sexlessness, until she saw the pleasure Abraham took in Hagar. Hagar's body became inescapable for Sarah. Then, in that early time of pregnancy, a thought formed. "She has a baby; I do not. She is intimate with my husband; I am not. So I will now deny to her what I do not have myself. I have nothing to lose by showing my vicious side to Abraham: he no longer loves me anyway." Sarah was then given further cause for envy. "God spoke to Hagar before He spoke to me: What did she do to merit this priority?" Sarah envied Ishmael too, in her identification with Isaac: "He is the elder son, and Isaac is his subordinate. I did love him, once. How could I not? This little boy, the fruit of my plan, if not my womb."

The paranoia? Toward Abraham: "His absence of care for me is an active ill will. I cannot trust him. He distances himself from me; he would discard me if he could. He does not care for me; I am a burden to him. He lavishes his attention on strangers; his sickly interest in them is a deliberate show of contempt for me. 'Look! The wishes of the merest passerby is of greater interest to me than any desire of yours.' That is Abraham's constant speech to me, expressed in his every action." As for Hagar and Ishmael, "They both laugh at me. I am nothing to them. They take their cue from Abraham. His disregard justifies their contempt. Hagar's status, Ishmael's very existence, are symbols of my worthlessness. These two are my open enemies; they conspire against me."

In the explanations that the envy and the paranoia offered for her suffering, they gave Sarah comfort. She had no cause ever again to be disappointed. But they also caused her to give up hope. They confirmed her isolation, her subordination, her worthlessness. "The promise is further evidence that I am the object of a universal ill will," she concluded. Hers was a laughter of the most mirthless kind: "I will take pleasure in the confirmation of the dark truth of my life." Sarah laughed alone—and as she heard her own laughter, she grieved. Her laughter was the playfulness of despair.[29]

And then—the *Akedah*. It cannot be considered without consideration being given to Sarah.[30] She could not have been tested as Abraham was tested. Had she been thus tested, she would have flatly refused the demand. She was Isaac's champion. That had become her vocation. Though she had weaned him, she had not surrendered him. The violence of the *Akedah* to Abraham was to his sense of the coherence of his *plural* loyalties (to God, to his son); the violence to Sarah was to her *sole* loyalty. The events of the *Akedah* took her beyond the limit of her paranoia. She died in the full knowledge of the failure of her life, broken-hearted, of course, but also broken-*minded*.

We must not forget Ishmael. Abraham is a father who wrecks his children's lives.[31] Ishmael has a certain robustness, a self-sufficiency. The horrible truth that his father had sent him away, thereby exposing him to mortal danger, does not sour his life, even though it limits it. He accompanies Abraham back from Moriah. When Abraham dies, he dutifully helps Isaac bury him.[32]

Postcrisis

Pose the question, How is Abraham to live creatively, beyond the *Akedah*? Only in a state of irony. This sole creative possibility is an impossibility, given Abraham's trajectory. Is this a third Abraham, an Abraham 3, a Kierkegaardian Abraham who embraces irony?

A Third Abraham?

I take my understanding of irony from the American philosopher and psychoanalyst Jonathan Lear; he takes his understanding of irony from the Danish philosopher and theologian Søren Kierkegaard. Kierkegaard's fundamental, ironic question is, Among all Christians, is there a Christian? The question asks of a collective whether any of its members live up to the aspirations that purportedly characterize it. That is, among all who understand themselves as Christian, is there anyone who lives up to the requirements of Christian life?[33] This is shocking. Kierkegaard was a scandalous writer, and scandal trailed in his wake.

Abraham's question is more scandalous still. He asks, Regarding God, is there God? We can see that this is an impossible question. God is God, as He chooses, whatever He does. So Abraham then formulates a second question: Among Abrahams, is there an Abraham? Who is he now? He was a critical intellectual, with a watchmaker conception of God; he was then a man of faith, with a personal relation to a benevolent God, in whom he could repose trust. But now—what is he?

Abraham cannot find excellence in the *Akedah*—he cannot remain the second Abraham. That would be to condemn himself to a second idolatry, worshiping God in the wrong way, the God as Abraham understood Him to be *before* the *Akedah*. The God of the *Akedah* is not that God.

All is obscure. His knowledge of God has been disrupted. He has no peace of thought; he has no fill of knowledge; the love and the fear of God collide in his breast; he no longer walks in God's presence, ever to observe His providence and on Him solely depend.[34] Indeed, Abraham has no idea what to do next, in the matter of God. He has lost the sense of what it means to be a man of faith. It is a moment of uncanniness.

The life and identity familiar to him since his emergence from the furnace is now unfamiliar. His fidelity to God has brought his service of God into question. He no longer understands what is demanded of him or what might be demanded of him. All previous understandings have fallen short of the demand just made of him. But reflection will not avail; he cannot think his way out of this puzzlement. He can't revive that bit of his Abraham 1 identity. Though the event offered further confirmation of God's decisive significance in his life, Abraham is no longer certain what God Himself signifies. He does not know whether he can now say, as he once would say, God is good—at least, not in the way that we seek to be good.[35] The God of pre-furnace Abraham 1 was the conclusion of an argument, a philosophical hypothesis; the God of pre-mountain Abraham 2 was personal and loved humankind.[36] And the God of *post*-mountain

Abraham 2? Abraham has no answer to this question, save that He is not as hitherto experienced. Divine terror has superseded divine grace and love, writes Joseph B. Soloveitchik.[37]

This is a catastrophe. Though Abraham chose alienation from Isaac over alienation from God, he is now alienated from his former sense of God. For all he knows, he is also alienated from God too. He has lost everything. He no longer has his son; he no longer understands God; perhaps he no longer has God.

The *Akedah* is an episode of radical and destructive violence in its threat, in what is perpetrated, and in the untimeliness of the miracle that ostensibly resolves it. For Abraham himself, it is the unsurpassable moment in his life. It is his trauma. He cannot get beyond the *Akedah*. Everything he does relates back to it. We must imagine it tormenting Abraham. It is his unresolvable, insurmountable crisis. It is not a transformative experience; it is a wrecking one.[38] His relationship with God was a personal one, in the strongest sense—fully singular. There was none other like it; there will be none other like it. It disclosed something of God's purpose for the world, something of God's form of existence. And then it ended. He has an experience of God-forsakenness. Worse still, grieving the loss of God, Abraham feared His return. God's silence is a burden; the prospect of His speech, a further burden. We must imagine Abraham in speculative address to an absent God. "You were my refuge in evil times, yet now the very thought of You is a terror to me."[39]

Just as significant that there are two Abrahams and not one, then, is that there are two Abrahams and not three. Abraham had reached the limit of his "beginnings." There is not a third Abraham, that is, in any creative sense. There is no third version of God that Abraham can preach; there are no further converts he can make. The post-*Akedah* God is not the Abraham 1 God, an abstraction, a deduction. Nor is He the Abraham 2 God, a Being of perfect justice. He is instead unreliable, remote. Post-*Akedah* Abraham no longer knows what his faith holds for him.

It is where he lives; but it is not his home. He is alienated inside his relation with God. In the fog of God's unintelligibility, he no longer knows how he would answer the question, Is God a moral agent, susceptible to moral praise or censure?[40] Abraham has to abandon all conversionist activity—all preaching, all *thinking*. The cosmos itself is once again an inhospitable place. His understanding has darkened.

But can he return to the orientation of the first Abraham, Abraham 1? No. This too is blocked. He cannot retrieve what has already been surrendered. He cannot return to autonomy. Nor can he complete Abraham 1's work, the full depopulation of the heavens, the booting out of the last remaining occupant, a reaffirmed revolt, finishing the job he started in Ur. That is impossible. There is no way back to Abraham 1, just as there is no way back to the moment when the God Abraham knew was close and benevolent or close and open to persuasion. This terrifying new knowledge of God is not knowledge Abraham wants.

Religion is not a theory, of course.[41] Wittgenstein entrusted to a notebook this reflection:

> It strikes me that a religious belief could only be something like a passionate commitment to a system of reference. Hence, although it's *belief*, it's really a way of living, or a way of assessing life. It's passionately seizing hold of *this* interpretation. Instruction in a religious faith, therefore, would have to take the form of a portrayal, a description, of that system of reference, while at the same time being an appeal to conscience. And this combination would have to result in the pupil himself, of his own accord, passionately taking hold of the system of reference. It would be as though someone were first to let me see the hopelessness of my situation, and then show me the means of rescue until, of my own accord, or not at any rate, led to it by my instructor, I ran to it and grasped it.[42]

The question arises, What happens when the passionately seized system of reference breaks into pieces in the believer's hands?

Does that sense of hopelessness return, or is something even worse, that deeper hopelessness occasioned when a restored hope has itself been shattered? This is Abraham's situation. He is in spiritual disarray.

Sarah

The death of Sarah dealt a blow to Abraham from which he did not recover.[43] His marriage to her had contributed some meaning to his life—not *all* of its meaning but not a negligible quantity and not contingent to his life's great purposes. He was who he was in part because of Sarah, in all the iterations of their union: in his marriage to her, in his separation from her, in his burial of her, and in their reunion in a shared burial place. Little of this, however, was apparent to Abraham himself.

She was his first interlocutor in Ur, then his partner in Haran, and then, through their long journeying in Canaan, the unwilling spectator to the collapse of their marriage, a collapse that began slowly and then picked up speed, until final ruin in Beersheba, that morning when Abraham stole out of the encampment. All this—interlocutor, partner, spectator—happened fully without thought on Abraham's part, equally when committed to thought in Ur, suspicious of thought in Haran, and trying so hard to do without it thereafter. His marriage prompted him to no reflection. Yet it was *so* promising as an object of inquiry. Not promising—*compelling*. His failure to think about his marriage was a failure as an intellectual, as well as a husband. Why did he not find momentum in their first exchanges? Why did he not allow the partnership in Haran to become a partnership in Canaan? (Did God get in the way?) Why did he not seek to stabilize the collapse at some point short of ruin—after all, even long-standing enmity is an intimate human relationship, with its own equilibrium.[44]

In his separation from Sarah, when she was in Hebron, and then before he had news of her death, he lived in her knowledge of his character. He recognized himself in his openness to his wife's knowledge of him. This was no period of glory for him. He was reminded of the two earlier separations, when she was held by Pharaoh and then by Abimelech, and the knowledge *those* separations gave to him of himself. *Those* were no periods of glory either. Skulking in palaces, the recipient of favors, fending off offers for Sarah—the worst kind of humiliation, the one not only self-chosen but requiring persistence. And the content of that humiliation? His inability to protect a family member, a willful failure, close to collusion with her tormentors.

When he learned of Sarah's death, he wept. The weeping was for her, for their marriage, and for himself. At that terminal moment, and for the first time, the mourning made him active in trying to understand the meanings of his attachment to her. It was a moment, that is, that held out the possibility of some development in him, some growth.[45] He experienced her absence, for the first time since the departure from Haran, as a *loss.* "What can I say about all this," he wondered. "What would I say to Sarah about it all, were she with me?" A phrase occurred to him, and he turned it over in his mind, as he made his way to Hebron.

He arrived within a day of her death. It was his duty to bury her; it was his honor to eulogize her. He was obliged to do the one; he wished very much to do the other. Her burial place was to be appropriate to her status as his wife and his superior as a prophet. It also had to be of a size suitable for his own remains. He wanted to be reunited with her in death. He knew the ideal location, the Machpelah cave, owned by a local Hittite, Ephron, son of Tzochar. A negotiation began with tribal leaders, in the course of which Abraham used the phrase that he had been mulling since his journey to Hebron: "alien and resident."

He had to negotiate for the plot, because he was not entitled to one as of right. "I am an alien and a resident among you," he said to the Hittites of Hebron. "Allow me the possession of a grave site, so that I can bury my dead." There was some back-and-forth between them. They wanted to make a gift to him of the site; Abraham insisted on paying a full price. He gave the negotiations the limited attention they required—formulaic deference, formulaic generosities, and so on. In the meantime, "alien and resident" expanded in his mind, until it reached the proportion of a general statement about him, an epitaph. Burying his wife, he pondered how he himself would be remembered when dead. As an alien and resident, he concluded. Alien and resident, existentially.

In that final illumination, in which the exchanges on a burial plot for Sarah evoked a strong sense of her presence, he arrived at a self-definition. Punctuate his statement to the Hittites like this: "I am an alien and a resident, among you." Or write it out algebraically: "I am [an alien and a resident] among you." Two separate propositions, then: (a) I am among you, and (b) I am an alien and a resident. This latter proposition is open in turn to two interpretations.

First, I am in part a resident and in part an alien. I am in part at one with my neighbors, living among them in mutual goodwill and cooperation; and in part, I am separate from my neighbors, in a posture of rejection, resolutely refusing any accommodation. I am aware of the issues on which I can compromise and what goods I can surrender; I am also aware of the principles that are nonnegotiable and the spiritual goods that must be defended at all costs. Call this "the separate and distinct parts" interpretation.

Second, I am a Jew fully divided against myself, both one thing and its opposite, an x and a not-x. Let us imagine Abraham reflecting, "I was Abraham 1, and then I was Abraham 2. I was committed to a life of inquiry; then I was committed to a life of service. I thought I was wholly committed to the one, until the furnace; and then wholly committed to the other, until the mountain. I now know that I hankered after faith when Abraham 1, as I hankered after autonomy when Abraham 2, and that I have never been able to bring the two into any happy, settled compact. On the contrary, I was at war with myself; such peace as I now have is in my intuition of a complete defeat." Call this the "divided against oneself" interpretation.

Soloveitchik makes the first interpretation. He asks the question, Is it possible to be "resident" and "alien" at the same time? "Is not this definition absurd since it contravenes the central principle of classical logic, that no cognitive judgment may contain two mutually exclusive terms?" No, it does not, Soloveitchik answers. "The Jew of old defied this principle and did not think of himself in contradictory terms."[46] Soloveitchik was good at giving accommodating, emollient answers to radical questions.

I make the second interpretation. The relevant division is not between the "Jewish" and "civic" aspects of a person but *within* the Jewish aspect. "I am an alien and a resident *inside my faith*," Abraham reflects. "There is no theodicy available to me. I can no longer preach God's higher wisdom; I can no longer defend God's cause.[47] He has become opaque to me; His purposes are mysterious. We no longer speak; God has broken off His discourse with me.[48] I have been promised this land many times, and yet, here I am, unable even to bury my wife without permission. Yes, I once was Abraham 1; and later, I was Abraham 2. What am I now? A person who contains the ruins of both Abrahams, a ruined person."

So much for the unspoken speech, as Abraham speaks aloud his words of praise and regret for Sarah. He tears these words out of himself, the expression of all his sorrow, a mourning that exceeds its immediate occasion. "Sarah" becomes the name for everything that he has lost, everyone whom he has lost. He promises to Sarah that he will follow her to the cave, that he will be buried alongside her.

That night he has a dream. He is lying in her arms, his head resting on her lap. Sarah gazes at him mutely, inquiringly.[49] The dream, a fantasy of care, acknowledges the alienation between them in the marking of its end. She is caring for him and puzzling over him, an object of solicitude *and* bafflement. But surely, she is greater than the sum of her solicitudes and her puzzlements over Abraham? This essential aspect of Sarah always eluded him, even in his dreams.

Decline

In this impasse, the passage of time without inner movement, Abraham's life sinks down to the merely incidental.

The post–Abraham 2 is no more than a person to whom stuff happens. His most intense experiences are recollections; his freshest emotions are of grief and remorse. He has lost God; he has lost his wife; he has no contact with his sons; he is without friends. His relation of loving-kindness toward the world does not avail him; it establishes no enduring friendships, no restorative partnerships; he is unable to comfort Isaac on the loss of his mother. Abraham's horizons shrink; there is a sense of dwindling, of weakness. Canaan becomes a region of sorrow.

He is very *busy*—but to little purpose. It is a grieving, blank busyness—*not* the contented, fulfilled busyness of the pre–Abraham 1, or the energetic, adversarial Abraham 1, or the dynamic, adventuring, imposing Abraham 2. A life full of activity and empty of progress: a further marriage (or remarriage), finding a wife for Isaac, miscellaneous further children. His most consequential act, his marriage to Keturah, is a circling back to an earlier moment in his life: he takes Keturah to be Hagar, just as he treats his new children as he treated Ishmael, to be exiled without inheritance, sent away from Isaac, fobbed off with gifts. "Abraham's eye was darkened, he saw joy no more."[50]

Reconciliation with Sarah is denied to him. And reconciliation with Isaac? Abraham sometimes wonders, "Can I say to my son, 'Give up your grief! Return to me, please. Let me love you as I once did.'" He broods, "Perhaps he will be pacified by my labors to find him a wife? Only a loving father would make such efforts, after all. Isaac will thank me, and we will speak, and I will explain, and all will be well again." But no. Isaac does not allow his father that chance. Instead, he avoids him, carefully ensuring that he and Abraham never come into each other's presence. He avoids Abraham's blessing.[51] It is only when his father lies shrouded, dead before him, that Isaac will place himself in proximity to this terrifying man—and then, only for a few moments. And even in this meeting that is not a meeting, with Abraham's body motionless at his feet, Isaac will tremble.

Abraham has stalled. His later years become merely circumstantial, of significance to him alone. There was a time—in Ur, in Haran, in Egypt, and for some time in Canaan—when it was correct to say of Abraham that he did not find his aim and vocation in the calm and regular system of his time, that he drew his inspiration from other sources, that his life was one of adventure, that he was in search of a hidden spirit whose hour (as he thought) was near, that he was the first to formulate the desires of his fellows, that he was driven to complete the task he gave himself, that his own happiness was of no concern to him and he sought only to attain his objective, that he challenged all the beliefs of his contemporaries, that he rose to honor by treating accepted values with contempt.

During this time, a period of his life corresponding to those years in which he was active as both Abraham 1 and Abraham 2, he was a world-historical figure, a far-sighted person who willed and accomplished not just his own ends but those that were necessary to history itself, understood as a force of progressive revelation. No more. He no longer has that status or anything close to it. And unlike certain other world-historical figures, who fall aside like empty husks when their end is attained, he became such a husk before that moment of completion.[52]

Essentially lifeless, spirit extinguished on Mt. Moriah, he subsists in a condition of general alienation and mental sunkenness. He is forlorn, listless. Dim sadness, and blind thoughts that he could not name, came upon him.[53] From perfect grief, wrote the poet, there need not be wisdom or even memory.[54] Abraham speaks to few people, and then, only briefly and inconsequentially. His requests, his responses, are limited to immediate, material concerns. He makes arrangements to leave to Isaac all his possessions. A certain sluggishness overcomes him, fitfully shrugged off with displays of activity, but to little purpose. He is brokenhearted.[55]

He has no projects; he offers no instruction; he has no one under his care. A sense of forsakenness hovers over him. His mind is drawn downward by the monotony of family life, by the absence of any life lived beyond the precincts of family, and by the burden of historic actions. He first experiences moments of forgetfulness; these moments deepen and lengthen, his consciousness then a mere registering of sensation; occasions of more elevated or intense awareness are conditioned by a certain confusion that causes him swiftly to retreat to his default lassitude.

In his last years, his decline consisted of a progressive weakening, without catastrophic incident. He suffered no illness or injury; no material want was left unsatisfied; no commotion was allowed to disturb him; he was finished, as the poet says, with both joy and moan.[56] For long stretches of time, he drifted between sleep and wakefulness; a drowsy calm settled on him, all thoughts and cares evacuated. Such was his state of contentless contentedness when death met him.[57]

Ishmael traveled from his home to bury his father. He found Isaac already there. Together, they laid Abraham to rest. *Of course* they attended on him, at this last moment: the death of one's father, as Freud wrote, is the most important event, the most poignant event, in a man's life (4:xxvi). They recalled his expulsion of one and his readiness to kill the other; they recalled his indifference to the death of his own father. He was as mysterious to them as God had become to him.

Abraham died homeless—that is, far from his place of birth, among strangers. God's promise in respect of the land had not been fulfilled; the land's inhabitants were not even aware that it had been made. Indeed, Abraham was careful never to mention it, in all his dealings with them. He was the first homeless Jew: many Jews after him would lead lives of similar dislocation and uncertainty.

And Abraham died godless—that is, no longer in God's company, level instead with the rest of humankind. Over time, Abraham gave up the hope of contact; he now saw no better, no further, than his fellows. He was therefore also the first godless Jew: but here, it would be centuries before other Jews experienced this alienation, though in their case without the grief of loss.

Further Interpretations

Further?

In part, because thus far, I have been interpreting the *Akedah* by retelling the story. The interpretations I now offer are formulated in the mode of hypothesis. First came my narrative account of the story; now come my six theories of it. As will become apparent, the narrative account does not altogether fit any of the theories, and the theories themselves do not cohere into one integrated, big theory.

And in part, because I am proposing my interpretations as contributions to that fund of interpretations built up across the millennia. This fund is ever growing, because Jews continue to think with and talk about the *Akedah*. We relate to each other the story, adding or subtracting from it as we choose, mixing speculation with narrative detail. We are captivated by its mysterious possibilities of exegesis and the extraordinary presence of its participants in our own lives.[58]

Polysemous Texts

There are texts that allow for several interpretations, of which more than one could be correct. This does not mean that there are not better or worse interpretations; nor does it mean that one can say *anything* one wants about a text. Still (and allowing these limitations), it is a property of certain texts that their meaning is irreducibly plural. These texts tend to draw out from us our best thoughts, prompting an active, creative response without finality.

When we pause from our reading, breaking off our interpretations, it is with the tacit acknowledgment that we have not quite captured the entire meaning of the text. We have not rendered it completely intelligible. We have worked hard to do it justice, but we have fallen short. Even with further engagements, fresh interpretations, our thinking remains inadequate to the text's brimming fullness of signification.

Texts of this kind evoke such wealth of thought because they themselves are products of much thinking, a thinking of genius.[59] What is the character of this thinking? It is perhaps best expressed with examples. Take the words "justice" and "love" in Shakespeare's great tragedy *King Lear* (ca. 1604–1605). We think we know what these words and their cognates mean; we use them all the time in our ordinary speech. If asked for definitions, we might say, love is what we hope for, and justice is what we demand. We might add that family life is impossible without the one and political life is impossible without the other.

Good enough, we might think. But not *really* good enough—indeed, not even *close* to being good enough. And we know this, because Shakespeare subjects the words to a more intense scrutiny, a higher order of examination. *King Lear* is a play in which these words take flight, volunteering meanings that surprise and elevate us.

There are only a few such texts that achieve this unbounded

expansion of meaning. The Torah is one such text, as the rabbis have many times insisted,[60] their "characteristic pluralism" in paradoxical explication of "the unity of the Revelation."[61] They hold it to be radiant with meaning, cryptic yet perfect.[62] For rabbinic culture, writes Michael Fishbane, the sense of Scripture is never predetermined; rather, everything depends on creative readings of its inherent, God-given possibilities.[63]

The *Akedah* is exemplary in this respect; it is also responsive to creative readings outside rabbinic culture. One fine Jewish critic, wholly external to that culture, observed that readers of the story are constantly finding something new to feed on.[64] In this spirit, I accept Abraham Socher's statement that the *Akedah* overpowers and confounds all interpretations.[65] What follows are the six readings that have helped me to make sense of the text. They are independent of each other; to accept one does not require one to accept any of the others.

There are seventy faces, or ways of interpreting, the Torah, says a Midrash. The Torah teacher Nechama Leibovitz once summarily rejected a student's interpretation of a verse. To the protest "What about the seventy faces of the Torah?" she replied, "Seventy, yes—seventy one, no!"[66] With texts such as the *Akedah*, the problem is more than a mere matter of limits on interpretive freedom. We live in the presence of such texts. The meaning we make of them contributes to the meaning we make of ourselves; misinterpret them and we misdirect our self-understanding. "We cannot be conscious of something in whatever way we wish," Levinas reminds us.[67]

I summarily reject, then, a received reading of the *Akedah* in which a test is set and passed, with celebrations all round. This reading, common among certain Jewish educators, is advanced in pursuit of a relentless, banal positivity. "So when times are hard,/We should try our best—/Who knows? These troubles/May well just be a test."[68] While polysemous meaning is a feature of all deeply serious writing, and the Torah is the model for serious writing,[69] this does not qualify as a serious reading of that most serious of texts, the *Akedah*.[70]

My six readings, by radical contrast, take as their common point of departure the discomfort that the *Akedah* causes to Jews.[71] To Wendy Zierler's complaint, "the *Akedah* seems to fail as a recipe for passing on religious convictions to living children whom we love,"[72] I respond, yes, of course it does. That is its purpose, or at least part of its purpose. Its "failure" is its triumph. It makes Judaism difficult.

Reading #1: Decision

We should concern ourselves with the type of decision that Abraham was called on to make, not the decision's content.

The fifteen-year-old Gershom Scholem announced to his German-Jewish assimilated father, "I think I want to be a Jew."[73] In an act altogether free of redundancy, a Jew decided to become a Jew.

On more occasions than they recognize, Jews are called on to make decisions about being Jewish. In the Second Temple period, say, while it was natural to be Judean in Judea, it was unnatural to be Jewish abroad. To raise a child as Judean in Judea was expected and required no special effort of will, writes Daniel R. Schwartz. To raise a child as a Jew in Egypt, Cyprus, Rome, or anywhere else in the Hellenistic-Roman diaspora, however, required a decision to do something that was not at all natural.[74] As then, so in the near-now,[75] and perhaps in the future too.

The *Akedah* is a parable about a certain type of decision, in respect of which Abraham is the ideal protagonist. Call it an "existential decision." This is a decision freely made, amid risk and doubt, in pursuit of the life purposes or projects one has given oneself. It often has a quality of stand-taking.

Though from the outside it presents as an exercise of choice, it is made under pressure of inner necessity. Rarely is it preceded by deliberation; calculations of relative advantage tend not to be made. The person making the decision, if challenged, is likely to say, "There is nothing else I could do" or "*Not* to have done that was just impossible." Absence of deliberation, however, does not imply absence of anguish. Catastrophes can flow from such decisions. They are likely to be agonizing; one's sense of oneself will take on a vivid fragility.

Abraham's decision was to act on God's command, in pursuit of his chosen purpose of complete submission to God's will. Abraham is the ideal protagonist to be faced with this type of decision, because of his great generosity and his adventurousness of spirit.

The Jewish philosopher and surrealist Benjamin Fondane asked the question, Is Abraham a figure of interest to believers only?[76] For sure, he is an exception. What use can we make of something so personal, so individual, a decision as the one he made, in response to God's demand? His act cannot be our act. Surely, he is not like us; he leaves us empty-handed; his answers are not ours.

Yes, indeed. Unless, that is, we too are exceptions; unless we too are ready to become individuals. For sure, this is risky. The only way to become an exception is to leave behind common sense, take a dark path, and chance losing our footing on it. Few do so voluntarily; most exceptions have exceptionality thrust on them by a predicament unresolvable by common sense or reason.[77]

On this reading, then, the point of the parable is not to invite a judgment about Abraham. It is instead to pose the question, How would *I* act if called on to make an existential decision, whatever the content of that decision might be, given my *own* life purposes? If I am a person who has chosen to be a Jew, under a certain conception of what it is to be a Jew, I may be called on to make a decision at the cost of my own life or another's.

Of course, the decision does not have to result in a sacrifice—Abraham's didn't. What is more, Jews are only rarely faced with *Akedah*-type decisions.[78] The essential point is that when these decisions *do* have to be made, reconciliation of the available courses of action is not possible, and the form of one's existence (if not one's life) is in the balance.

Interpretations of the *Akedah* that concern themselves with the details of the binding of Isaac thus miss the parable's greatest challenge. We should read the story itself as no more than an instance of one kind or model of a trial. It is this model, not the instance, that we are called on to ponder.

This reading, or something close to it, is proposed by Maimonides. The purpose of the *Akedah* is to provide us with a model to be followed. The story itself is merely the means by which the model may best be presented.[79] The *Akedah* is thus a prophetic parable or *mashal*. By identifying the story's literary form, Maimonides indicates how it is to be interpreted. "My remarking that it is a *mashal* will be like someone removing a screen from between the eye and a visible thing" (Guide, I. Introduction, III.24).[80] The parable tells a story in order to teach us about a certain kind of decision we might be called on to make. We experience both the call and the decision as we follow the story, placing ourselves in Abraham's position and then in Isaac's position, pondering what equivalent call might be made to us, what decision we ourselves would then make.

The literary form, the parable, typically has an atmosphere of implication; it is enigmatic; it operates on more than one level; it tends toward the paradoxical. The *Akedah* is an exemplary parable. It is a "dark saying" (Proverbs 1.6).[81] Parables are constitutively polysemous texts because they *both* proclaim a truth as a herald does *and* at the same time conceal a truth like an oracle.[82] The most compelling parables are charged with a spiritual energy. Some parables have an additional "thought experiment" quality. "Just suppose," says the philosopher,[83] using thought experiments when the ordinary way of doing philosophy isn't enough. They hope that guided contemplation of an invented scenario will provide new knowledge when argument alone cannot. The thought experiment cannot, no more than the parable, be substituted by an argument without loss.[84]

Reading #2: Scission

The Akedah affirms a principle of scission, the cutting of family ties in favor of other commitments.

The command "Go" (*lech lecha*) is spoken only twice in the Torah, each time to Abraham. He is told to leave for a land yet to be specified (Gen. 12:1); he is then told to leave for a mountain yet to be specified (Gen. 22:1). Why this singular pair of commands? Here is one explanation: to effect Abraham's severance from both father and son, and so from the vertical ties of family, in favor of a more complete attachment to God. In Genesis 12:1, he must abandon his father; in Genesis 22:1, he must sacrifice his son.

There is a sentimental reading of the Abraham story that runs like this: Abraham is "the supreme symbol of the Jewish family,"[85] a family that becomes a nation. A closer reading of the story finds a family tearing itself apart on the promise of nationhood. In the founding generation alone, a father and two brothers are left behind, a nephew is lost, a son and mother are cast out; this son and six others are excluded from the family line—that is, Terah, Nahor, and Haran; Lot; Ishmael, Zimran, Jokshan, Medan, Midian, Ishbak, and Shuah.

Of all these scissions, the *Akedah* is the worst. Abandonment of father? Terah has another son to care for him. Expulsion of eldest son and mother? Ishmael and Hagar have each other. The six sons? They receive gifts. But sacrifice of younger son? Isaac is alone and without hope of life. One meaning of the *Akedah*, then, lies in its extreme affirmation of this principle of scission. As Soloveitchik puts it, writing of Abraham, "the chosen person severs his affiliation with his clan and friends, he deserts everybody in order to give himself up to his new friend, God."[86]

Parallel to the breaking of the family, there is a break with the concept of family, understood as the primary locus of identity, the primary focus of loyalty. Identity, restated as communal membership, now attaches itself to the larger group, made up of converts and unexcluded family members. Loyalty, restated as religious piety, now directs itself toward God, in whose service the faithful live. And the reward? The nation that derives from Abraham's "seed" will "possess the gate of its enemies" (Gen. 22:17).

These are simplifications, of course; I indicate a direction of travel only. The journey is not completed in the Abraham story itself, nor could it ever be, because that would make of Judaism a mere cult.

This double demotion of the familial that the Abraham story effects, the privileging of fidelity to God over duty to parent and child and of membership of the yet-to-be-formed nation over membership of one's family, works itself out across ensuing millennia in the life of study and literary activity,[87] and in the revolutionary life, forms of existence to which Abraham's own life choices give exemplary weight.

The case against family has four parts.

First, family hierarchies, the very order of time, often generate injustices. In such cases, sons must be given priority over fathers, and younger brothers over elder brothers.

Second, family itself is an obstacle to the achieving of worthwhile goals. Families exasperate when they refuse to stand aside.[88] They must understand their place, which is not the top one. A Mishnah confirms their subordinate place, by reference to the family member least likely to welcome it. If you find two lost items, one belonging to your father and one belonging to your teacher, tending to the teacher's item takes precedence. And why so? Your father merely brought you into this world; your teacher, who educates you in the wisdom of Torah, will bring you to life in the World-to-Come (Bava Metzia 2.11).

Third, "family" is the synecdoche for *all* inherited attachments that must be sloughed off to allow the fullest self-realization. God commands Abraham, "Get thee out of thy *country*, and from thy *kindred*, and from thy *father's house*, unto a land that I will shew thee: And I will make of thee a great nation, and I will bless thee, and make thy name great; and thou shalt be a blessing" (Gen. 12:1–2).

Last, loyalty to family is either loyalty to the wrong group or the wrong kind of loyalty. That is, either the loyalty should be to another group (say, a political party or nation) or it should be to an impersonal value (say, the greatest happiness of the greatest number) and not to any group of people at all.[89] Abraham's virtue of *chesed* is an early formulation of this impersonal value. In its humanity, it accords to an unknown passerby the respect God Himself commands;[90] in its universalism, it withholds from family members all special favors (yes, to protest on behalf of the innocent of Sodom, if indeed they exist; no, to protest on behalf of Isaac).[91] The object? To move beyond the circle of intimacy to the realm that matters, the ethical, to live like Abraham, that is, hospitably, in a tent with flaps open on all sides.[92] Precisely to drive this point home, Maimonides insisted that Abraham came to kidnapped Lot's aid *only* because Lot "shared his beliefs" (Guide, III.50).[93]

These aspects converge on religious conversion and then on radical politics, of course. The Jewish revolutionary Jesus[94] preached separation from family, as did the Enlightenment philosopher Jean-Jacques Rousseau[95] and the Russian anarchist Sergey Nechayev.[96] All radical attempts to remake humankind are ultimately assaults on the family, proposes Yuri Slezkine, and all of them fail or dissimulate.[97] Abraham's career is the obscure, unacknowledged starting point of these attempts. The *Akedah* gives this starting point its quality of utter rupture.

Reading #3: "Patch-Up"

Oscillations between reason and faith are punctuated by "patch-ups," provisional reconciliations that meet immediate needs. Abraham's sacrifice of the ram is the first such patch-up.

Abraham's life is typically structured by reference to ten tests. I propose another structure, one that divides his life into two parts, each one terminating in a crisis. The first crisis is the mirror of the second crisis. Though a divine intervention is decisive in both, in the first, an urgently solicited miracle resolves the crisis, while in the second, a most unwelcome anti-miracle initiates it. ("Anti-miracle"? I mean the divine suspension of a universally applicable law but for a destructive purpose, rather than a redemptive one.) Though each crisis is of an ordeal endured and a death averted, the initiator of the first one is a human ruler of divine pretensions, while the initiator of the other one is God Himself. That is, God does not intervene in the second crisis to protect against a lethal danger; He *originates* it.

Once again, we can interpret the *Akedah* in the context of a longer period of Abraham's life. The lesson of the furnace? Critical reason is inadequate in the living of one's life. The lesson of Moriah? Faith is dangerous to life itself. I propose Abraham's life, in its A1 and A2 iterations, then, as the third of my six readings. We turn to faith when critical reason exposes its limitations; we retreat from faith when it puts in jeopardy what we are inclined most to value in life. Abraham's life, under this aspect, becomes the prototype of *every* Jew's life, in its unstable, combustible, unresolved combination of interrogation and submission, challenge and deference, free thinking and worship. We oscillate between the two, devising solutions certain to fall short of full reconciliation. They are patch-ups—improvisations that do not bear the closest scrutiny but are good enough. And by "good enough," I intend the highest praise.

The *Akedah* is the model story of this patching up.

To recapitulate, as Abraham and Isaac climb the mountain, Isaac asks his father, "Where is the lamb [*seh*]?" Abraham replies, "God will provide the lamb my son." It is both an evasion and a true statement, depending on how the sentence is punctuated. Add a comma after "lamb," and it is an evasion; add a colon, and it is the truth. The angel appears and tells Abraham not to harm Isaac. No reference is made to any lamb; no instruction is given to complete the sacrifice.

When the angel has finished speaking, Abraham looks up and sees a ram (*ayil*)—that is, it is a male adult sheep, not an infant sheep of unidentified sex. He decides to make a sacrifice; and he decides to use the ram. It is an improvisation, the outcome of contradictory motivations. There are no qualities associated with a ritual practice present; there is no conscientiousness in respect of detail. What Abraham does is very far indeed from what Freud termed the "stereotyped character" of rituals (9:119); there is no privileging of the fixed over the spontaneous, of rule-following over originality of action.[98]

What drives the decision?

First, though it has the appearance of an independent decision, it has a constrained quality. While the act itself is uncommanded, its object is to express a still greater subordination to God. It is a supererogatory sacrifice, performed in pursuit of more perfect service, in advance of any actual command to like effect. In its initiative taking, it is the defeated residue of Abraham 1's critical reason, his mind in inventive prostration before God.

Second, there is the desire to follow through the physical motion of sacrifice, to trace the downward arc of the knife, to drive it home. Abraham had set out that morning to make a sacrifice; he will not return without having made one. God *will* be honored this day. He thinks, "A fresh sacrifice is not forbidden. I was not told to leave the mountain straightaway; it is open to me to kill the ram. God will not *object*." He senses in himself this desire, to finish what he has started, a desire not to be denied. In this limited respect, when finishing the interrupted act, the identity of the creature under the knife is irrelevant. And yet, how *can* it be irrelevant to Abraham? How can he overlook the fact that the table occupied by the ram was only minutes earlier occupied by his son?

Third, it is a recoil from human sacrifice. *This* is how sacrifices should be made, by killing an animal, not a person! The sacrifice is hastily made, as if to expunge the impression made on the collective mind of the antecedent acts in respect of Isaac. Forget all those acts—the deception, the tying up, the raising of the knife! From now on, Abraham will make sacrifices on *these* new terms, where human participation is limited entirely to the performing of sacrifices. Never again will he be required to kill another person, least of all, a child of his own. (Of course, God has *not* given Abraham such an assurance; it is instead merely Abraham's own resolution. But why rebel now, after everything that has just happened?)

Fourth, it is amends for the attempt on his son's life, something akin to a guilt sacrifice. "I was ready to take your life; I will make a symbolic sacrifice of my own life, killing a ram that will stand for me." How do we intuit this motive? The clue is in the word *ayil*, which means "strong man, leader, chief" as well as "ram." Abraham himself is precisely a "chief," a "leader." By this symbolic self-extinguishing, he pays the price for what he has done *and* ensures that he will never be able to do anything like it again. He becomes a dead man, without agency. He returns imaginatively to the moment of the furnace, but this time without praying for deliverance.

It is in the complexity of this tangled, divided motivation that Abraham works out his patch-up. The sacrifice of the ram is made in *response* to a most terrible act of faith. This impromptu act, an improvised one that is wholly his own, making use of a ram since no lamb is available, both not quite on the mark and even richer in significance, driven by the need to make sense of what has happened, is the first and most extreme patch-up in the spiritual life of the Jewish people.

Reading #4: Failure

Jewish religious life must negotiate unavoidable failure.

There is a reading of the *Akedah* that runs this way: to fear God is to be in a state of unconditional submission to His will; God wished to ascertain whether Abraham lived resolutely in this state; He devised a test for this purpose; the test consisted of giving Abraham the most powerful reason to abandon the state; the reason made killing his son the condition of remaining in the state; passing the test would mean staying in the state, notwithstanding this powerful reason; Abraham passed the test, at which point his hand was stayed; the outcome was a triumph for Abraham.

There is a problem with this reading, however.

We can take it for granted that the instinct to protect one's children is a "truly natural law, universally and permanently imprinted in us."[99] That is to say, the instinct is constitutive of human life. To violate it as Abraham did, *especially* as Abraham did, with an active menacing, is to tear at the fabric of one's humanity.

The point can be expressed more abstractly. To be a human being is, among other things, to have human instincts; among those instincts is the instinct to protect one's children; to live in a state of fear is a mode of human existence. Now, if that mode requires readiness to kill one's own children, human beings cannot live in it without a continuous and active repudiation of their human character. They prove the fear, while losing the title of human being. Or they affirm the title, while failing to prove the fear (by refusing to kill their children). Their ineligibility is their eligibility; their eligibility is their ineligibility.[100]

Bring God into the formulation. He demands of human beings that they must live in fear of Him. They can only do so by ceasing to be human beings. God cannot make this demand without self-contradiction, because the demand that human beings live in a state of fear is demanded of them as human beings. God's self-contradiction is Abraham's unsolvable dilemma. He could not pass the test. He could not refuse God; he could not kill his son. Failure was thus written into its framing. No decision other than the wrong decision could be made; no course of action other than the wrong course of action could be pursued.

And yet, Abraham is not a tragic figure. A tragic Abraham would confront the command's essential feature, which is to demand the *impossible* of him. He would be divided between the demand of an imperious God, oppressively present to him, and the prospect of an absent God, orphaning Abraham, leaving him bereft—that is, divided between two terrors, the terror of submitting to the demand and the terror of resisting it. He can do neither, and yet he must do one.

This is not our Abraham. He is *not* torn apart by irreconcilable imperatives. He is not Sophocles's Antigone, say, torn between the duty to respect political authority and the duty to honor family pieties, attacking what is also immanent in her, gripped and shattered by something intrinsic to her actual being.[101] For Abraham, it has to be God, only and always God. He knows that he ever runs to the source of the one true life, as the poet writes; that his only hope is to see the Lord, his King; that apart from Him, he fears and worships nothing; that to him, time is nothing but compliance with His will; that if God will not be with him, he is nothing.[102]

That Abraham does not recognize, did not experience, his response to God's demand as requiring the making of a tragic choice does not mean that it wasn't that kind of demand—that is, to choose between two courses of action, both of which require the making of an intolerable sacrifice. It didn't cease to be tragic just because Abraham was oblivious to its tragic character.[103] That he missed this essential aspect was itself a failure on his part. He does not choose; he merely acts. In this perspective, the *Akedah* is a moment of evacuation of agency, the very reverse of tragedy's intensification of agency. This radical failure to notice, this willed blindness, this protractedly robotic motion, both ensured that he was able to live beyond the *Akedah* and limited that life to the inconsequential, the petty, the routine.

The *Akedah* winds up to the highest pitch of tension the problem in Judaism of failure. This is typically understood to be a failure by Jews in consequence of their delinquency or their incompetence. In a faith self-constituted as a community of learners,[104] there will always be dunces; in a faith exacting in ritual and moral demands, there will always be backsliders. It is said that Jews nonetheless know how to accept their failures because they know that they will be redeemed and that God will master His anger and be reconciled with His people. Israel coexists in failure with its God, writes Michael Wyschogrod.[105] So far, so commonplace.

Not so readily acknowledged, however, is the possibility that failure is written into Jewish practice, that to be a Jew is precisely to fail at being a Jew. Perfection is both demanded of us and yet impossible to attain.

Maimonides explains how one may "arrive at a very high degree of perfection." He is very ready to use this language of "perfection." A "saintly man" disposed to perform praiseworthy deeds, for example, is "more perfect" than the man of "self-restraint," who does so by "subduing his passions and fighting against his longings." And yet, though one "attains perfection by acquiring every possible moral and mental virtue," which only Moses achieved, even he failed to "comprehend the true essence of God," because his "human intellect still resided in matter." This is a necessary human failure, a limitation constitutive of humankind. Our reason is unable to comprehend Him. To try to grasp the truth of the divine essence is not a correct, not an appropriate, undertaking (Eight Chapters, 41, 44, 52–53, 77, 78).

That Maimonides's ideal of perfection is itself untenable is a second problem. The ideal assumes that we live in an epistemically closed universe, one in which complete knowledge is possible. Remove this untenable assumption, and the realizability of the ideal collapses.[106]

Even a perfect observance of Jewish law is impossible. A remark of Haym Soloveitchik's touches on this version. The Haredi quest to achieve a perfect religious observance, he writes, must fall short of success. Spiritual life is an attempt to play music that is better than it can be played.[107] Soloveitchik means, very specifically, *Jewish* spiritual life. Every performance of a Jewish life will end in failure. And in this respect, human deficiency is *not* the cause. If Jewish law is indeed like music, the failure is written into the score.

Is there any doubt, then, that Jews cannot be "perfect"? Certainly, any Jew who aspires faithfully to obey every single halakhic law will fail.[108] And certainly, the proliferation of ancillary laws, devised to limit the risk of violation of primary laws, raises to the level of near certainty the risk of *repeated* violation of the law.[109]

Abraham represents a horizon of holiness that we cannot reach. If he failed, so must we. Indeed, every Jew participates in Abraham's own failure, which thus becomes exemplary.

Reading #5: Trust

Abraham is troubled by a possible lack of openness to God and tests himself with a trust game.

Failure is the outcome of the *Akedah* on the third reading; it is the premise of the *Akedah* in my fourth reading. In the moment before the command to sacrifice, Abraham is harsh with himself for his less-than-perfect openness to God. He still has an instinct to challenge, to question God, to ask for proofs, to puzzle over promises; he is ready to hold God to standards of his own intuiting, standards that may be alien to Him. This is the problem to which the *Akedah* is the solution. It is a trust game in which the stakes are as high as can be imagined. Abraham will commit to an undertaking that he must then trust that God will abort.

Proverbs counsels, "Trust in the Lord with all thine heart; and lean not unto thine own understanding. In all thy ways acknowledge Him, and He shall direct thy paths. Be not wise in thine own eyes: fear the Lord, and depart from evil" (3:5–7). This is Abraham's challenge.

I take the following passage from an account of trust games: "Trust is revealed when an agent performs an initial sacrifice, that is, an action which, depending on the reaction of another agent, might be detrimental to the first agent's own interests. You put yourself in somebody else's hands. Trust is repaid, and the second agent is revealed to be trustworthy, if his or her reaction offsets and compensates the first agent's sacrifice." A trust game is devised by the first agent either to test his or her own trust in the second agent or that agent's trustworthiness. The game requires a "sacrifice."[110]

Throughout the post-Haran period of Abraham's life, he had been working hard on showing unconditional faith, unconditional obedience, unconditional trust in God. Whenever challenged to do so by given circumstances, however, he would fall short. He would experience what Wittgenstein called an "irritation of the intellect,"[111] a grating question that would not leave him alone. He would demand proof; he would express skepticism. When the occasion seemed to require action, he would act: remove himself from a famine-blighted land, misrepresent his connection with Sarah, argue for a city's wicked inhabitants. While the forms taken by this action would vary (a journey, a lie, a protest), they were united by a common stance. "I determine my course of action; I am in charge of my life; I look to my own resources to meet life's trials." And then to his embarrassment, Abraham would find that this self-reliance was not quite enough. The journeying did not save him; the lies saved neither him nor his wife; the protest did not save the city. God intervened, after indulging the displays of self-reliance, of independent action, of protest.

Or so Abraham pondered. Taken together with that embarrassing demand for proof (the covenant of the pieces) and that skeptical response to the promise of a son, these incidents had had a somewhat demoralizing effect on Abraham. He had become distressed by what he identified as his doubts, distressed beyond reason by what he identified in himself as faithlessness, distressed most of all by a reflex of independence that he thought had faded to nothing. In consequence, he had developed a bad conscience.[112] It seemed to him that he had not made himself inward with the lesson of the miracle of the furnace. Did he think of it now as a mere event, something inert, a detail in his life, long left behind? Had the miracle been lifesaving, yet not life changing? Abraham worried that this was so. Had he been rescued but left untransformed? Free to live but not liberated into a life lived on utterly different terms?

Following deep meditation, the severest introspection, in a spirit of extreme self-chastisement, he devised a test for himself, one that would establish the completeness of his faith. He rejected the thought of testing himself by abandoning a son, exposing him to lethal peril. That he had already done. He resolved to go further. He would set out to kill another son, and he would do it himself, as a sacrifice to God. Abraham whispered to himself, "I will raise my hand to my own son in the confident and certain knowledge that He will save him. Nothing bad will happen! I will stab downwards toward my son's neck confident that God will arrest the movement, just as others fall backward toward the ground, confident that their loved ones will catch them. It will end well. I will be an example to the world. My gesture will be a display of faith unparalleled in human history."

If the express demand of the test is "Put Isaac to death," the implicit demand is "Demonstrate that Abraham 1 is *already* dead." Abraham knows that he must put himself to the test. *He* is the author of the test, not God. "Affirm my obedience to God and extinguish my autonomy of Self; affirm my membership of the community of the faithful and repudiate my given family; affirm the found pieties of my religious life and extinguish the given pieties of my family life; affirm my intellectual humility." And do all this even if it is self-defeating: affirm the purity of the religious undertaking, even at the price of its future.

We must not think of this as a decision in pursuance of an already established, settled relation of trust in God. It is not "trust," that is, in the sense of "a confident, centered eagerness to greet what comes." It is not outgoing, ready and glad, an openness to God independent of any "particular resolve or volition."[113] Not at all. It is instead a darker, despairing, willful, even perverse act that Abraham plots. His self-test is a final, desperate *performance* of trust, a gamble, in repudiation of a life not yet trusting enough.

There are two textual clues that hint at this reading of the test as devised by Abraham himself. First, a sacrifice is amends-making, one made in respect of a fault. In the formulation of the commentator Shlomo Yitzhaki (1040–1105), commonly known as "Rashi," "*korbanot* are *kapporah*" (sacrifices are atonements).[114] So the question is, What is Abraham's fault? It is his continuing, if residual, commitment to critical reason, his lack of humility, an inadequate fear of God.[115] Second, Abraham is never told where to go. In Genesis 22:1, God says that He *will* tell him ("one of the mountains I will designate to you"); in 22:3–4, Abraham *already* knows ("the place that God had designated to him"). But nowhere is the telling itself related. So how did he know? Either God told him in a second, unrelated vision (which would be very odd), or else Abraham chose the place himself. And if he chose the place, why not the test itself?

There is an alternative version of this reading. As with the first version, its premise is that Abraham brings the test on himself. Unlike the first version, it does not hold that he also devised it himself. In this second version, in consequence of the Sodom episode, Abraham has acquired a certain taste for challenging God. It is the merest, the faintest, of taste—but still, the taste. A perfect conviction of God's justice? A shadow has been cast over it. And then, in consequence of the birth of Isaac, God's prophecy has been fulfilled. Abraham is thereby freed of the anxiety that he will not merit its fulfillment. And so the test becomes necessary; it is in the character of a challenge Abraham has prompted by his own state of mind (the shadow, the new peace of mind).

One might think that only a fanatic would act thus, to suppress his own skeptical, critical impulses. The sacrifice is itself the sin in respect of which a guilt-sacrifice is required. But what does that make of the *Akedah*? A text that celebrates such tendencies or exposes them to critical scrutiny? This question is addressed in my final reading.

Reading #6: Warning

The Hebrew Scriptures contain texts that open to question its own normative religious principles.

Begin with some witnesses to a certain comprehensiveness of address in Jewish texts. One writes that the Torah is an answer to ultimate problems of existence *and* it is a challenge to all answers, *including* its own. The second one writes that Judaism is a systematic program for cultivating submission to God's will *and* a cold shower for the innate religious fanaticism of the human soul. The third writes that the Bible exceeds the doctrines that have been built on it.[116]

When a political or religious tradition contains materials that invite a searching, foundational challenge to its values and positions, materials that constitute warnings against itself or against received versions of itself, we may say that the tradition incorporates an element of "autocritique."[117] Judaism contains an abundance of autocritical texts. The *Akedah* is one such text; Job, a revision of the *Akedah*, is an obvious second;[118] it is easy to summon others to mind.[119] These texts are not to be recuperated as "difficult," retrieved from uncompromising challenge by strategies of "educational translation."[120] Instead, in their very extremism, they call into question, even stand athwart, standard religious thinking. They make room within normative faith for pain, doubt, and negativity.[121]

The *Akedah* is a narrative reductio ad absurdum of three normative Jewish values, typically expressed as counsel. We are enjoined to (a) submit to God's will; (b) rely on God's goodness; (c) put faith above ethics. In consequence of the extreme pressure to which the *Akedah* subjects these values, three *counter*values become visible. They affirm the merit of (a) readiness to contest God's will; (b) stalwart self-reliance; (c) asserting the sovereignty of ethics. Though these countervalues are rarely expressed as counsel, they become vividly present to every reader of the *Akedah*.

I think of the *Akedah* as the text in which these values and countervalues receive in their unequal coexistence their first and still clearest expression. The *Akedah* exhibits the values in a harsh light; it allows narrative space for the countervalues to be heard.

CONTESTATION, NOT SUBMISSION

There is a reading of the *Akedah*: It is the text that forbids child sacrifice. It marks the moment at which Judaism parted company with the pagan world. The *Akedah* is thus taken to be a story of two commands: the first, to sacrifice Isaac; the second, to prohibit the sacrifice. The greater weight is given to the second command. We esteem Abraham's attentiveness to the voice that led him back to the ethical order, in forbidding him to perform a human sacrifice, as the highest point of the story.[122] We read the *Akedah* as a story about how the prohibition was achieved. We understand it as warning us against the practices of *other* cultures—specifically, against the practices of sacrifice and idolatry. This is a well-known, even familiar, reading.[123] Call it the "anti-sacrifice reading."

The theological objections to human sacrifice are well known. Offered with the magical intention of currying favor with a deity or divine power through gifts, these sacrifices disregard the natural causality of empirical events. Further, no human being can impose his or her will on God or influence God's thoughts or intentions.[124] What God demands is love, not immolation; the *Akedah* purges the idea of the holy of violence and evil. God's justice, truth, love, and grace are revealed to be inalienable; divinity does not mean horror.[125]

In short, the reading understands the first command as limited, while understanding the second command as universal. The first command did not define a new duty (contrast the command to circumcise); it had a specific objective; it was related to one person only. The second command was general in application. A one-off command to sacrifice is thus followed by a general prohibition; it is as if "Sacrifice your son!" was followed by "Sacrifice no one!"

In the story's passage from first to second command, a developmental account of religion is intimated. The *Akedah* is not about the command to offer a sacrifice, then, but the command to desist from it. Maimonides made the general point in the first chapter of the volume of the *Mishne Torah* concerning foreign worship; Ernst Cassirer related the point to the *Akedah* itself. In its beginnings, he wrote, prayer and sacrifice are the only ways by which humans can communicate with their gods. That is an elementary need and tendency of human nature, which can never be completely destroyed. But the *form* of sacrifice and its meaning undergoes a slow and continuous change. In Judaism, the first decisive step is the abrogation of human sacrifices. Not humans but God Himself makes this step. He refuses to accept the sacrifice of Isaac and substitutes the ram that is offered in his stead.[126]

Read thus, the *Akedah* anticipates Moses's command, "When you enter the land the Lord your God is giving you, do not learn to imitate the detestable ways of the nations there. Let no one be found among you who sacrifices their son or daughter in the fire" (Deut. 18:9–10). The purpose of the *Akedah* story, then, was a first statement of a new norm, the prohibition of human sacrifice, and the substitution of animal sacrifice. The ways of the pagan world were rejected.[127] The episode "stands at the liminal moment when human sacrifice ceases to commend itself as the proper means of expressing religious devotion."[128]

When Jews of ancient times practiced human sacrifice, they did so in utter repudiation of their faith. The prophet Jeremiah, speaking in God's name, protested, "They have built shrines to Baal, to put their children to the fire as burnt offerings to Baal— which I never commanded, never decreed, and which never came into My mind" (19:5). Ezekiel says something similar: "When you offer your gifts and make your sons pass through the fire, you defile yourselves with all your idols, even to this day" (20:31). We can register in many places the *Tanakh*'s profound recoil against the offering of children as a sacrifice pleasing to God.[129]

There are two challenges to the anti-sacrifice reading, the standard one and a more interesting one.

The standard one disputes that the *Akedah* brings human sacrifice to an end and infers its persistence from the prophet Micah's condemnation of the practice. According to this challenge, then, when proposed by Jews, the anti-sacrifice reading is deformed by self-admiration. "Look what an advance in civilization we made!"

It is a compelling challenge, for sure. The second command patently does *not* take the form of a general prohibition. The angel does *not* say, "Sacrifice no one!" Further, Abraham is expressly blessed for his readiness to kill his son.[130] The first command lingers; it is not altogether erased. Certainly, the *Akedah* cannot be taken to mark the transition from human sacrifice to animal sacrifice, if only because the story of Cain and Abel makes plain that the Torah regarded the latter practice as belonging to the earliest forms of ritual.[131] And the prophet Micah intimated that it persisted even among Jews in practice of their own faith, at least as they understood it. He made a vehement protest: "Wherewith shall I come before the Lord, and bow myself before the high God? . . . Shall I give my firstborn for my transgression, the fruit of my body for the sin of my soul?" (6:6–8).

The anti-sacrifice reading has an answer to this challenge, though. Aaron Koller provides it, in his sophisticated and thoughtful book on the *Akedah*, *Unbinding Isaac* (2020). God's command to Abraham reflects His sincere desire for human sacrifice. It is tempting to God, and tempting to His servant, that the most precious possession be offered as a sacrifice. Abraham correctly understands this desire of God's and dutifully obeys. Later, and just in time, Abraham understands that the command has been superseded by a more powerful one, against sacrifice. This second command teaches that children cannot be mere adjuncts in someone else's religious experience. One person's religious fulfillment cannot come through harm to another person.[132]

The more interesting challenge has a normative thrust. Against the reading of the *Akedah* as a text that prohibits child sacrifice, it offers a reading that finds in the text an affirmation of sacrifice as a spiritual value. It denies that the *Akedah* concerns Abraham alone; it reads it instead as related to the nature of Jewish religiosity, in the most general sense.[133] For this purpose, "sacrifice" is subject to two revisions.

First, substitutive practices are adopted. The principal chain of substitutions runs like this: Abraham substitutes a ram for his son on Mt. Moriah; in the First and Second Temples, which occupy this site, animal sacrifice is the focus of ritual activity;

after the destruction of the Second Temple, study takes the place of sacrifice but keeps its ethos and drive and something of its sacral power.[134] (There is also a subsidiary chain of substitution that runs like this: sacrifice your firstborn; redeem him with a payment.)[135]

Second, human sacrifice is affirmed but in the version of *self*-sacrifice. Sacrifice ceases to be the transfer of a living thing from the human to the divine realm and instead becomes the giving up of a vital interest for a higher cause.[136] The *Akedah* is read as a foundational story of parallel self-sacrifices in this second sense, Abraham and Isaac each volunteering what is most precious to him.[137] They sacrifice their futures.[138] In grimly rhapsodic language, J. B. Soloveitchik affirms sacrifice as an "iron law" in Jewish history. It is humanity's affair, he writes, whether the sacrifice consists of physical agony or of spiritual surrender. God wills humanity to choose the altar and the sacrifice. Abraham sacrificed Isaac not on Mt. Moriah but in the depths of his heart. He gave up Isaac the very instant that God asked him to return his most precious possession to its legitimate master and owner. There was no need for the physical sacrifice, since experientially Abraham had already fulfilled the command.[139] Sacrifice is a cornerstone of Judaism; the command of the *Akedah* was never canceled by God.[140]

It is precisely at this point, when the anti-sacrifice reading is overrun by this more interesting challenge, that the first countervalue breaks cover. David Hartman, in express opposition to his teacher J. B. Soloveitchik, deprecates sacrifice and champions contestation, by deploying "Sodom-Abraham" against "*Akedah*-Abraham." Sodom-Abraham is an empowered man of faith, whose moral intuition is as vital to him as his belief in God. *Akedah*-Abraham, however, is passive, acquiescent to God's demands, accepting of his own finitude, incapable of deciphering God's will. Abraham contained dichotomous realities, self-assertion and self-denial.[141]

As a mode of reasoning, the *Akedah* demands that we sacrifice our intellect and intuition, everything we know and cherish as a human being, in deference and obedience to the word of God. It sustains a sclerotic conservatism: "If we change anything, everything will collapse."[142] To Hartman, *Akedah*-Abraham is a warning, not a guide.[143]

SELF-RELIANCE, NOT RELIANCE

The anti-sacrifice reading does not just warn against strange worship; it also affirms God's goodness, the benevolent interest He has in us, the very foundation of any theodicy, any account of God's justice as it operates in the world. Rav Ami said, "There is no death without sin; were a person not to sin, he would not die. And there is no suffering without iniquity" (Shabbat 55a). To this general proposition, Jews add that God loves Israel. He is with Israel in times of trouble; God always responds to Israel's need.[144] God's goodness can be relied on.

The *Akedah* exposes this reliance to withering scrutiny. The value does not survive consideration of the irreversible harm done in the story to Abraham himself and to the people closest to him. The *Akedah* contains a warning to us about God. He is not consistently benevolent. This warning is later taken up by Isaiah. Speaking through His prophet, God declares, "I form the light, and create darkness: I make peace, *and create evil*: I the Lord do all these things" (45:7; italics added).

We know the questions addressed to conventional theodicies. Why did God create a world in which natural disasters occur, in which the virtuous can suffer and the evil can prosper, often at the expense of the virtuous? And having done so, why did He not intervene to remedy unmerited suffering, unmerited benefit? Call this "the puzzle of omission."

The answers given to these questions are equally well known.[145] We should adopt an extended perspective; the domain of divine justice is the world to come; the apparently righteous may not truly be righteous, while the apparently flourishing wicked may either not be wicked or not be flourishing; the vulgar desires of the wicked bring strength to the vital current of all people, the average and the saintly;[146] God does not *intend* for the virtuous to suffer (we shouldn't muddle "immediate" with "general" providence); suffering commonly follows nature's operation; we have free will; we suffer for our own good; God tests us, to increase the reward ultimately due to us; God has withdrawn from the world (*tsimtsum*). Sholem Aleichem's Tevye speaks the folk wisdom of the Jewish people: "There's no arguing with God, and you can't tell Him how to run this world of His."[147]

So far, so familiar. The puzzle of omission is difficult but not impossible to address.

The *Akedah* raises a different puzzle, however. It is unrelated to any specific law against child sacrifice. How is it that God Himself performs acts that cause the innocent to suffer? This is not a scene setting or framing puzzle of omission. It is instead a puzzle of *com*mission. The puzzle does not arise when God creates conditions in which the wicked are able to injure the innocent; it arises when God Himself injures the innocent. Indeed, how could it *not* puzzle, this disordering, injurious intervention by God in the world's affairs?

"I gave them *laws that were not good* and rules by which they could not live," says the prophet Ezekiel in God's name. "When they set aside every first issue of the womb I defiled them by their very gifts—that I might render them desolate, that they might know that I am the LORD" (20:25–26; italics added).[148] How are Jews to respond to laws that are not good, laws that mandate child sacrifice? The prophet leaves the question open, as a challenge to his Jewish audience.

The Talmud relates an exchange between God and Moses about the great Rabbi Akiva. Moses says, "You have shown me Rabbi Akiva's Torah, now show me his reward." God replies, "Return to where you were." Moses witnesses Akiva's flesh being

weighed in a butcher shop in Rome and understands that he
has been tortured to death by the imperial authorities. Moses
challenges God, "Master of the Universe, this is the Torah, and
this is its reward?" God replies, "Be silent; for such is My decree!"
(Menachot 29b). In the set of facts that prompted this story,
the agents of the suffering were the Romans. The question put
to God was, Why did you *allow* evil? The *Akedah* prompts a
more radical question: Why did you *perpetrate* evil?

There is a Midrash that also has a bearing on our topic.
A man sees a building in flames. He ponders, "Is it possible that
the building lacks a person who has control over it?" The building's owner looks out and says, "I am the owner." In the same
way, says the Midrash, when Abraham pondered, "Is the world
without a guide?," God looked out and said, "I am the guide."[149]
That is to say, though God may be slow to extinguish the fire,
He did not cause it; He is not an arsonist. The *Akedah* prompts
the question, Did not God there play the arsonist's part, requiring Abraham to burn his own house down?[150]

The *Akedah* returns us to an essential solitariness. "Theodicy" reveals itself to be no more than an intellectualist simplification, a mechanical formulation. The world is *not* a just place;
the arc of the universe does *not* bend toward justice. Danger
comes from God, not only from humankind.[151] God is *not* to
be trusted; He does *not* submit to morality's discipline.[152] We
are alone.

RELIGION *AS* ETHICS, NOT *ABOVE* ETHICS

The *Akedah* is typically read as affirming religion above ethics.
Yeshayahu Leibowitz (1903–1993) made this reading the cen-
terpiece of his theology. On Mt. Moriah, all human values were
annulled and overridden by fear and love of God. The *Akedah*
is humanity's absolute mastery over its own nature. Humanity
overcame its materiality, that is, its physical nature. This includes
all the benevolent sentiments as well as conscience; all the fac-

tors in humanity's makeup that an atheistic humanism regards as "good." In the morning prayers, we find the request, "Compel our *Yetzer* [inclination] to subject itself to You," a request meant to apply to our benevolent as well as evil inclinations. It was Abraham who first burst the bounds of the universal human bondage—the bondage of humanity to the forces of its own nature. The daily performance of the mitzvoth represents the motivation animating the *Akedah*.

Leibowitz would insist that the duties of faith take precedence over all human needs, interests, and values, even of those divine promises embodied in visions of the future! Faith is in conflict with human nature; it demands that we suppress our human sensibilities. Judaism rejects the primacy of the ethical as an autonomous category. Abraham is required to assume the service of God even when it is dissociated from all human needs, feelings, and values. The Torah cannot be reduced to moral principles. True devotion to religious values is totalitarian. The *Akedah* is the highest expression of religious devotion, the supreme value before which all human considerations must be set aside.[153] These are the arguments of a fanatic, although Leibowitz was not a fanatic.

By radical contrast, Levinas makes the simple affirmation, "Ethics is not simply the corollary of the religious but is, of itself, the element in which religious transcendence receives its original meaning."[154] The prophet Isaiah tells us that the religious is at its zenith in the ethical movement toward the other person, that the very proximity of God is inseparable from the ethical transformation of the social, that this transformation means the abolition of domination and servitude. "At the heart of the Infinite, where the intellect dwells, there is an independent man, master of his fate, who communicates with the Eternal, in the clear light of intellectual and moral action."[155] It is the accomplishment of the ethical that accomplishes the religious.[156] Levinas's conception of the "ethical other" is itself

(Samuel Moyn suggests) a secularized theological concept. He does more than redefine religion as ethics; he denies that it has any other content.[157] God is the master of justice; He judges in the open light of reason and discourse.[158]

Reading somewhat against the grain of the story, Levinas therefore associates Abraham's "Here I am" with "love, subjectivity and ethics." It submits to "the glory of the Infinite," by "ordering me to the other."[159] The fear of God, with which the story ends, is not to be opposed to the love of Isaac but rather to be interpreted as "fear for the other man."[160] For Levinas, then, there is no "beyond good and evil" in Judaism; if there is to be any "suspension," it must be of the "religious" in the name of the "ethical."[161] The temptation to go above the ethical must always be resisted.[162] God appears in the ethics and justice of the relation of one person to another, in the one for the other.[163] "The ethical order does not prepare us for the Divinity; it is the very accession to the Divinity. All the rest is a dream."[164] That Abraham obeyed the first command is merely "astonishing"; that he obeyed the second command is "essential."[165]

Each one us must decide whom we are with, Leibowitz or Levinas. Are we ready to submit our religious beliefs and practices to ethical scrutiny?

The *Akedah*'s exploration (alternatively, the explorations it prompts) of these three values and countervalues has become central to Jewish inquiry. Is sacrifice *truly* the highest spiritual value? Can God *truly* be trusted? Should we *truly* elevate religion above ethics? These questions are Judaism's challenges to itself. Astonishingly, the *Akedah* allows them without thereby violating the boundaries of Jewish religious self-understanding. It constitutes a moment of autocritique[166] and thereby warns against seeking from Jewish faith the merely consolatory.

5

◆◗◆◗◆

"Abraham, Abraham"

The Abraham story affirms and advances that tendency in Jewish thinking, and thinking about Jews, to think dichotomously—that is, to organize the thinking into mutually exclusive or contradictory pairs. To structure the world in terms of binary oppositions is, of course, a process intrinsic to human thought in general.[1] What is distinctive about the tendency under review in this chapter is its content and perhaps also its special intensity of application.

Dichotomous Judaism

Dichotomizing has become a standard move, responsive to Scriptural duplications (say, the two accounts of Creation[2] or the Almighty's two names in the *Akedah*),[3] rabbinic perspectives (say, the rabbinic houses of Hillel and Shamai), communal divisions (say, between secular and religious Jews), and the brute facts of geography (Israel and Diaspora). We do not need to look far to find practitioners of this dichotomizing.

The nineteenth-century Jewish historian Heinrich Graetz is one such practitioner. He set the seventeenth-century philosopher Spinoza both against *and* with the false messiah Shabbtai Zvi, because while the one was the "diametrical opposite" of the other, *both* "worked hard for the destruction of Judaism."[4] He set the eighteenth-century philosopher Moses Mendelssohn against the founder of Hasidism, Baal Shem Tov. He set Judaism's philosophical tendencies against its mystical tendencies, and he set the dispersion of the Jews, "with its attendant cosmopolitan existence," against the Talmudic system, "whose purpose is to isolate Judaism."[5] He defines Diaspora existence as studying and wandering, thinking and enduring, learning and suffering; the persecuted, oppressed Jew coexists with the earnest, scholarly Jew.[6]

The late twentieth-century Jewish historian Yosef Haim Yerushalmi added to these dichotomies one that sets premodern Jewish self-understanding against modern Jewish self-understanding, expressed as "anti-historical memory"/"history." As a professional Jewish historian, he writes, "I am a new creature in Jewish history."[7]

Joseph B. Soloveitchik was another dichotomizer, illuminating with his binarisms some oppositions constitutive of Jewish existence.[8]

For Martin Buber, dichotomizing was almost a reflex: no other people, he wrote, has begotten such base adventurers and betrayers or such exalted prophets and redeemers. The two dominant human types who wage the struggle of Judaism's internal history are the prophet and the priest. The prophet wants truth; the priest, power. They are eternal types in the history of Judaism. In Hasidism, what Buber termed "underground Judaism" was "victorious for a while over the official kind." There is ever a battle between the priests and the prophets, the rabbis and the heretics, the law of the halakha and the popular Aggadah and the world of mysticism.[9]

Freud cited this tendency to spin out pairs, this dichotomizing, in defense of the improbable arguments in his last work, *Moses and Monotheism* (1938). Jewish history, he wrote, is familiar to us for its dualities: two kingdoms into which the nation divides, and so on (23:52). He then added his own somewhat bizarre dualities:[10] two religious inaugurations, one in Egypt and one in Meribeth-Kadesh, and two religious inaugurators, both named Moses, one an Egyptian, the other a Midianite priest, one rationalist, and one inspired, obscurantist.[11] Freud fully embraced contradictions, constructing his science of the mind out of them.[12]

The dichotomizing is not limited to the internal organization of Jewish life. To grasp the weight of the dichotomizing tendency in Jewish thinking, we must add further dichotomies, ones that set Jewish thinking against non-Jewish thinking and ones in which Jewish elements and non-Jewish elements coexist in a greater whole. The first is foundational to Judaism; the second, mostly characteristic of Jewish life lived in modern times.

As to foundational dichotomies, Maimonides writes, regarding the instruction to be given to a convert, "We inform him of the fundamentals of the faith, i.e., the unity of God and the prohibition against the worship of false deities" (MT Forbidden Intercourse 14.2). This is not mere definition by negation; what is negated has itself a determinate character. The dichotomy produces a double definition of Judaism, one positive (what it is), the other negative (what it is not). The master dichotomy has many metonymic iterations: "Jerusalem"/"Athens," "Hebraic"/ "Hellenic," "God of Abraham"/"God of the Philosophers," and so on. "Two nations are in your womb," God tells Rebecca, Isaac's wife (Gen. 25:23). The nations, derived from the sons Jacob and Esau, will be locked in mutual enmity forever.

These foundational dichotomies were complicated by modernity. Jewish affiliations and interests came to incorporate, to the despair of many tradition-minded Jews, "non-Jewish" elements. Modernity ruptured Jewish "totality."[13] Among the precursors of this radical, transformative development were the philosophers Benedict Spinoza and Moses Mendelssohn, their double formation in medieval rabbinic and early modern Christian cultures indicating the path taken by the generality of Jews in the decades and centuries that followed. This was never a simple matter. The liberal version assigns confessional existence to private spaces and political existence to public spaces. Well formulated in two slogans, "A Jew at home, and a man outside" and "For the Jews as individuals, everything, for the Jews as a nation, nothing!,"[14] this version is as inadequate for Jewish life (which has a strong national aspect), as it is intolerable to antisemites.

It is as if, when reflecting on our Jewish condition, the dichotomy is the unavoidable, necessary form in which we must work through our perplexities. Levinas, responsive to just this sense of inner necessity, writes, "The very fact of questioning one's Jewish identity means it is already lost. But by the same token, it is precisely through this cross-examination that one still hangs on to it."[15]

We may propose, then, the dichotomy as a Jewish cultural institution.[16] And yet, it does not stand unchallenged. It is instead vulnerable to two distinct forces, the one a drive toward the unifying of binary formulations, the other a drive toward complicating them.

So first, the dichotomy as cultural institution coexists with that *other* Jewish cultural institution, the principle of unity.

What makes Judaism distinctive is its resistance to all *theological* dualisms in favor of God's unity (Guide, II.31). "The Lord is God; in the heavens above and the earth below, there is no other" (Deut. 4:39). In the early centuries of the Common Era, Judaism accordingly found itself in conflict with Gnosticism, which distinguished between the hidden and benevolent God, the God of the "illuminate" whose knowledge they call "gnosis" and the Creator and Lawgiver, whom they also call the Jewish God and to whom they attribute the Hebrew Scriptures. The term "Jewish God" was abusive and meant to be so. As Gershom Scholem explains, the Gnostics regarded as a misfortune for religion this confusion between the two Gods, the higher, loving one and the lower, merely just one.[17]

Behind this principle of unity is a drive *toward* unity, as a value good for all contexts. It holds the promise of peace, the reconciliation of all contradictions, the solution of all questions, the elimination of all dissent. Let the following statement stand for the drive in its sunniest, most affirmative iteration: "The religious man of any age transcends divisions, subsumes contrasts into harmonious emotion, and exists in unmediated closeness to God, the world, and other Jews." The achievement, writes the author, is "a single, unified felicific state." Much internal conflict turns out to be pseudoconflict or spurious conflict or not conflict at all; the actual conflict that survives this analysis is a defective state that can be overcome.[18] I am skeptical.

It is better, perhaps, to think of this drive as an ungovernable desire, ever at risk of self-frustration. "The greatest intellectual temptation in my life," writes Elias Canetti (relevantly, in 1944), "the only one I have to fight very hard against is: to be a total Jew. I would like to be named Noah or Abraham." Abraham, of course. But Noah? He was not a Jew; he was instead the ancestor of all human beings—not a Jew at all then, still less a "total Jew."[19] Canetti names the temptation and resists it in a single thought.

Let me now turn to the second force that works, with greater subtlety than the first, against the dichotomy as Jewish cultural institution. Unlike the drive to eliminate all dichotomies, this force both affirms and subverts them; it restates them, that is, but in a compromised or otherwise ragged state.

Sometimes this is because the relation between the polarities is more spectral than binary, not facing each other in antagonism but connected to each other by infinite gradations. To the great Jewish scholar Harry Austryn Wolfson, say, there were Hellenizers and Hebraizers, Hellenic and Hebraic tendencies, *inside* Judaism.[20] And certainly, not every dichotomy is reducible to an "either/or."

Sometimes this is because there is typically an inequality between the terms, the second term being the disfavored one. Sometimes a fundamental dichotomy, it is said, will collapse in messianic times (sacred/profane; Jew/Gentile).[21] And sometimes it is because what presents as dichotomous turns out to be non-antagonistic aspects of a single phenomenon.[22] Ostensibly dichotomous terms might even be impossible to disentangle (say, the philosophical/the mystical).[23]

Sometimes, a dichotomy is accepted so readily, with such flippancy, that it prompts a recoil, a refusal to accept that things can indeed be that effortlessly easy. I am thinking here of the answer that Levinas gave to the question, "How have you harmonized these two modes of thought, the Biblical and the philosophical?" He replied, with what he must have intended as a magisterial insouciance, "Were they supposed to harmonize?"[24] Who would not respond to this performance with the murmured dissent, "Yes, they were. How could you think otherwise?"

Last, some dichotomies are historically conditioned. They comprise terms that are not dichotomous in all periods. The dichotomy between Aggadah and halakha, stories and rules, narrative and law, is a good example of such a dichotomy. It is no more than a modern scholarly construct, says Isadore Twersky. It is not a reality of Jewish intellectual history for Talmudists, who mix the two freely and naturally, while recognizing essential generic differences.[25]

To this Jewish dichotomizing, in all its diversity and complexity, I add the pair Abraham 1/Abraham 2. Or rather, I add one further version of Abraham pairs. There are two others, each rooted in an episode in Abraham 2's life:

- *Abram/Abraham*: Circumcision affirms his direction of travel, following the departure from Ur. Already estranged from his place of birth and his father's household, he is now physically estranged from all males, save for the male members of his family and household. He is no longer as the generality of male humankind. He takes a new name, to mark this moment of confirmatory alienation and confirmatory intimacy of association with God.
- *Sodom/Akedah*: Abraham challenges God in one episode and submits in another episode. In the absence of proper consideration of Abraham 1's career, these contradictory responses have excited an immoderate interest among commentators. As we saw in chapter 4, David Hartman proposes them as a strong dichotomy. We must choose between the Sodom paradigm and the *Akedah* paradigm, he writes. We cannot have both. We cannot both suspend *and* affirm our ethical values.[26]

These pairs sit inside the one paradigm of Abraham 2, Abraham the man of faith. The first one is not a dichotomy at all. Rather, it affirms an identity of character. The name may have changed, he may now be circumcised, but Abraham is the same man as the one told to leave Haran. The second dichotomy is a limited one: the challenge and the submission are to the same God, and the challenge itself is punctuated by much deference. "Behold now, I have taken upon me to speak unto the Lord, which am but dust and ashes." "Oh let not the Lord be angry, and I will speak." "Behold now, I have taken upon me to speak unto the Lord." "Oh let not the Lord be angry, and I will speak yet but this once" (18:27, 30, 31, 32).

My version of the Abraham pair constitutes a more radical dichotomy. It gives equal weight to both the pre-Torah and Torah periods of Abraham's life. It makes light of the name change, taking it to be nothing more than a token of God's covenant with Abraham, just as circumcision is nothing more than a token of God's covenant with Abraham and his descendants. And it takes the Sodom paradigm to be a partial, limited return of the repressed Abraham 1 paradigm. The meaning of the Sodom challenge is to mark the limit that Abraham 2 reaches, in the reliving of his Abraham 1 life of open contest.

The Two Abrahams

Abraham endures forever, Abraham Joshua Heschel wrote, and we are Abraham.[27] I would rewrite this formulation. *Abraham 1* and *Abraham 2* endure forever, and we are *both* of them. Every Jewish life is two lives, the lives of the two Abrahams.

Abraham 1

The appearance of Abraham 1 was an event in history: it is the first appearance of the self-authored human being. It had an epochal significance, the introduction or *re*introduction of monotheism to the world. It was an axial moment.

Abraham's relations with his father became wholly negative; his relations with his mother were practically nonexistent. He actively, openly rejected his father not once but twice: the first time in Ur, with his public, destructive act of disrespect, the breaking of the idols; the second time in Haran, with his similarly public abandonment of Terah, a broken and infirm old man. The absence of any reference in the Torah to Abraham's mother supports the "self-originating" understanding of Abraham. (The rabbis improvised various names for her: Amtilai in Bava Batra 91a and Atudai in *Pirke de Rabbi Eleazer*; the pre-rabbinic, earlier Jubilees gives her name as Ednah.) It is as if he had no mother at all. To be the first father, it is necessary that he himself was not a son.

Abraham complicated the then-given understanding of what

it was to be a father. In his life, a certain *competitiveness* between God and fathers was initiated. Indeed, Abraham offers an extended lesson to humankind: fathers are not to be worshiped. He does not worship his father; he is not a father to be worshiped. The depopulation of the heavens includes the expulsion of ancestors. They are not to be worshiped. They have no powers, not even in life, independent of God's will. They have no authority, other than allowed by God, moment by moment. The One Father is not to be confused with fathers. When God commands Abraham to depart from Haran, he is precisely *not* endorsing Terah's commitment to Nimrod. We know this because God both withholds that destination ("a land I will show you") and requires Abraham to leave his father behind.

It is against the following argument, then, that Judaism would set itself and in respect of which the *Akedah* lays the ground: "What are the stories of the gods? What are our feelings when we believe in God? They are feelings of awe before power, dread of the thunderbolts of Zeus, confidence in the everlasting arms, unease beneath the all-seeing eye. The feelings of guilt and inescapable vengeance, of smothered hate and of a security we can hardly do without. We have only to remind ourselves of these feelings and the stories of the gods and goddesses and heroes in which these feelings find expression, to be reminded of how we felt as children to our parents." The author continues, "When a man's father fails him by death or weakness how much he needs another father, one in the heavens."[28] But what if the father has failed the son not by weakness or death but by an act of violence against him, one initiated (on this account) by the most powerful father of all?

Maimonides writes, "Abraham our Father was the first to make known the belief in the Unity, to establish prophecy, and to perpetuate this opinion and draw people to it" (Guide, III.24). He defined the ideal form of the Jew's relation to God. Judaism is the struggle against idolatry. Abraham invites by his example

Jews to resume, to continue, the struggle that started in a shop in Ur several millennia ago. Jews have declared this commitment. Maimonides made himself the heir to this struggle.[29] The idols themselves change; idolatry itself is a constant. Rejection of idolatry is typically taken to be the sum of Judaism's identity, understood in negative terms (MT Avoda Zara 2).[30]

Here is Maimonides again: "The first intention of the Laws as a whole is to put an end to idolatry, to wipe out its traces and all that is bound up with it, even its memory as well as all that leads to any of its works" (Guide, III.29). The Jewish tradition makes affirmation of the unity of the one God the reverse side of rejection of idolatry—one can't have the one without the other, is the argument. It is before all else a project of self-purification. The struggle is against deformations of Judaism. This is the great project of Maimonides, writes James Diamond: to purge his tradition, both rabbinic and biblical, of its magical, mythical and superstitious elements. It is work for each generation. With Abraham's death, there was a deterioration once more toward idolatry, to the point where Abraham's descendants could barely be distinguished from their idolatrous counterparts in Egypt. And so on.[31]

The struggle against idolatry, which begins with Abraham, is a campaign for every generation. One of the first uses made by the new political mythology of Nazism was to combat Judaism, wrote Ernst Cassirer. This was not surprising. Judaism had, from its very beginnings, attacked and rejected all those mythical elements that had once constituted religious thought. The classic expression of this rejection was the prohibition against graven images. It represented a complete break with mythical thought, which has imagery at its very core. To deprive myth of imagery is to ensure its decay. Myth is anthropomorphic in its essence, and through it, we can never find God's true nature. Anthropomorphism leads to idolatry, not to religion, Cassirer concluded. The deification of nations is the same idolatry as that of natural things.[32]

What is the elevated life according to Abraham 1? Commitment to a life of intellectual dissent, that is, finding one's vocation in critical engagement with one's society; to stand for the principle of human creativity within that society; to define oneself at some distance from established positions, to say "no" to all worldly authorities. If philosophy is still necessary, wrote one of Abraham's successors, it is so only in the way it has been from time immemorial: as critique, as resistance to the expanding heteronomy. Even if only as thought's powerless attempt to remain its own master, it will convict of untruth, by their own criteria, all fabricated mythologies. It is incumbent on philosophy to provide a refuge for freedom.[33]

For a radical restatement of Abraham 1's vocation within Jewish life, we have to wait until the Haskalah, the Jewish Enlightenment, and specifically for the arrival of the Polish-German Solomon Maimon (1753–1800). He was sunk in the Jewish life of his place and time: its people, benighted; its scholars, obscurantist and despotic. Maimon then reasoned his way toward Enlightenment thinking, becoming the interpreter and interlocutor of Kant and the author of works of philosophy and of an autobiography.

"I left my people, my homeland, and my family," he explained in his autobiography, "to seek the truth." In this appropriation of Abraham 2's career, he defined his life as a successor to Abraham 1. The restatement of vocation is in the modifications to the language of God's *lech lecha* command. Maimon did not leave at the direction of another; his object was not unspecified land but as yet unascertained truth; he was fully alone. The leaving was as much an assertion of independence as Abraham's leaving was a gesture of submission. The German Enlightenment publicist and novelist Karl Phillip Moritz praised the au-

tobiography. It shows, he wrote, how powers of thought can develop in a human mind under even the most oppressive conditions and how a true drive for knowledge can't be scared off by obstacles that seem impossible to overcome. Maimon's opening move in this endeavor was the same as Abraham's, thinking freely about the fundamental laws of the religion of his fathers (as he wrote). We are all Epicureans, all *Apikorsim*, now, he declared.[34]

Hannah Arendt understood Maimon to be the first of his type. People such as Maimon contributed most to the spiritual dignity of their people. They were great enough to transcend the bounds of nationality. They were bold spirits. They understood Jewish emancipation as the admission of Jews as Jews to the ranks of humanity. They achieved liberty and popularity by the sheer force of imagination. As individuals, they started an emancipation of their own, of their own hearts and brains. Though excluded from formal society, they truly did not desire for its embrace. In the arena of politics, they become rebels.[35]

Abraham 2

Philo, the first-century Jewish allegorizer of the Torah, reads the phrase in the opening verse of chapter 12, "leave your land, birthplace, and father's house," as "body, senses, and reason." That is, only when Abraham had left his "reason" did he "begin to become acquainted with the powers of the living God."[36]

In the Abraham story, prayer is the hope of God, and vision is the evidence of God. Prayer precedes vision; vision is the reward for prayer and, on occasion, a demand exacted by answered prayer. Abraham's first prayer is also his last: with Abraham freed from the furnace, God is now his interlocutor. Abraham does not call to God; he hears Him. Abraham's God-directed words are not requests; they are responses. He is not a conjuror of divinities: he cannot summon God. He has to await His arrivals and then wait upon Him. When Abraham consults his mind, it is not for purposes of reasoning but in order to entertain his visions.

Abraham 2 is the Abraham of "I am but dust and ashes" (Gen. 18:27), the Abraham so admired in the Jewish tradition. A person who "takes up no space, and does not seek anything, and does not need anything," explained a Mussarist. "And so he does not have need of jealousy or hatred, for no one stands in his way, and he does not become angry, and he does not become proud, and he does not have the craving to fulfill his appetites and his desires for pleasure."[37] This is the Abraham who pleads for the wicked of Sodom and waits on travelers. Another Mussarist (glossing Maimonides, glossing the Talmud) wrote, "One who is not compassionate cannot truly be of the seed of Abraham our father."[38]

Though we find Abraham 2 avatars everywhere in the Jewish tradition, Judah Halevi (ca. 1075–1141), a poet and a physician—and then a theologian, defensively—is more than representative. He may be read as drawing out all the implications of Abraham 2's position. Speculation and reasoning do not give God pleasure, he writes in his masterwork, *The Book of the Kuzari* (1130–1140). The work rallies to Judaism. It champions Judaism against philosophy, using philosophy's language. It speaks up for a "despised religion." It has an antirationalist tone; it is hard on intellectuals. It is a philosophical fiction, a polemic in favor of Judaism's truth claims, a literary work of antiphilosophy, a set of dialogues that has monological force. "I was asked to state what arguments and replies I could bring to bear," writes Halevi, "against the attacks of philosophers and followers of other religions, and against Jewish sectarians who attack the rest of Israel."[39] Across several conversations, a rabbi triumphs in his undertaking to convert the Khazar king to Judaism. It is conventional to set up as a dichotomous pair, Halevi and Maimonides, the *Kuzari* and *The Guide of the Perplexed*, antirationalist and rationalist works, contending for the superiority of revelation and reason, respectively. The convention unravels on examination.[40]

The myth of philosophy is that we can know based on our native powers alone and that God is a conclusion only reached at the end of inquiry.[41] Philosophers are overrated: There are no prophets among them. Philosophers will always let you down. They will abandon a position if it no longer seems to them to be rationally defensible. Their faith is always subject to their reason. Reason chooses those whose natural gifts are perfect, that is, philosophers. The divine influence, however, singles out those who appear worthy of being connected with it, such as prophets and pious men.[42]

Our intellect, sunk in matter, cannot penetrate to the true knowledge of things, except for the grace of God, by special faculties that he has placed in the senses. To the chosen among His creatures, He has given an inner eye that sees things as they really are, without any alteration.[43] Those who speculate on the ways of glorifying God for the purpose of His worship are much more zealous than those who practice the service of God exactly as it is commanded. The latter are at ease with their tradition; their soul is calm like one who lives in a town, and they fear not any hostile opposition. The former, however, are like a straggler in the desert, who does not know what may happen.[44]

We embrace what intellectuals despise: miracle, signs, wonders. We can say, "We believe in the God of Abraham, Isaac, and Jacob, who led the children of Israel out of Egypt with signs and wonders; who fed them in the desert and gave them the land, after having made them traverse the sea and the Jordan in a miraculous way; who sent Moses with His law and many prophets thereafter to confirm it with promises to the observant and threats to the disobedient. Our belief is comprised in the Torah."[45] The philosophers, on the other hand, posit a God who has no will, is without likes or dislikes, and is beyond all desire and intention.

Human reason is out of place in matters of divine action, on account of its incapacity to grasp them. Reason must rather obey, just as a sick person must obey the physician in applying his or her medicines and advice. Suspicious of the distaste that spiritualizing philosophers expressed toward all things physical, Lenn E. Goodman writes that Halevi prized language and imagination in all their materiality and cherished the warmth of the soul's attachments.[46]

There was an excuse for the Greek philosophers. Science and religion did not come to them as inheritances. Aristotle exerted his mind, because he had no tradition from any reliable source at his disposal. He meditated on the beginning and end of the world but found as much difficulty in the theory of a beginning as in that of eternity. Had he lived among a people with well-authenticated and generally acknowledged traditions, he would have applied his deductions and arguments to establish the theory of creation, however difficult, instead of eternity, which is even more difficult to accept. The theory of creation derives great weight from the prophetic tradition of Adam, Noah, and Moses, which is more deserving of credence than mere speculation.[47]

Abraham bore his burden honestly—the life in Ur Kasdim, emigration, circumcision, the removal of Ishmael, and the distress of the sacrifice of Isaac—because his share of the Divine Influence had come to him through love, not speculation, writes Halevi. Abraham observed that not the smallest detail could escape God, that he was quickly rewarded for his piety and guided on the right path, to such an extent that he did everything in the order dictated by God. How could he do otherwise than deprecate his former speculation? When divine power showed itself to him, he gave up all his speculations and strove only to gain God's favor. Halevi celebrates Abraham's abandonment of philosophy.[48]

We do not need to rest with a medieval poet. There is the

early twentieth-century Jewish thinker Franz Rosenzweig and the mid-twentieth-century Jewish thinker Michael Wyschogrod. Rosenzweig was a translator of Halevi. Philosophy is a special type of temptation, he argued. A proper relation with God no more depends on a theory of God than a proper relation with a person depends on a theory of humankind. Philosophy starts from something valuable, "wonder," a sense of the miraculousness and mystery of the existence of the world, of humans, of God, but breaks off to demand an answer. The sense of wonder is immobilized. This insistence on an answer is a disease, *apoplexia philosophica*. No person is immune from this disease's attack, which is born of suspicion, impatience, a wish for certainty.[49] Rosenzweig, who began his masterwork, *The Star of Redemption* (1919), with the slogan "In philosophos" (Against philosophy), found in Abraham's "Here I am" the exemplary response of humanity to God. "Now, called by his name, twice, in a supreme definiteness that could not but be heard, now he answers, all unlocked, all spread apart, all ready, all-soul, 'Here I am.'"[50]

For Wyschogrod, the Jewish people are intelligent beyond all measure but are not philosophic. Philosophy is a tradition that will continue to remain foreign to Judaism. The God of the Bible is a person; He has a personality, has emotions and plans, has weaknesses, insecurities, and neuroses, and makes calculations that sometimes succeed and sometimes fail. Against this simple fact, Jewish philosophy has marshaled all of its resources. Philosophers of Judaism do not understand that Jewish existence is embodied. Gefilte fish, bagels with lox and cream cheese, the smell of chicken simmering in broth—these too are Judaism. This embarrasses our philosophers—they would much prefer discussion of Judaism's ideas, its theory of humanity and God and particularly its ethics, for which they have the highest respect. But for the body of Israel, these things are not primary.[51]

For neither thinker, of course, is philistinism the preferred alternative to philosophy. The philistine, says Rosenzweig, can scarcely be considered a perfect specimen of health—rather the contrary.[52] Though it is "difficult" to speak of "Jewish theology," says Wyschogrod, there is no problem at all in speaking of "Jewish thought."[53] And there is no problem either, Levinas would add, speaking of "wisdom."[54]

What Do These Abrahams Have to Do with Each Other?

Why does the Torah account of Abraham's life start in Haran? Certainly *not* because the Torah is concerned only with "highlights," not "details," as has been suggested.[55] Nor is it because it follows the "well-known principle," "the Torah elaborates in certain cases and is brief in others,"[56] which is not a principle at all but merely states the problem. The medieval Jewish commentator Nachmanides (1195–ca. 1270) had a better suggestion. The Torah does not want to deal at length with the opinions of idol worshipers, he wrote, or go into detail on the disputes between Abraham and the Chaldeans.[57] That is, it didn't care to be more precise. A first approximation would do, adequate to the function of establishing a boundary. As to what might lie beyond it, of what possible interest could that be? Mere follies, both vicious and simpleminded. Nachmanides was onto something, certainly. But there is also the character of Abraham 1 to consider.

Abraham was a mere infant of three years when God became known to him, asserts the Talmud (Nedarim 32a). Relying on the most whimsical reasoning,[58] it thereby dismisses the philosophical Abraham of the midrashim, who found his way to God at forty. This Abraham, Abraham 1, would have to wait for many centuries, until Maimonides's *Mishne Torah*, to bring him back to Jewish consciousness (MT Avodah Zara 1).

Suppose a dialogue between the two Abrahams, one that takes place before their respective crises. Abraham 1 begins, as of course he would.

Abraham 1: "My motto is, 'Interrogate the given!'

"I rely on the Jewish philosopher Husserl. Husserl is most Jewish in his interrogation of the 'given,' which is central to his phenomenology, its 'magic word.' Husserl's philosophy, his science of phenomenology, endeavors to return to and attend to 'givenness' in all its forms. And then to work beyond it.

"We are children of the world, the world of nature and the world of culture. It is not just my world but the world of others too. It is the world in which we live 'our normal, unbroken, coherent life.' This is our *Lebenswelt*, our 'life-world.' There are two ways in which we engage with the world, natural thinking, or 'the natural attitude,' and philosophical thinking, or 'the philosophical attitude.' These are two very different versions of 'waking life.'

"Lived experience is 'given.' We are awake to this world. It is the 'naturally, normal one.' It takes cognition for granted. It is a world in which 'people live, work, judge, evaluate, converse; a world of people, animals, tables, clothes, of red and green, hot and cold,' and so on. We are marked by our dealings with others in relation to institutions, laws, morals, customs, and so on. Members of a group (state, church, etc.) know themselves as its members. The natural attitude has a certain naturalness, straightforwardness, naiveté. It is 'common sense.' The world is 'simply there for me,' spread out in time and space. This is a general, unquestioning acceptance of the world, everything that is taken for granted. We swim in the flow of the world's 'givens.' We are in the rhythm of the world, running its natural, practical course. The natural attitude is the normal, everyday attitude of human beings prior to any skeptical questioning. It is captivating. And there is a natural wisdom and knowledge.

"The philosophical attitude is a 'completely different sort of waking life.' It demands a 'total change of interest'; it 'breaks through the normality of straightforward living'; it is 'founded on a particular resolve of the will.' This is the philosophical attitude. It puts the achievements of knowledge and thus the world itself in question. It is a 'universal and radical reflection' and must be 'carried out with the greatest self-responsibility.' It has as its object 'the actual and highest truth.' Such persons are 'self-thinkers,' autonomous, self-critical philosophers, who subject their beliefs to the most radical scrutiny. This placing in question all hitherto-existing convictions, which forbids the taking in in advance of any judgment about their validity, must be undertaken at least once in a person's life. Then, though my whole life of acts—experiencing, thinking, valuing, and so on—remains, and indeed flows on, it is no longer before my eyes as 'the' world but is instead a 'phenomenon.'[59]

"It is for this reason that while I can be a model, you can only be that lesser figure, an authority. You cannot introduce people to God, so that they may experience Him as you did. You can only ask others to accept your witness. They must trust your testimony. You advocate for a religion based on nothing better than hearsay.

"Far worse, you will never know the joy of *beginning*. In your fidelity to faith, your *meta*-faithfulness, you imprison yourself in the logic of others—of the Other. You have surrendered your inner freedom by denying humankind's greatest capacity, which is to start something new. This is Hannah Arendt's great insight, born of her immersion in the study of the totalitarian form of life. 'Over the beginning, no logic, no cogent deduction can have any power, because its chain presupposes, in the form of a premise, the beginning,' she writes. 'As terror is needed lest with the birth of each new human being a new beginning arise and raise its voice in the world, so the self-coercive force of logicality is mobilized lest anybody ever start thinking—which as the freest and purest of all human activities, is the very opposite of the compulsory process of deduction.'"[60]

Abraham 2: "Your last point, in its extravagance, does not merit a response. As for the rest, be clear: I do not stand upon hearsay. Personal experience of the Divine Presence is still possible. Indeed, there are witnesses to that Presence in every generation. God is a living force for countless people. To become an Abraham, to be God's friend (Isa. 41:8), is within everyone's reach.

"There are limits to argument, limits to reason. Investigating these limits has been the work of philosophy since the eighteenth century at least. Reason does not have the strength to draw a person toward God. Reason's criticisms of faith are implicit in faith itself; it merely presents faith with its own thoughts; faith finds room for these thoughts, while Reason finds its entire purpose in them.[61] While faith incorporates Reason's content, Reason itself falls short when addressing faith. Philosophers themselves understand that religious commitment requires something experiential and not merely intellectual. As one philosopher, who is also a Jew, said, 'If I met a person who had been a die-hard atheist and who one fine day came to believe in God simply on the basis of a metaphysical argument, I do not know what I should think. If the belief in God were simply a belief in the strength of a certain philosophical argument, and that was all that was going on, I would say this was not belief in God at all but a metaphysical illusion.'[62]

"You have no piety. You think humanity is nothing but an indifferent accident on the surface of being.[63]

"Let me return to your rather grand motto, 'Interrogate the given!' I ask you, Do you allow *nothing* to the given?"

Abraham 1: "A great deal. For Husserl himself, the 'given' is not to be refused. There are distinct modes or 'manners' of givenness: memory, fantasy, perception, and so on. Indeed, the 'given' is the ground of all creative endeavor. As a result of the activities of specialized groups (artists, scientists), the common-sense world comes to be extended. Science is thus an iteration of the natural attitude, a set of theoretical extensions of common sense. Natural knowledge makes strides, progressively taking possession, at first existing for us as a matter of course and something to be investigated—its content, its elements, its relations, its laws. Of course, so busy is it producing results, advancing from discovery to discovery, that it finds no occasion to raise the possibility of cognition as such.[64]

"Let me return the challenge: Do you take *everything* for granted? Is your 'faith' anything more than a conviction of certainty combined with a poverty of proof?"[65]

Abraham 2: "No. Just as expertise in doubting is not acquired in days or weeks, so faith is a task for one's entire lifetime. Nothing is to be taken for granted.[66] If I may borrow a formulation of Augustine's (yes, I read widely too), 'To believe is nothing other than cogitating in a state of assent.'[67] The state is itself hard-won. Our people will have doubts: of course they will! What thoughtful person does not entertain doubts?[68] What is more, what thoughtful person holds principles of faith to a higher standard than that of plausibility? It is understood, in matters of religion, that the plausible is about as good as it gets.[69]

"The Torah is not an inheritance (Pirke Avot 2.17). To be a Jew, one must be a Jew by choice, even if one is also born into the Jewish faith. It is not enough to have a Jewish mother; indeed, it is not even necessary to have a Jewish mother. One must become a Jew oneself. The Torah is not simply given. It has to be taken possession of, and this requires work. By studying the Torah, we make it our own. It becomes our law.

"Many Jewish voices testify to the truth of the *Pirke Avot*'s words. The Maharal of Prague (1525–1609) taught that the Jew is born incomplete and may only be completed through study and the keeping of the mitzvoth. In becoming inward with the law, one realizes oneself as a Jew. This has been affirmed repeatedly across the generations. Martin Buber, for example, taught that each generation must struggle with the Torah in its turn and come to terms with it. Every person must read it as if it were entirely unfamiliar, as thought, it does not present itself as ready-made. Nothing may be prejudged.[70] And there are other Jewish witnesses to this truth. *Of course* there are—it is fundamental to Jewish life.

"Jewish existence precedes Jewish essence; being Jewish is always a work in progress.[71] When we are born, we are not yet fully human. Only if we actualize our intellectual potential do we actually become human beings. Maimonides understands this as 'perfecting' ourselves intellectually. The 'ultimate perfection,' he writes, is to become rational *in actu*, fully rational. The Torah has come to bring us this perfection (Guide, III.27).[72] If we seek to elevate ourselves without its resources, however, we will merely uncover the nakedness of our minds.[73]

"As with the Jewish soul, so it is with the Jewish nation. The beauty of the promised land is that it promises new promises. In order for the air to be breathable in Zion, it must leave room for actions and desires; we must have to surpass it in turn; it must not be a paradise. Immobilized paradises promise us nothing but an eternal ennui.[74]

"What is more: We champion the moment of creativity in our understanding of the Eighth Day. Let me quote the late Rabbi Sacks: Adam and Eve ate the forbidden fruit on the sixth day; they stayed in Eden on the seventh day; they were exiled into the world on the eighth day. God took pity on them and showed them how to make light. We light a special candle at Havdalah, not just to mark the end of Shabbat but also to show that we begin the workday week with the light God taught us to make. The Havdalah candle marks the beginning of human creativity, which is parallel to Divine creativity, and its symbol is the eighth day.[75] We say, 'On the eighth day God saw what *He* had not created. And it was good.'[76]

"You muddle philosophy with thinking. Doing philosophy is not the only way to think. There are other—dare I say, better—ways to think. We all have minds, and we put them to use to serve our greater purposes. Though my purpose is not your purpose, it is as reflective as your purpose. It is also more productive than yours. My faith provides you with a reservoir of incentives to philosophical endeavor.[77] What does your critical thinking offer in return?

"I do not pretend that we do not have our limitations, our blind spots. I readily concede that we struggle with how to address 'outside books.' The Mishnah says that people who read such books have no place in the World to Come (Sanhedrin 10:1). But what are these books? What categories of writing, what authors, are forbidden? Halevi counsels, 'Let not the wisdom of the Greeks beguile thee. It has no fruit, only flowers.'[78] Flowers are beautiful and should be appreciated, but in the right way. Yet, what is that way? We debate these questions among ourselves, and there is no resolution to our investigations.[79]

"You take more for granted than we do. You too have your prejudices, but yours are more difficult to dislodge, because they are maintained by an imperturbable, complacent self-esteem. You overvalue self-interrogation, a banal, slavish worship of self-invention for its own sake, often leading to a self-deceived originality, an affair of mere eccentricity, of contrarianism. In your admiration for the transgressive, you disregard the possibilities of the creativity of the encounter with the given. You are scoffers, you Abraham 1 types.

"In your overestimation of autonomy, you risk sliding into viciousness, into a selfish immorality. Ethics puts limits on autonomy. Levinas, one of our philosophers (yes, we Abraham 2s have our own philosophers!), wrote, 'Ethics forbids my natural will, in its murderousness, putting my own existence first. It redefines subjectivity as a heteronomous responsibility to my neighbor, in contrast to that autonomous freedom to act as I please.'[80] You champion freedom, but you sanction violence.

"Levinas regards philosophy as 'the temptation of temptation.' It is a merciless demand to bypass nothing, he says, a refusal to undertake anything without knowing everything, an all-encompassing curiosity. Any act not preceded by knowledge is regarded as naïve; it deprecates the generosities of pure spontaneity. We should not overlook a certain unsavory joy of knowledge, its immodesty, the abdications and incapacities peculiar to it. The demand for truth that legitimates this curiosity can find purer paths![81]

"What is more, and here I will pause (not stop), faith in its ideal form is for you pure interiority, and so, wriggle as you may, you cannot get past the primordial importance in Judaism of the prescriptive (yes, Levinas again!),[82] where philosophy is left speechless, resourceless, useless. What does it have to say about consecrated rituals, about community practices, about the small and large duties of a revealed faith? Nothing!"

Abraham 1: "That is very unfair—for so many reasons!

"You simplify the *Pirke Avot* passage so that you can appropriate what you find attractive in my position. Contrary to what you say but *not* contrary to *Pirke Avot*, the Torah is not an inheritance for a further, second reason, utterly opposite to the first reason. What, I see you wondering, is this reason? It is this: the Torah is not an inheritance (let me repeat the phrase) *precisely because it has already made us*. It is constitutive of our mode of existence. It forms us, regardless of our wishes and regardless of our efforts.

"The Torah is not just our starting point. It travels with us. We can never leave behind its strategies, its orientations, its way of thinking and arguing. We can no more escape its presence than we can live outside our own bodies. Indeed, we do not want to escape it; it is our Torah as much as it is yours. One among us, for example, reads it as promoting just that philosophical enterprise of questioning idealized by the Greek philosophers in their notion of the 'examined life.'[83]

"And of course, we acknowledge too that, in addition to the 'Chain of Tradition' in which the Torah was transmitted from Moses to Joshua and then to the Elders and so on (Pirke Avot 1), there is also that no-less-solid chain of rote practices and uncon-scious repetitions, compelling processes of which we remain un-aware but that exercise an extraordinary hold on all of us Jews.[84]

"This is true too of the ties of family, religion, and nation. For Jews, can these ever be separate ties? Certainly, I do not think of them as just so many restraints to cut through. While we may experience them as restraints, they are *our* restraints. They make us who we are; we cannot just skip out of them.[85] I am quite aware that people cannot simply decide, as a sover-eign act, to be anything or anyone they want to be.[86] There are limits to self-invention. And costs too. We will always pay a price for our freedom.

"*I* do not reject family! Have you forgotten? The *Akedah* will be *your* crisis, not mine!

"I will go further. Let me surprise you by returning to Hannah Arendt, in order to adopt a remark she made to Ger-shom Scholem, when defending her book *Eichmann in Jerusa-lem* against his objections.[87] 'To be a Jew,' she insisted, 'belongs for me to the indisputable facts of my life, and I have never the wish to change or disclaim facts of this kind. There is such a thing as basic gratitude for everything that is as it is; for what has been *given* and not *made*.'[88] You might have expected Arendt to dismiss what is 'given,' as everything that is conventional, un-reflective, clichéd, and so on. But no! Here she is saying some-thing altogether different. The 'given' is a gift, worthy of eliciting gratitude—certainly, the gift of Judaism, of Jewish peoplehood."

Abraham 2: "Well, in the same spirit of convergence, if not reconciliation, let me make four points.

"First, we both affirm God's unity. We each reject the an-swer typically given in our times to the question, Why does humankind suffer? That answer was, if only an incomplete one, that the gods are agents of our misery and need to be placated with praise and with gifts, with sacrifices both animal and human. The gods are cruel and must be appeased. You destroyed this knowledge, substituting it with the knowledge of one God, remote and indifferent; I destroyed this knowledge, substituting it with the knowledge of one God, close and engaged.

"Second, we share a horror of idolatry. We are agreed, I believe, that idolatry is the worst thing. It is no surprise that the rabbis say that anyone who repudiates idolatry is called a Jew (Megillah 13a). In Yeshayahu Leibowitz's succinct definition, idolatry means adoring something that is not God, raising it to the rank of a Godhead and enslaving oneself to it.[89] I am sure you can find statements to similar effect among your own authorities.

"Third, every Jew is a compound made up of elements of *both* of us. We need each other; each one of us is incomplete without the other. 'Abraham' is the exemplary Jew in this respect. As the Midrash says, 'He is the one who both tears apart and sews together again.'[90] I grant you that Abraham 1 / Abraham 2 is a useful distinction. But you have a tendency to elevate it into an absolute dichotomy, and this is wrong. You would make us, Abraham 1 and Abraham 2, each other's enemy. On examination, we are interwoven and interdependent, even entangled.[91] Oppositions are better treated as dialectical, coloring each other, historically evolving or even collapsing as conditions change. They are only useful if we acknowledge their limits as heuristic tools.[92]

"Last, we share a common fate. Nachmanides wrote that God symbolically did to Abraham all that was destined to happen in the future to his children. He paraphrased a Midrash, which is even blunter: 'Whatever happened to Abraham happened to his children.'[93] Abraham as a whole, that is: the Abraham of Ur and the Abraham of Canaan, the Abraham of the furnace and the Abraham of the mountain."

Abraham 1: "I appreciate what you say, though I don't appreciate the jibe about my 'own authorities.' In intellectual matters, I defer only to the authority of Maimonides and then only in respect of his counsel *against* such deferences.[94] You might say that my sole 'authority' is the man who denies the authority of 'authorities.'

"Perhaps I should now just shut up. But I can't quite manage to do that. So instead, I will challenge you on two of your points.

"As to idolatry, I notice you omitted Leibowitz's concluding words. Idolatry, he added, includes any conception of the divine whose contents are human categories or values. (He was paraphrasing and endorsing Maimonides's position.) I'm very happy with that—but are you? Out goes pretty much all of the Jews' folk religion, as well as much of its liturgy.

"And as to compound, well, it all depends on the proportions, doesn't it? I imagine you would give the larger quantity to your version of Abraham. I cannot concede that. Indeed, you haven't so much found common ground *with* me as more precisely identified the ground of contention *between* us. But there's a bigger point to make. You think that a stable compound is possible. That's in itself a difference between us. There are no ideal quantities that would make for a stable Abraham.

"I will affirm the following, however. We are both 'Abraham' in one very fundamental sense. We were both called to leave our natural state and go to a faraway place.[95] My call, which came from within me, demanded that I separate myself from the practices of my ancestors; your call, which you believe came to you from outside yourself, demanded that you separate yourself from the land of your ancestors. In each case, we answered that call willingly and in a spirit of glad, elevated adventure."

Abraham 2: "Thank you for that. And by the way, I wasn't attacking you when I referred to 'authorities'! You don't deny, surely, that there are thinkers to whom you defer? For someone to whom argument is everything, you are immoderately sensitive to criticism.

"Now to the issue between us. Your critical reasoning risks

becoming nothing more than a prejudice. And unless you acknowledge some limits to critique, unless you allow that some positive value is at least theoretically open to a person, a value that has no trace of the idolatrous, you will be consumed by mere negativity. A life cannot be lived in a state of permanent critical interrogation of everything! True intellectual formation comes through developing a specific tradition.[96]

"Nor, by the way, can I let pass your reading of *Pirke Avot*. On the one hand, I admire it as corrective to my own reading, which I accept had an unconscious quality of ingratiation. I wanted to show you that you're not the only intellectual on the team. Well, so be it. But your reading is too extreme. It too is a simplification. There *is* an element of competence required to practice our religion. It can't just be all unconscious processes. It's not all 'given'!

"If you are not careful, you will end up aligning yourself with those 'psychological Jews' who insist on their 'inalienable Jewish traits,'[97] while disavowing any commitment to Judaism itself or even to the Jewish people."

Abraham 1: "The work of disenchantment is without end. It is a noble, elevated undertaking. Nothing has a natural right to last, other than reason and equity. All else lives by mere variety of disease.[98] We must commit ourselves to an unceasing enmity toward these diseases. It is an unceasing labor, the work of philosophers and free spirits, and when it is effective, its successes are to be measured in a long, dense succession of demolitions, destructions, downfalls, and upheavals.[99] And then a sweeping away of the debris of the phony and the meretricious.

"The work requires alert, suspicious minds. It is a project that can occupy a life. Institutions, faiths, whole cultures, all need a cohort of such minds to ensure that they stay honest—stay within *touching* distance of honesty. Convictions should be allowed no greater status than hypotheses, and even then, they must remain under our supervision, we practitioners of mistrust.

"The work is also exhilarating. There is joy in escaping the bondage of system and habit, of family maxims, class opinions, and national and religious prejudices; in allowing tradition only as a means of information; in seeking the reason of things for one's self and in one's self alone; in seeing through the form of things to their foundation; in having recourse to the individual effort of one's own reason.[100] I pity you that you have never known this joy.

"The inauguration of my project in Ur represented an immense progress in intellectuality, allow me to say; it was an advance in civilization of the greatest consequence. Jews can derive much pride from this achievement. We are all sons and daughters of questioning, philosophical Abraham. Here, I borrow language from one of Judaism's greatest sons, Sigmund Freud (23:64–65, 114), even though for reasons of his own, obscure to us, he credited the achievement to Moses, rather than to me.

"At the beginning of Jewish communal existence, it has been written, there stands a pointedly singular figure, reminding all Jews thereafter that their tradition did not arise from some already-meaningful, clear, and demarcated point of origin but instead arose through a wrenching break with everything that was given, everything that was already in place.[101] It is to me that reference is being made here, of course: I am that singular figure. And what I represent continues to be a horizon of aspiration for all Jews—or should be.

"But to return to the Abrahamic work of disenchantment, I want to argue that it stands against two deplorable tendencies in your thinking.

"First, the tendency to deprecate reason—an '*Akedah* of the intellect,' to borrow a phrase.[102] Philosophy itself is used to critique reason, to undermine it, to expose its pretensions, its predisposition to exceed its limits and veer into nonsense. Absurd formulations of Judaism are proposed, such as Isaac Breuer's 'not a religion of unreason, but a religion that transcends reason.'

What does that even mean? If anything at all, it is a formula to distract from your mental paralysis, one induced by theories of evolution, cosmology, Bible criticism, and so on.[103]

"Second, the tendency to treat Jewish 'difference' as constitutive of Jewish existence—to suppose a 'Jewish Will,' an 'ontological' Jewishness, a 'Mensch Yisrael.' This language is hateful to me. It is a further disparagement of reason, by giving primacy to a sham Jewish 'Being' over universal human capabilities.[104]

"Both these tendencies live in your favorite sage, Judah Halevi. Though he did not originate them, he was the first to give them coherent, combined expression. They then recur in Jewish life, with each exponent aspiring to write his or her own *Kuzari*."

And so it continues. These exchanges have been going on, after all, for millennia. Banteringly familiar, sometimes relaxed, sometimes vehement, each Abraham knows the other's arguments so well that for economy of use, they could be given numbers.

Neither Abraham convinces the other, but it is not hopeless. Both Abraham 1 and Abraham 2 have a notion of the sacred. At bottom, their quarrel is about whether the sacred is best understood as an expression or an experience, as a representation or a presence.[105] Each has a paternal regard for the other. Abraham 1, of course, thinks of Abraham 2 as his successor, if not his heir; Abraham 2 sees his own childhood in Abraham 1.

They need each other. Without an Abraham 1 element, Abraham is a fanatic, a dogmatist, a zealot; without an Abraham 2 element, Abraham is deracinated, subversive, purposeless. As with Abraham, so with Jews generally, surely?

Yet there is a glibness about resting here. It disregards the conflict, including the history of the conflict, between the Abrahams. Today, Jewish life has too much Abraham 2 and not enough Abraham 1. But there is no perfect balance. We lurch in one direction, and then we lurch in the other, leap-like acts of existential irresolution, though equilibrium is ever the ambition.[106]

The great Moses Maimonides (1138–1204) is the best possible companion for us when we seek to reflect on these unending, anxiety-inducing lurchings.

Maimonides

Start with Maimonides's Abraham, "the rationalist par excellence."[107] With him, we meet both Abraham 1 and Maimonides himself. "I followed conjecture and supposition; no divine revelation has come to me to teach me, nor did I receive what I believe in these matters from a teacher" (Guide, III.Introduction). This is the philosopher speaking, but it could have been the patriarch's voice we heard. Maimonides's identification with Abraham was intimate, personal, elevated. He named his son Abraham, binding in the closest possible association patriarch, philosopher, and son: two Abrahams enfolding one Moses.[108]

Abraham 1 is especially vivid in Maimonides—not for Maimonides mere first approximations of paganism or of Abraham's campaign against idolatry in the early years. Maimonides instead relates a whole history of religion, from a first knowledge of God through to a polytheism that he identifies as the faith of Abraham's time. The Chaldeans, he writes, affirmed the eternity of the universe; they attributed miracles to magic and chicanery. It was against all this that Abraham contended, thereby disclosing the Law's essential purpose (Guide, III.29–30; Mishne Torah, Avoda Zara 1).

In Maimonides's work, then, we might say that Abraham 1 is the best version of Abraham 2.

Consider circumcision. In the constituting of Judaism, Abraham makes two contributions. As Abraham 1, he contributes a new, defining mental disposition: critical, self-interrogating, adverse to the worship of false gods. As Abraham 2, he contributes an equally new, equally defining physical adjustment, small but consequential: the cutting of the foreskin. All Jews will thereafter be identified by this disposition; all male Jews, by this adjustment. The question arises, Are these two contributions to be given equal weight?

Judah Halevi challenged the philosophers among his people: consider how little circumcision has to do with philosophy! Notwithstanding how very hard to perform this command was at Abraham's age, he subjected himself and his household to it. Circumcision was constituted as the very sign of the covenant. It was also, when first performed on an infant, an anticipation of the *Akedah*; it remains an allusion to the *Akedah*, vivid though unwelcome in every father's mind at the moment of *brit*. To Halevi, it serves the further purpose of a rebuke to all Jews of a philosophical bent, liable to privilege intellectual inquiry over communal membership, mind over body. It is the body's identifying marker, not the mind's reasoning, that makes a Jew (at least the male Jew).[109]

We may concede that the Abraham of Ur would never have concluded that he had to circumcise himself. Circumcision is the answer to no question, the outcome of no process of reasoning. What does circumcision have to do with Abraham 1? Nothing. *What*, then, does circumcision have to do with philosophy? At most, surely, to function as philosophy's Other. A circumcised philosopher? Absurd! Not at all, rejoins Maimonides. Circumcision both affirms the principle of the golden mean and makes intellectual life possible. It is philosophy's visible marker and serves philosophy's purpose:

- *Golden mean*: Circumcision is Aristotle inscribed on the body. Sexual intercourse should neither be excessively indulged nor wholly obstructed. Did God not command, "Be fruitful and multiply"? The penis is weakened by means of circumcision but not extirpated by excision. This is in accordance with the principle of keeping the mean in all matters, writes Maimonides (Guide, III.49).
- *Sublimation*: Circumcision makes intellectual life possible by

weakening the penis and diminishing the desire for sexual intercourse. "When only the desires are followed, as is done by the ignorant, the longing for speculation is abolished." Circumcision is God's "gracious ruse" to make a nation of philosophers out of the Jews. "He forbids everything that leads to lusts and mere pleasure" (Guide, III.33, 49).

No less than any other Jewish practice, circumcision defers to reason, insists Maimonides.

Solomon Maimon wrote of Maimonides, "It was not his particular doctrines that had the largest influence on my progress, but rather his noble audacity in thinking, acknowledging no limits except those of reason; a love of truth before all else; and his firmness of principle and methodological rigor in deriving truths from zealotry and superstitions."[110] In his sovereign commitment to pursuing an argument wherever it took him, Maimonides was an exemplary intellectual. He deprecated dependence on "traditional stories" and considered reliance on "authority" ill-advised. Only by "the way of speculation" could a person acquire "true knowledge" (Guide, III.23). The legitimacy of philosophy in religion was not the issue, writes Isadore Twersky. Rather, the issue was the legitimacy of religion without philosophy.[111] Maimonides celebrated those moments of "manifest agreement between Scripture and philosophy"; he took those other moments, when "at first blush, the sayings of the philosophers and the rabbis" seem "to contradict one another," as a challenge; he was "convinced that our law agrees with Greek philosophy" (at the least, in respect of free will) (Eight Chapters, 8).

Heschel made the point with his customary lyricism. For Maimonides, all knowledge becomes cognition, all knowing thinking. Thinking is existence itself. The human soul is realized in the activity of thinking. To live in the kingdom of reason is an imperative. The love of thinking was the fundamental motif of Maimonides's life; he approved only of a faith practiced in thinking. He related to thinking as to something personified. Every act of thinking was the reception of a revelation for him. The uninterrupted effluence of the divine entered thinking. The mystery of thinking was the most penetrating experience of his life. Immortality for him was the eternal life of the spirit in the process of knowing.[112] To develop Heschel's account, it is only in thinking, in all its arduous, unpredictable creativity, that one encounters God. Immobilizing thought into dogma imperils this encounter. Keeping one's conclusions provisional, open to revision, is the only way to remain open to God.

Take the question, A created world or an eternal world? Call this the "What world?" question. Maimonides makes the following argument in Part II, section 25, of the *Guide*:

1. Once we believe that the world was created, all miracles become possible and the Law itself becomes possible, and all questions that might be asked on this subject vanish. This is because providence itself is but a constant reenactment of Creation.[113]

2. On the other hand, the belief in the eternity of the world—that is, that the world exists in virtue of necessity, that no nature changes, and that the customary course of events cannot be modified—destroys the Law in its principle, gives the lie to every miracle, and reduces to inanity all the hopes and threats that the Law has held out.

3. This, then, is a reason for recoiling from that theory. This is why estimable people have spent their lives, and others will go on spending their lives, investigating this question. For if it were proved that the world is created, all the objections of the philosophers to us would fall to the ground.

4. However, if philosophers would succeed in providing a proof for the world's eternity, the Law in its entirety would become void, and a shift to other opinions would occur. Everything is bound up with this problem. Give it, therefore, your most earnest consideration.

The meaning is plain: the eternity of the world is an open question, and one should investigate it, whatever the consequences.

Plainness of meaning is not standard in Maimonides, however. There is a teasing quality, for example, to the opening sentences of his "Essay on Resurrection,"[114] a pair of quotations from Proverbs. Here is the first one: "Sincere are all the words of my mouth, there is nothing tortuous or perverse in them; they are all of them straightforward to the man of understanding, and right to those who find knowledge" (Prov. 8:8–9). And here is the second one: "A man of sense conceals what he knows, but fools proclaim their folly" (Prov. 12:23). How can *both* quotations govern what follows? How can the essay both "straightforwardly" state Maimonides's position *and* conceal it? And yet the stakes could not have been higher. The essay was written in response to an accusation of heresy from no less a figure than the head of the Talmudic authority in Baghdad.

The *Guide* opens with a defense of contradictions. "One of seven causes should account for the contradictory or contrary statements to be found in any book," he writes. As to the seventh cause, "in speaking about very obscure matters it is necessary to conceal some parts and to disclose others." On occasion, this means "proceeding on the basis of one premise in one place" and proceeding on the basis of the "contradictory premise in another place." "In such cases, the vulgar must in no way be aware of the contradiction; the author will use a device to conceal it" (I.Introduction). This is not something Maimonides wishes to celebrate. He does not say with Whitman, "Do I contradict myself?/Very well then I contradict myself,/(I am large, I contain multitudes)."[115]

David Hartman formulates the "paradox of Maimonides" in Abraham 1/Abraham 2 terms (without saying as much): while he, more than any other Jewish philosopher, mediated the halakhic way in which traditional Jews serve God (the A2 position), his theological, spiritual, and psychological views appear to undermine the very beliefs and religious attitudes that traditional Jews regard as sacred (the Abraham 1 position). This is the reason, Hartman proposes, that Maimonides continues to fascinate us. How is it that the person who was responsible for shaping the structure and ethos of Jewish normative practice was committed to a conception of God, history, and philosophy that, to many, threatened its very foundations?[116]

Consider, then, another fundamental question: An unknowable God or a personal God? Call this the "What God?" question. It is binary: a separate God (equivocal predication, immutable, static relation with the world, etc.) *and* an involved God, the two approximating to Abraham 1's conception of God and Abraham 2's conception of God, or "the God of the philosophers" and "the God of the patriarchs." Judaism has both conceptions.

Maimonides is candid: "*On the one hand*, there is a demonstration of his separateness from the world and of his being free from it, and *on the other*, there is a demonstration that the influence of his governance and providence in every part of the world, however small and contemptible, exists" (Guide, I.72). This major contradiction then generates further, subsidiary contradictions:

- *Prayer*: Pray to a God fully separate from us, indescribable save negatively, and with whom we can have no relation, in language that affirms His involvement in the world, His positive attributes (He is "great, mighty, and terrible"), and His care for us? Silent meditation is best, Maimonides suggests, quoting Psalms, "Silence is praise to Thee" (65:2) and "Commune with your own heart upon your bed, and be still" (4:5).[117] One obstacle notwithstanding, he could equally have quoted Emily Dickinson: "I worshipped—did not 'pray.'"[118]
- *Imitatio Dei*: Seek to emulate a God who cannot be described and with whom no qualities are shared? The duty to imi-

tate God defines the ideal of human conduct. "The utmost virtue of man is to become like Him"; "we should make our actions like unto His." However, there is "absolutely no likeness whatever in any respect between Him and the things created by Him" (Guide, I.35, 52).

Maimonides proposes of the major contradiction that the *character* of this "governance and providence" is "hidden from us," because of the "inadequacy" of our "faculties" (Guide, I.72). This is an evasion, of course. A Maimonides scholar, Marvin Fox, who agrees that "we cannot say that we do not know and leave it at that," praises Jews who are able to "retain both the language of worship and the truth about divine attributes." These Jews inhabit "a single system," one that accommodates the demands of "both religious piety and philosophical truth." They live these contradictions in a state of "dialectical tension," "keeping them in balance," notwithstanding that "affirming opposed statements about God" is "an offense to the intellect." Maimonides is the very model of such Jews. He "teaches us the great art of balancing" inconsistent propositions, truth claims, practices, and beliefs.[119]

Another Maimonides scholar, Kenneth Seeskin, writes, "Maimonides' thought is difficult to classify. There is Maimonides the defender of tradition and Maimonides the thinker who sought to reshape it, Maimonides the student of Aristotle and Maimonides the critic, Maimonides the believer and Maimonides the sceptic. Which is the real Maimonides?"[120] Seeskin both states the problem and retreats from it: the problem is not one of *classification*. Maimonides led his readers in quite a dance. "There is not one of Maimonides' Thirteen Articles which was not rejected by leading lights in the history of Judaism," wrote the philosopher Leon Roth, "*including Maimonides himself.*"[121]

Consider this possibility. What if Maimonides was fully, radically divided—divided to his root, "hopping between" positions,[122] without prospect of reconciling them? What if the corpus of his work is one great demonstration of the necessity and the impossibility of precisely this unity? The thought that this *might* be so explains the widespread unease with which the *Guide* was received in the Jewish world and the attacks on the work launched by distinguished (and not so distinguished) elements within it. Concessions to reason create dangers for faith.[123]

Now consider the alternative possibility, that Maimonides maintained these divisions in a state of tense equilibrium, a constant, reflective self-steadying, achieved in part by a negative theology that requires a generous resort to paradox. The contemporary philosopher Hilary Putnam (1926–2016) calls this theology the "path to a redemptive antinomy," because while it denies that God exists in the sense that anything else exists, it does not give any other, positive content to God's existence.[124]

Either way, would that not make Maimonides the philosopher *for* the Jews, *of* the Jews? Would he not then be the guide for people who live in a condition of permanent perplexity,[125] of continuous inner restlessness, conflict, tension? Not to guide them *out* of it but to guide them on how to live *in* it, to guide them, that is, *not* by devising a map for general use but by demonstrating how *he* does it. Not that this demonstration can be imitated, of course. To conceptualize Judaism as both code *and* philosophy, and in doing so produce those works of systematizing and speculative genius, the *Mishne Torah* and the *Guide* respectively, is not an undertaking open to many others.[126]

Putnam wrote about Jewish dividedness in language unavailable to Maimonides:

> As a practicing Jew, I am someone for whom the religious dimension of life has become increasingly important, although it is not a dimension that I know how to philosophize about, except by indirection; and the study of science has loomed large in my life. In fact, when I first began to teach philosophy, back in the early 1950s, I thought of myself as a phi-

losopher of science. . . . Those who know my writings from that period may wonder how I reconciled my religious streak, which existed to some extent even back then, and my general scientific materialist worldview at that time. The answer is that I didn't reconcile them. I was a thoroughgoing atheist, and I was a believer. I simply kept these two parts of myself separate.[127]

Putnam later commented on this passage, "I had come to accept that I could have two different parts of myself, a religious part and a purely philosophical part, but I had not truly reconciled them. Some may feel I still haven't reconciled them. I am still a religious person, and I am still a naturalistic philosopher."[128] He was helped toward reconciling these two parts, he said, by teaching a course on Jewish philosophy. It led him to the view that "theorizing about God" is beside the point. Yet a sense of predicament remained, on the one hand, feeling attached to the Jewish tradition and, on the other hand, being unwilling to turn his back on modernity.[129]

The Jewish Agon

Abraham 1 does not accept that religious belief can be founded on the evidence of religious experience, not even on a vision, that most certain and intense version of a religious experience.[130] Yet what is left of Judaism without the teaching obtained by visions? Abraham 2 fears that Abraham 1 has scoffing, skeptical tendencies that can get out of control, overrunning faith, disabling religious practices.

Of course, "Abraham 1" and "Abraham 2" are ideal types, abstractions from the empirical Abraham, who was never quite entirely 1 or 2 but instead always both, in uncertain, shifting combinations, the accent on the one and then on the other. "When" 1, he was *never* fully and only the curious, speculative philosopher, trusting nothing, allergic to all certainties; "when"

2, he was *never* altogether the sublime undoubter.[131] Taking many things on trust is necessary if one is to function as a person at all; critical thinking is unavoidable when first encountering a text or tradition that claims authority.[132]

Abraham 1 versions will always be in want of a saving miracle; Abraham 2 versions will always live in the shadow of an impossible command. Moriah overwhelms furnace. It is as if we are being told, "You insist on Abraham 2, and you want to push Abraham 1 to the margins? Then you have to take Moriah; you cannot just have the furnace. If you insist on a personal God, then you must take him in his *Akedah* moods too."

Abraham 1 challenges us, "Dare to know!" Abraham 2 demands of us, "Fall on your face!" (Gen. 17:3). Can these two imperatives be reconciled? They are contained in the two stories about Abraham that everyone knows. The first is the breaking of Terah's idols; the second is the binding of Isaac. Yet while one is nowhere in the Torah, the other has a central, even decisive place in it. What are the implications for Jewish life of this asymmetry? Does it reflect a discomfort within the Jewish tradition with the radical character of Abraham 1's challenge? The authority of Argument; the authority of God. Take the argument wherever it leads us; follow God wherever He directs us. How can one *live* both? This is the Jewish agon.

This experience of dividedness *as a constant* is standard among modern Jews. It goes under different names, and it is diverse in its content. But it's there, as is the promise, elusive, if not chimerical, of wholeness. The dividedness is complex. We need to separate out its two levels:

- *Level #1*: In his life, Abraham 1 says to us, "Think for yourself, as I have learned to think for myself." In *his* life, Abraham 2 says to us, "Follow me, as I have learned to follow God."
- *Level #2*: In his crisis, Abraham 1 divides: "If my appeal to

God fails, I will indeed die; but if the appeal succeeds, I will die as Abraham 1." In *his* crisis, Abraham 2 divides: "I cannot follow God, and yet I must follow Him; in His command to me, He conceals Himself from me."

On the first level, competing, incompatible appeals are made to us; on the second level, dismal prospects are opened up to us.

It is on the third or "meta" level, that further level that combines these two other levels, that Jews typically lead their lives— or those Jews, at any rate, who combine the self-divided Abraham 1 *and* the self-divided Abraham 2, that is to say, those Jews who incorporate both critical reasoning *and* faith in their makeup, while also acknowledging the limitations of the one and the impossibilities of the other. Benjamin Fondane wrote that consciousness will not be relieved of its division with itself.[133] There need be no gloominess about this judgment; creativity begins in dividedness.

Coda

The Abraham Story in the Jewish Tradition

The Torah, the primary document of revelation,[1] contains the first biography of Abraham. It is the source, the point of departure, for all other accounts of Abraham. The first book of the Torah, Genesis, begins with Abraham's lineage and place of birth (11:26–28) and then goes straight to the command to leave Haran. Thereafter the story follows the course described in chapters 3 and 4 and closes with the 175-year-old Abraham's death, "old and satisfied" (25:8).

The story has been intensively studied, and the studying has produced many interpretations. If we ask why this is so, many reasons suggest themselves.

We might point to the divine provenance attributed to the Torah as a whole. *Of course* we would want to ponder God's communications with us. Every single word stands inside the principle, "For it is no vain thing from You" (Deut. 32: 47).[2] The words have "a maximum density of signification, a saturation of sense of signification."[3] We might also point to the status of the Torah as a work of instruction ("Torah" means "teaching"). If we are to derive lessons from the text, if it proposes laws for us to follow, we need to establish precisely what these lessons teach us, what these laws require of us.

We might, too, have a sense of it withholding part of its meaning. We might think of it, that is, as cryptic. For sure, in respect of many of the Torah's stories, we will want to know more of what went on than we are told in the text itself. We will want to see into the stories' depths.[4] What is more, the further our historical environment is removed from that of the Scriptures, the more some readers will bridge the gap through "interpretive transformations."[5]

And we might point to the vowel-free text, noting that the choice of vowels a reader makes, required if the text is to be read at all, is *already* an act of interpretation.[6] The Torah was written without the use of capital letters, periods, commas, or any other kind of punctuation. Even where a sentence began or ended, James Kugel explains, was often a matter of opinion: it all depended on how one interpreted it.[7]

And of course there are the Torah's intimations, its silences, its elaborations, its ostensible redundancies and duplications, its anachronisms and its contradictions, that call for explanation. "Woe to the person who says that this Torah has come to present an ordinary story in ordinary words," warns the *Zohar*.[8]

The ground idea of this coda is that there are two active, current Jewish discourses regarding the Abraham story. By "discourse," I mean something like "voice." To the English poet and devotional writer John Donne (1572–1631), the Bible was God's voice. "If I take knowledge of that voice," he writes, "and fly to thee, thou wilt preserve me from falling."[9] The Bible's voice, of course, is made up of many different voices. A "discourse" has this same composite quality.

The discourses that concern me here interpret God's own discourse; they add their voices to His voice. They are responsive to the story as related in Genesis (11:26–25:10), the foundational account. They address it with elaborations, additions, and glosses. One of the two took its name in the aftermath of the Second Temple destruction (though it traces its origins to Judaism's own); the second one refuses any one name and is less than two hundred years of age. The first discourse defends against three challenges to its integrity (see below); the second discourse assumes these challenges, incorporating them in its own voice. My book is an instance of this second discourse.

The first discourse is rabbinic. It has an obscure origin in the Second Temple period; it emerges across the catastrophic years between the destruction of the Temple in 70 CE and the collapse of the Bar Kochba Revolt; it comes to creative maturity between 200 and 600 CE (when it produces the Mishnah and the Babylonian Talmud); it governs Jewish life thereafter for well over a millennium; and it is still with us. These rabbinic texts of late antiquity, Menachem Fisch writes, represent a unique record of a unique intellectual enterprise.[10] In this discourse, the Abraham story is accorded the foundational status the Torah invites, Abraham himself is the focus of much idealizing attention, and the *Akedah* is taken to be a triumph.[11] That is, I read these accounts as being conditioned by a certain apologetical or "recuperative" stance toward Abraham. I call this the "JR" discourse.

The second discourse is nonrabbinic and emerges in the modern period, across the seventy or so years between the publication of Solomon Maimon's autobiography in 1792 and the publication of Mendele Mocher Sforim's story "The Little Man" in 1864. It does not have the same coherence as the JR discourse. Its productions constitute a class that is also an anticlass. While the first discourse can comfortably be designated "rabbinic," the second discourse resists any affirmative adjectival naming. None of the available candidates is satisfactory: "secular," "heterodox," "modern," "literary," "psychological," or "self-designated" Jew. I therefore give this nonrabbinic discourse the arbitrary designation "JX." Writers who use this discourse pursue a Jewish vocation. I read the JX accounts of the Abraham story, such as they are, as mostly possessing a marginalizing, even dismissive character. There are important exceptions to this tendency, however.

To complicate the picture, I briefly take in another Jewish discourse, "Second Temple Judaism," which preceded the JR discourse. And I also identify three challenging *non*-Jewish discourses that precede the JX discourse: (a) the Christian; (b) the Enlightenment; (c) the academic. The Christian discourse is concurrent with the rabbinic one. The Enlightenment discourse comes just before the JX discourse and contributes to its emergence. The academic discourse is concurrent with the JX discourse and exercises some influence on it. Though each of these three discourses has its own integrity, I do not consider them in their integrity. Instead, I regard them only insofar as they bear on the JR and JX discourses.

Once the rabbis had overcome the objections of the Karaites (repudiators of the Talmud, champions of the personal interpretation of Scripture), their authority remained essentially unchecked until the middle of the nineteenth century. Thereafter, the JX writers, by modifying our understanding of what it means to be Jewish, provided materials to answer the question, Can the Jews as a people survive the waning of rabbinic Judaism?[12]

The JR Discourse

Pre-rabbinic Judaism

"Second Temple Judaism" refers to the period between the return from first exile in Babylon in the sixth century BCE and the destruction of the Second Temple in 70 CE. The Jews enjoyed various forms of self-government in these "postexilic" times, all falling short of full sovereignty. The Judaism practiced in this period was in many respects different from the Judaism in later centuries. Cult and pilgrimage were its defining features.[13] The Temple was the central institution, one of the largest structures in the Roman world. In this period, synagogues, local places for worship and study, began to appear.[14]

There was neither a uniform corpus of texts nor a coherent body of generally affirmed theological ideas. The conception of a specific set of writings, "the Bible," did not exist before the end of the period. Instead, there were distinct sets of books considered sacred by various religious communities and sects. The Five Books were the agreed core and were taken to be writings from the ancient past, esteemed for that reason among others. Some academics have gone so far as to write of Judaisms, not Judaism. In Second Temple Judaism, it has been proposed, what we find is "everything and its opposite."[15] This goes too far. There were regional variations, but common to all were circumcision, kashrut, and Shabbat. The period was marked by sectarianism, a self-conscious pietistic self-differentiation among Jewish elites and subelites, especially in Judea. In addition to the sects, there were also small, barely institutionalized groups associated with individual charismatics. There were no shared criteria that allowed a person to identify which forms of Judaism were the right ones.[16]

Scripture was on nearly everyone's mind, writes James Kugel.[17] "How I love your Torah; I speak of it all day long" (Ps. 119:97) might have been the motto of all the Jewish communities and sects in the period. Biblical interpreters became a central force in postexilic society. They looked to ancient texts for messages relevant, even prescriptive, for their own day. A sizeable literature was written in the centuries when the Second Temple stood: histories, stories, legal texts, wisdom literature, translations, and works of Scriptural interpretation (commentaries, retellings). Available literary forms of the time were borrowed and put to Jewish use. The boundaries were blurred between Scripture and interpretation, between interpretive rewriting and commentary, and between acknowledged authorship and the attribution to Patriarchal or other Scriptural figures of non-Scriptural materials.[18]

This creativity was the consequence of a diversity of forms of Jewish life. The Dead Sea Scrolls, a collection of writings found at Qumran, near Jericho, was the product of communities in the region; the philosophical and exegetical works of Philo were the product of Alexandrian Jewish life. The Alexandrian Jewish writers had no interest in recounting the tale of Troy, the labors of Hercules, or the Greco-Persian wars; their heroes were Abraham, Joseph, and Moses, and they appropriated Hellenism to the goals of rewriting biblical narratives.[19] The Abraham story was in all regions, for all sects and groups, a common focus of interpretive activity:

- Jubilees rewrites Genesis and Exodus, adding and subtracting as the author pleases. Abraham begs his father to give up idol worshiping. "My father," Abraham says. "Here I am, my son," Terah replies. Abraham later leaves Haran with Terah's permission. "Go in peace," Terah says. In Egypt, Sarah is taken from Abraham by force. Job elements are added to the *Akedah*. In heaven, a Satan figure, "Mastema," says to God, "Behold, Abraham loves Isaac, his son. He is more pleased with him than everything. Tell him to offer him as a burnt offering upon the altar." At the end, God tells Abraham, "I have made known to all that you are faithful to Me."[20]
- Pseudo-Jubilees, a text from Qumran, relates a version of the *Akedah* in which Abraham frankly acknowledges to Isaac that he is to be the lamb for the sacrifice. Isaac replies, "All

that the Lord has told you so shall you do." The fragments
of text identify God's audience as "angels of holiness" and
"angels of Mastema."[21]

- Philo (ca. 20 BCE–50 CE), the Alexandrian Jewish philosopher, interprets the Abraham story both "literally" *and*
"allegorically," providing an "open explanation" for "the multitude" and an "esoteric explanation" for the "few." In "On
Abraham" and "On the Migration of Abraham," Philo explains that "Haran" is "the abode of the outward senses,"
that "Pharaoh" is a figurative representation of "the mind
devoted to the body," and so on. Abraham blamed himself
severely for his former life, years passed in blindness. Later,
he regarded no life so pleasant as one lived without association with the multitude; he loved the solitude that is
dear to God. When he was bidden, he took no thought for
anything—not clansmen or blood relations or country or
ancestral customs or home life.[22]

- In the *Jewish Antiquities* (93–94 CE), Josephus characterizes
Abraham as a man of ready intelligence, persuasive with his
hearers, and not mistaken in his inferences. He had loftier
conceptions of virtue than the rest of humankind and was
determined to reform the ideas then current concerning
God. He went down to Egypt in order to hear what its
priests said about the gods. Abraham judged it just to obey
God in all circumstances, since all those to whom He is
benevolent survive through His providence. Abraham explains to Isaac, "You were born out of the course of nature;
leave it now, not by sickness or war but amid prayers and
sacrificial ceremonies." After the reprieve, father and son
embrace and return home to Sarah, where they "live in
bliss."[23] This fairy-tale version of the *Akedah* is nearly three
times the length of Genesis 22.

- 4 Maccabees, a philosophical work written in Greek and
concerning the relations between "devout reason" and "the

emotions," references the *Akedah* as a precedent for self-control in the face of violent death. "Remember whence you came, and the father by whose hand Isaac would have submitted to being slain for the sake of religion," Jewish martyrs to Seleucid persecution counsel each other.[24]

(In its heterogeneity of religious positions, its diversities of nationality, language, and literary form, Second Temple Judaism writing shares features with JX discourse.)

And then came the period of catastrophes, the worst of which being the destruction of the Temple in 70 CE. It brought to an end an entire native Jewish political, social, and cultural order. The Temple's plundered riches were transported to Rome. Jews were expelled from Jerusalem. The city was renamed Aelia Capitolina; the region, hitherto Judea, was renamed Syria Palestina. We may assume that the Jews of this catastrophic time would have been asking fundamental questions. As Robert Eisen formulates the questions, Had the covenant with God been broken, and was this the reason for their suffering? And if the Covenant was still in effect, what explained the catastrophes that Jews were experiencing?[25] Had God been defeated?[26]

Rabbinic Triumph

Let us imagine a pious Jew, committed to his religion, contemplating the destruction of the Second Temple. A religion based on sacrifices cannot function without a place in which to perform them. Is Judaism to be mourned or reconstructed? And if the latter, precisely how? With what materials, what fresh perspectives? Notwithstanding the long tradition of opposition to sacrifices elsewhere than in Jerusalem, the Jews could have decided, but did *not* decide, that with the destruction of the Temple, sacrifices would now be made by each community, wherever located.[27] Alternatively, they could have committed, but did *not* commit, to mourning the destruction, thereby fashioning a merely commemorative religion.

Instead, another course was adopted, a practice of substitution. Let study substitute for sacrifice and pilgrimage, let rabbis substitute for priests, let village synagogues substitute for the Jerusalem Temple. In consequence, the Jews came to be defined as a religious community; they practiced the exegesis that is spiritual life.[28] The rabbis projected to the traumatized, dispossessed Jews a rallying authority. A Patriarchate in Tiberias was established. A remnant of the Judean clerisy, "a coalition of priests and sectarians,"[29] continuing the line initiated by the Pharisees, assumed the title "rabbi" and acquired ascendancy in the Jewish population. In addressing the consequences of Israel's loss of temple, city, and land, the rabbis are an example of how a defeated people endures the end of an order.

A period of immense intellectual creativity followed. It ran from the completion of the Mishnah (200 CE) to the completion of the Babylonian Talmud (600 CE), the works that constituted the initial canonical statement of rabbinic Judaism. In addition to these texts, the Tosefta, the Jerusalem Talmud, and compilations of Scriptural exegesis known as midrashim were compiled. Judaism itself was restated. This is the Judaism as we still know it. The heterogeneity of what went before was written out of Judaism's self-understanding. What persisted of it was dismissed as heretical or sectarian.[30] Although Second Temple Judaism passed the Hebrew Scriptures on to rabbinic Judaism, then, it did not pass on its own literary productions. The rabbis formulated a new Judaism under pressure of an emergent rival faith, Christianity. They sought to demonstrate the antiquity and permanence of their tradition,[31] and in doing so, they rewrote history. They projected their own authority with such compelling force that it became unchallengeable in the Jewish world. Whoever disagrees with one's rabbi, affirms the Talmud, is as one who disagrees with the Shekhinah, the divine presence (Sanhedrin 110a).

All of this has a bearing on the rabbis' interpretations of the

Abraham story. God's providence had to be upheld. Embattled and diminished, dispirited Jewry's morale had to be maintained.

Rabbinic Recuperations

The rabbinic readings of the Abraham story are made under the sign of recuperation.[32] That is, they are readings that explain or smooth away textual difficulties; they tame texts, blunting the shock they deliver; they limit possibilities of meaning; they neutralize the texts' subversiveness; they rewrite them in more innocent terms, reducing them to harmlessness.[33] They sanitize, but they do not censor;[34] they are "benevolent interpreters."[35] Though the rabbis sometimes have to work very hard on their recuperative readings (for example, to justify Abraham's abandonment of Terah),[36] the readings always possess dignity and a measure of cogency. The interpretations are apologetic, but they are rarely fanciful or forced. They apply a version of the charity principle, interpreting ostensibly questionable conduct by reference to the most elevated possibilities. In their self-understanding, the rabbis are engaged in the pursuit of truth, not damage limitation.

(Of course, I am speaking here of a dominant tendency. Such is the diversity of rabbinic voices within this discourse that dissenting, nonrecuperative assessments can also be found. Further, recuperative readings are also to be found in Second Temple–period texts.)[37]

The essential question that the discourse addresses can be formulated thus: How to define Abraham's greatness?[38] The question was given several answers, each tending to support a larger rabbinic objective. There were three such objectives in which Abraham played a material part: (a) asserting the centrality of study; (b) defending God's justice; (c) rebutting Christian positions.

Let me take them in turn.

First, there is study. Rabbis engage in the religious study of their religion,[39] thereby setting an example to all Jews. Abraham was enlisted in this enterprise. It was said that he studied in Yeshiva, that he kept the Written Torah and the Oral Torah, that Eliezer studied with him (Yoma 28b). It was said that he wrote a tractate *Avoda Zara*, containing four hundred chapters (Avoda Zara 14b) and the "Book of Creation," the *Sefer Yetzirah*. The rabbis played with time as though with an accordion, judged the great Jewish historian Yosef Haim Yerushalmi (1932–2009). They went against the very grain of the Written Torah, which is firmly anchored in historical realities and in which there is a genuine flow of historical time and of the changes that occur within it.[40] History itself, the Jews' unbearable, catastrophic history, disappeared in the rabbis' hands.

Moreover, the rabbis made study a sublimation of sacrifice. The substitution of the ram for Isaac was the type of the substitution of the study of sacrifice (and study generally) for sacrifice itself. When we study, we repeat the *Akedah*, not at the moment of offering Isaac but at the moment of offering the ram. The *Akedah* became the insuperable horizon of Jewish existence.

There was an antimartial thrust to rabbinic thinking. "Heroism" is not demonstrated on the battlefield. "Who is the hero of heroes? One who transmutes foe into friend."[41] The Talmud complains that Abraham should not have taken his disciples into battle against the kings. They were "Torah scholars," whose service was to God, and their lives should not have been risked in combat (Nedarim 32a).

By contrast, little was made of Abraham 1, who represented the alternative not just to priestly authority and sacrificial cults but also to rabbinic authority and the pious study of authorized texts. The rabbis were wary of the centrifugal force of intellectual inquiry. Even rabbinic academies could not altogether substitute for a single Temple or rabbinic inquiry for priestly service and a single set of ritualized transactions.

Now for the second objective, defending God's justice. The

destruction of the Temple, the loss of Jerusalem, called into question Divine providence. Reassuring answers had to be found, and Torah stories that supported the questioning had to be neutralized. This is more than that undertaking Wyschogrod characterizes as "calming the atmosphere without extinguishing the fire."[42] The *Akedah* had to be interpreted as a story that *fortifies* theodicy.

- *Death not sought*: God merely ordered Abraham to reserve his son for sacrifice, wrote the ninth-century rabbi and philosopher Saadia Gaon. When the reservation had been completed—the fire and wood in place, the knife raised—God said, "Enough! I do not want any more from you than this!"[43] God at no point desired or intended that Abraham kill Isaac. Rashi was ready to depart from the plain meaning of the text, writes Michael J. Harris, to affirm this proposition.[44]
- *No harm*: God knew that Abraham could withstand the test; "He tests only the righteous."[45] As for Isaac, the fundamental difference between the biblical report and the account reshaped by Jewish teachers from the second century BCE onward, explained Geza Vermes, concerned Isaac's active role in the drama. His willingness to be sacrificed was transformed into a redeeming act of permanent validity for all his children until the arrival of the Messiah.[46]
- *If harm, not by God (or his agent, Abraham)*: In the murderous time of the Crusades, Jews cast themselves as Isaacs, while their oppressors took God's part and Abraham's part. "[The crusaders] bound their sons as Abraham bound Isaac his son," wrote a chronicler of the murder of Mainz's Jews in 1096. "They received upon themselves with a willing soul the yoke of the fear of God rather than deny and exchange their religion for an abhorred offshoot."[47]
- *If by God, a test of faith*: To the moralists (*ba'alei ha-musar*), the *Akedah* was a fertile text for the inculcation of religious

and ethical values. The *Akedah* teaches that everything must be sacrificed to God, if need be; how much more, then, must humans be willing to give up their lusts for God. Moreover, whenever humans have an opportunity of doing good or refraining from evil, they should reflect that perhaps God is testing them at that moment as He tested Abraham.[48]

• *And to the advantage of all subsequent generations of Jews*: "This deed," wrote Hasdai Crescas (ca. 1340–1410), "was a kindness to our entire nation."[49] From the order of morning prayers: "Master of the Universe, just as Abraham our father suppressed his compassion to do Your will wholeheartedly, so may Your compassion suppress Your anger from us." A few lines later, Jews pray, "We are Your people, the children of Your covenant, the children of Abraham, Your beloved, to whom You made a promise on Mount Moriah; the offspring of Isaac his only son who was bound on the altar."[50]

Given the material facts of Jewish existence, while the objective of defending God's justice was of the greatest moment to Jews, it was also the most difficult to achieve. It is therefore not surprising that more sober readings of the *Akedah* were also proposed. The Mishnaic treatise *Pirke Avot* itself hints at one such reading. "With ten trials was Abraham our father tried, and he endured [*ve'amad*] them all; to make known how great was the love of Abraham our father." The critical word is *amad*. It has a range of meanings, from (at the highest) "passed" to "survived" (at the lowest), with intermediate meanings of "withstood" and "endured." Commentators tend to take the meaning of *amad* at its highest and build from there their account of the test as a complete triumph for Abraham. *Pirke Avot* is somewhat subtler and more open-ended, however. It can be read as saying no more than that Abraham did not so much pass the test as get past it. It didn't flatten him. He lived beyond it; he subsisted.

The medieval chroniclers did not always draw back from

challenging God. They did not challenge Him as a perpetrator, for sure; but they did challenge Him as a culpable bystander. "Has there ever been an *Akedah* like this in all the generations since Adam? Eleven hundred *akedot* took place on a single day, all of them comparable to the binding of Isaac. For him, the world shook. Will You remain silent for these eleven hundred, O Lord?"[51] The medieval Jewish imagination was fully open to the horror of the command. "If Abraham had had a hundred bodies," wrote a fourteenth-century commentator, "it would have been right for him to give them all up for Isaac's sake. This act was not like any other act, this trial was not like any other, and nature cannot bear it, nor the imagination conceive it."[52]

It must have seemed to some rabbis that the *Akedah* was better excluded from theodicy discussion. This was Maimonides's position. In his reading of the *Akedah*, the question of God's justice simply does not arise. He does *not* make the innocent suffer in order to increase their reward; God does *not* test a thing to ascertain what He did not hitherto know. To hold that God behaves otherwise is to deny that He is "a God of faithfulness and without iniquity." It is to make of Him a criminal. Only "ignorant fools in their evil thoughts" could think that God would behave as is commonly represented in accounts of the *Akedah*. "How greatly is He exalted above that which such people imagine" (Guide, III.24). Yeshayahu Leibowitz's suggestion, that Maimonides "is the re-embodiment of Abraham" in the moment of this ultimate test, can only be correct in the context of Maimonides's (and not Leibowitz's) understanding of the *Akedah*.[53] As Aaron Koller points out, in the name of Maimonides, while the first command to Abraham only qualifies as an instance of the seventh level of prophetic experience, the second command is an instance of the eleventh, highest level (Guide, II.45).[54]

We can state a rabbinic rule: Defend theodicy first and Abraham second. If criticism of Abraham serves the defense of theodicy, Abraham will indeed be criticized. This is the mean-

ing of both the Egypt story and the Timna story. Egyptian enslavement was the outcome of Abraham's untrusting flight to
Egypt; Amalekite assaults were the outcome of Abraham's rejection of Timna. We are responsible; God cannot be blamed. This
is the "harsh moral" of the tales.[55] After all, what is theodicy if not
a defense of God's honor, a recuperative move on *His* behalf?

Last is the objective to rebut Christian objections and thus
to maintain Jewish morale. Christianity was a challenge to Judaism, though never an existential one. The Jewish response tended
toward the dismissive, until displays of disrespect became dangerous. "It is generally accepted," wrote Nahum Glatzer, "that a number of Talmudic interpretations and Midrashic homilies are the
result of polemics against Christian teachings, or attempts to
strengthen the faith of those Jews who were exposed to Christian
propaganda."[56] The Abraham story was a central site of Jewish-
Christian controversy.[57]

Against Christian appropriations, the rabbis celebrated Abraham as a source of national pride, as a witness to Jewish excellence (e.g., in opposing idolatry: Avoda Zara 3a), as a person of
great spiritual and physical courage;[58] and as a Torah-observant
Jew. (This last was also to encourage Jews to greater observance
themselves.)[59] He was "perfect," a person "over whom the evil
inclination had no sway" (Baba Bathra 17a). He fully merited
God's favor, which his descendants have inherited. Heinrich
Graetz, amplifying this rabbinic position, commended the *Akedah* to his readers as "an act which shed everlasting glory upon
all Abraham's descendants."[60]

The rabbis were quick in Abraham's defense, then. God ex-
empted him from the duties owed to parents;[61] Abraham did not
lie about Sarah to Pharaoh or Abimelech (Zohar 1:140b);[62] alternatively, Sarah was not at risk in Egypt because she was accompanied by an angel;[63] if Hagar had walked straight, the skin of
water that Abraham had given her would have sufficed until she
reached an inn (Rashbam);[64] Abraham did not lie to Eliezer and

Ishmael (Moed Katan 18a); Isaac consented to the sacrifice; and so on. Judaism was not to be outdone by Christianity.

The rabbis took a complex position regarding Abraham in response to Christian claims about Jesus. Our Patriarchs were also perfect, *especially* Abraham, the rabbis argued. But then against the Christians, the rabbis insisted, the Patriarchs were not divine. As Samson Raphael Hirsch many centuries later wrote, "The Torah does not hide from us the faults, errors and weaknesses of our great men, and this is precisely what gives its stories veracity. Their faults and weaknesses do not detract from their status as great men. We must never attempt to whitewash the spiritual and moral heroes of our past. They do not need our apologetics."[65]

Christians praised Abraham as a person of faith in direct communion with God. A pre-Torah Jew, he did not need the scaffolding of ritual laws. Against this Christian claim that Abraham was righteous though he did not have the Law (indeed, that he was righteous even before circumcised), the rabbis responded, "No! Abraham observed *all* the mitzvot, *all* the commandments!" (Yoma 28b).[66] The deploying of Abraham in support of the centrality of study and the deploying of him against Christian appropriations thus converged.

The Abraham story continues to be read thus today, in large parts of the Jewish world.[67]

Three Challenges

There are three challenges to the JR readings of the Abraham story that we must take into account, not least because in their combined force, they contribute to the formation of the JX discourse.

The Christian Challenge: Appropriating, Superseding

Stories about Abraham circulated in the early centuries of the Common Era. Hitherto, Abraham had been the exclusive concern of the Jews. Now, however, the early Christian Church had taken him up. In the hands of Paul, writes Jon D. Levenson, the identification of Jesus and Isaac assumed an especially forceful and far-reaching statement.[68] Jesus was the "new Isaac."[69] The *Akedah* "profoundly shaped early Christian self-understanding, theology and practice."[70] The Abraham story as a whole had an immense appeal to the Christian imagination. It was, for example, a crux in the intra-Christian debate, faith versus works.[71]

Philo was claimed by the Church as its own and was given a posthumous baptism.[72] His partially allegorical readings were taken as mandate for the Church's own allegorical readings. Transitional texts, neither declaredly Jewish nor declaredly Christian, were composed, a bridge between Jews and Christians. The *Testament of Abraham*, say, written by a Jewish-Christian, perhaps,[73] but shorn of all Jewish detail, related God's efforts to manage the death of "my friend Abraham, my beloved."[74] Last, and most consequentially, fresh interpretations of the Abraham story were proposed (above all, of the *Akedah*),[75] in retellings and in interpretations of Torah verses. The *Akedah* was a special favorite of Christian art.[76]

The essential message to Jews was, "Your history is now our history. Christ is the true heir to God's promises, the church is the true Israel. The Abrahamic covenant trumps the Sinaitic covenant."[77] The Jews, dispossessed of their Temple, were now to be dispossessed of their descent. Every word of the Torah was given a Christian meaning; the Torah itself was appropriated for the Church's use. The Torah made sense only insofar as it prefigured Christianity. "The rest of it—a great deal—was deafness, blindness, forgetfulness. A previously non-existent book, called the Old Testament, was created out of an old one, the Torah."[78] It fragmented into a series of isolated prefigurations, figural prophecies, of Christ.[79]

This strategy of appropriation was pursued by various means:

- *Typologies*: The Torah's characters, tropes, narratives, and prescriptions were read as just so many anticipations of Gospel characters, narratives, and prescriptions.[80] Jesus dies figuratively many times over in the Torah. The Scriptures contain nothing other than God's promises (Hebrew Scriptures) and the testament of God in Christ (New Testament). The smallest details in Torah narratives were dragooned in advance of this project, without any regard to coherence. The three men who appear to Abraham are a prefiguration of the Trinity.[81] The wood carried by Isaac *and* the bush in which the ram was entangled are types of the Cross on which Jesus was crucified.[82] And so on. "The Old bears witness to the New."[83]

- *Processes*: Christ's purpose was to fulfill God's promises made in the Torah. The last-moment substitution of a ram was enlisted in support of this argument. What was unfulfilled in Isaac, because he did not die, though was readied for sacrifice on the altar, was fulfilled on the Cross.[84] (In Christian tradition, the *Akedah* is known as the sacrifice, not the binding, of Isaac.)[85] "Isaac did not suffer," explained Melito of Sardis (d. 180), "for he was a type of the passion of Christ." Isaac, the Torah, and the Jewish people merge into a single type for him, "a preliminary sketch" of "what was to come" but now "useless," "worthless."[86]

- *Preemptions*: It was not enough to maintain Jesus's descent from Abraham; it was also asserted that Jesus antedated him. "Your father Abraham rejoiced that he was to see my day; he saw it and was glad," Jesus tells the Jews. They are made to reply, "You are not yet fifty years old, and have you seen Abraham?" Jesus then responds, "Truly, truly, I say to you, before Abraham was, I am" (John 8:56–58).

- *Preferences*: That the God of Israel tends to favor the late born over the firstborn, Levenson observes, is a point of venerable antiquity among Christian theologians. In those circles, it reflects the anxiety of the self-designated "new Israel," the Church, relative to the "old Israel" that it claims to supersede, that is, the Jewish people. Divine favoritism toward late-born sons, of course, is attested too many times in the Hebrew Scriptures to be a mere coincidence.[87]

Appropriation, then—*literally*. In *Dialogue with Trypho* (ca. 155–160), the apologist and martyr Justin addresses his Jewish interlocutor, "The scriptures are not yours, but ours."[88] Some went even further: "The divine prophets lived according to Jesus Christ."[89] Jesus "was not unknown to Abraham, whose day he desired to see," wrote Bishop Irenaeus (ca. 130–202). Abraham "saw in the Spirit the day of the Lord's coming." By "an announcement made to him," he "learned that the Son of Man would be a man among men."[90]

To these moves should be added both the endlessly deployed "letter/spirit" dichotomy and a resourceful interpretive opportunism:

- *Dichotomy*: "The letter kills, but the spirit giveth life," says Paul (2 Cor. 3:6). This was one central Christian interpretive axiom and informed much anti-Jewish polemicizing.[91] It underwrote a general condemnation of Judaism, giving Christianity a general permission to take its place. Among its applications, it identified Torah pairs (say, Hagar and Sarah) with "letter" and "spirit" functions, thereby affirming Christianity's superiority independent of any predictive typologizing.
- *Opportunism*: In relentless exercise of self-mandated "imaginative freedom,"[92] Christian exegetes piled up proofs for their faith, regardless of even the loosest rules of interpretation. For example, Paul noticed that Abraham was declared righteous (Gen. 15:6) *before* the command to him to circumcise himself (Gen. 17:10). This must mean, Paul inferred, that Abraham is "the father of all who believe" (Rom. 4:11).

"We, brethren, as Isaac was, are the children of the flesh" (Gal. 4:28). Paul would spare nothing, wrote Shalom Spiegel, until he had converted everything he had learned from rabbinic instruction into a proclamation of the blood of the crucified Jesus.[93]

The general intent, as Erich Auerbach explains, was to strip what was named the Old Testament of its normative status and to interpret it as a mere shadow of things to come.[94] An early Christian writer imagined God addressing Abraham: "It suffices for you that you have been honoured by being the type."[95] Or as the Church Father Athanasius put it, "When Abraham offered his son, he was worshipping the Son of God."[96] The anonymous fourth-century *Vision of Paul* supposed that Abraham, when in heaven, himself took on "the likeness of Christ."[97]

In the sacred history of Pauline Christianity, Levenson explains, Abraham played a critical part. The history comprised three stages: righteousness without the Torah (Abraham); sin and death through the Torah (Moses, Sinai); the restoration of righteousness without the Torah (Christ). Of all the figures in the Hebrew Scriptures, Abraham ranked the highest, then. He served as proof that faith could be detached from deeds and reckoned as self-sufficient. Christians, not Jews, therefore were the true heirs to the promises made to him by God.[98]

Most Jews met these provocations in indifferent or intimidated silence, though a few bold spirits engaged the Christians in polemic. The mute and the vociferous were united, however, in their refusal to be impressed by Christian claims,[99] which became a source of great exasperation to the early Church. This is why, I suspect, their appropriations, themselves violent, were often related in stories that were themselves conditioned by an atmosphere of violence:

- *John 8*: In this Gospel account, Jesus accuses the Jews of seeking his death. "If you were Abraham's children, then you would do what Abraham did. As it is, you are looking for a way to kill me, a man who has told you the truth that I heard from God. Abraham did not do such things." "Ye are of your father the devil. He was a murderer from the beginning." The Jews take up stones to cast at Jesus, but he escapes them.

- *Acts* 7: Stephen, a deacon in the early church in Jerusalem, is on trial before the Sanhedrin, who condemn him to death by stoning. In his speech of defense, he denounces his Jewish judges and relates Abraham's story in a version that departs from and thereby undermines the Torah account.

The violence testifies to that impulse in early Christianity to incorporate in the new religion everything of the Jewish/Israelite past that could usefully be incorporated into it and utterly to annihilate the rest.[100]

Abraham was a special focus of attention for the theologian and bishop St. Augustine (354–430). Following St. Paul, he takes Abraham to be the spiritual father of all Christians.[101] In his major work, *The City of God* (426), he retells the Abraham story in full, adding his own running commentary. He praises Abraham: "O, what an excellent man he was, in his use of women!" Abraham is further to be praised because "he immediately believed that his son would rise again when he had been sacrificed." In the burnt offering, "Christ was signified."[102] In the polemic *Against Faustus the Manichean* (ca. 398–400), Augustine takes "the righteousness of Abraham's faith" to be "an example to us." He defends Abraham against Faustus's criticisms, mere "impudent misrepresentations." So, for example, Abraham did *not* sell Sarah to Pharaoh and then to Abimelech; he was assured by God that Sarah would not suffer violence or disgrace. For Abraham to sacrifice his son of his own accord would have been shocking madness; to do so at the command of God proves him faithful and submissive.[103]

Artists and sculptors gave visual, material effect to the Christian practice of *separating* Abraham from postbiblical Jews and *linking* him to New Testament figures. Regensburg Cathedral contains a very striking confirmation of the violence of the separating. Among its devotional artworks, worshipers are able to contemplate both a statue of the sacrifice of Isaac and a *Judensau* group, three Jews in intimate contact with a pig.[104] As to the relating, an early fourteenth-century French illustration, for example, depicts the Christ-Logos extending a hand to Abraham, who stands in a prayerful posture, his back to the concealed three angels whom he has been entertaining. In a mid-fifteenth-century English alabaster carving, a seated Abraham supports between his legs a crucified Jesus.[105]

As the Church developed, divided, won new adherents, multiplied institutions, and acquired powers undreamed of by the first Christians, it contented itself with relying on the accounts of the Abraham story written in those first centuries. There were few further elaborations of the Abraham story of consequence. Church thinkers were content to take the Abraham of Paul and the Fathers, broadly speaking.[106]

The next major event in the Christian reception of the Abraham story came many centuries later, with the Danish philosopher Søren Kierkegaard's *Fear and Trembling* (1843). This important text is commonly read as making its essential argument in a verbless sentence, one with the cadence of a chant or slogan: "The teleological suspension of the ethical."[107]

If a case is to be made in mitigation of the Christian appropriation of the Hebrew Scriptures, then that case must rely on *Fear and Trembling*. That it is a Christian appropriation of the *Akedah*, however, there can be no doubt. Kierkegaard takes Abraham to be a Christian before the fact.[108] His wisdom is his foolishness, his strength is his vulnerability, his courage is his resignation. Abraham is the "knight of faith," the very model of Christian chivalry,[109] and the story of the *Akedah* itself is as mediated by

Hebrews 11.[110] As I argued in chapter 4, this is not the Jewish interest in the *Akedah*, an interest that never leaves the realm of the ethical. This makes the embrace of Kierkegaard by some JR writers somewhat embarrassing;[111] JX writers are not so susceptible to him.[112]

So commonplace is this Testamental relating of "Old" to "New," so deep in the culture is this assumption that the two make a single whole, that every opportunity should be taken to prize them apart. Especially welcome, then, if only for this reason, is Leibowitz's setting of the *Akedah* against the Crucifixion. The *Akedah*, the highest symbol of faith in Judaism, and the Crucifixion, Christianity's highest symbol, stand in opposition to each other, he proposes. In the *Akedah*, human values and divine promises are shunted aside before reverence for God and love of God. In the Crucifixion, by contrast, the deity sacrifices his only son for humanity. This is the great difference between theocentric religion, in which humanity strives to serve God, and anthropocentric religion, in which God fulfills humanity's need for salvation.[113] Judaism and Christianity are not to be muddled; "Judeo-Christian civilization" is an ideological fiction.

The Enlightenment Challenge: Disparaging, Refuting

In a statement that held true for six hundred years after it was made, Maimonides affirmed of Abraham that no one was antagonistic to him or ignorant of his greatness (Guide, III.29)—until, that is, the period of the Enlightenment.

Immanuel Kant's essay "What Is Enlightenment?" (1784) is indispensable to understanding Abraham 1's distinctive achievements; the essay should be taught in every Jewish school. And yet, when Enlightenment authors addressed the Abraham story directly, they tended to lose themselves in denigrations—Kant included (to the immense pain of his Jewish admirers).[114] They were indifferent to Abraham 1's independent reasoning; they proposed a refutation of Abraham's rational theology; they offered many mocking, satiric disparagements of Abraham 2's life; they condemned the Abraham of the *Akedah*.[115]

Enlightenment thinkers took Socrates as their model of the critical intellectual, persecuted for his commitment to free inquiry, an exemplary and symbolic forebear of the *philosophes* ("the poor Socrateses").[116] It could have been Abraham. The critique of unreason in the shape of superstition and prejudice, enthusiasm and fanaticism, tradition and authority, and the drive toward autonomy of thought and responsibility, which were Enlightenment projects,[117] was Abraham's own project in Ur. Pierre Bayle, in his *Dictionary Historical and Critical* (1697–1702), came closest to this Abraham when he described Abraham's exile from Ur as "perhaps the first instance of banishment for religion's sake."[118] Abraham was not given credit for reasoning his way to God, even though his achievement in this respect was a commonplace in Second Temple and post–Second Temple texts available to Enlightenment circles.[119]

The *Dictionary* contains a terse account of the Genesis story. The falsehoods and groundless traditions relating to Abraham are so numerous as to try one's patience. What exploits has he not been made to perform against idolatry? How many sciences and how many books have not been attributed to him? Such are the dreams of the rabbis. Bayle cites Philo, Josephus, and Maimonides and refers to the Talmud, along with various Church authorities. Bayle, who had an extraordinary interest in and knowledge of Judaism,[120] criticizes the "superstitious cruelty" of Terah, in "acting the part of an informer against his own son."[121]

The great Voltaire, the "most admired and dreaded writer of the eighteenth century,"[122] had little time for Jews. His entry on Abraham in his *Philosophical Dictionary* (1764) has four targets: the historicity of the Scriptural account; Abraham's behavior toward his wife; Abraham's religious inheritance;[123] the Jews' contribution to civilization. The entry is typical of Voltaire's contradictory attacks on the Hebrew Scriptures as both discredited and scandalous; he rejects its authority and draws on it for his antisemitic polemics.[124] He mocks commentators who strive to "justify Abraham's conduct and reconcile his chronology." The Jews, a "little people, new, ignorant, rude, lacking in the arts, copied as best it could" the "ancient peoples" among whom they lived. "And these are our fathers!" exclaims Voltaire.[125] That is, these are the people from whom Christian Europe traces its spiritual descent![126]

As for the Abraham of the *Akedah*, Kant would have counseled him to reply to God's voice, "That I ought not to kill my son is quite certain. But that you, this apparition, are God—of that I am not certain, and never can be, not even as this voice rings down to me from the visible heaven." The moral law within prevails over mere external directions, especially when of unreliable provenance. Whoever pretends that a proposition is true because it is present in one's own mind and that this truth comes from nowhere but God is a liar or an enthusiast (that is, a person who seeks to free claims from any critical appraisal).[127] Judaism itself is garments without a person, a church without a religion. They must throw off these garments, the garb of the ancient cult. Kant took the *Akedah* to discredit Judaism; the "New Atheists" (Dawkins, Hitchens) took it to discredit religion as such.[128]

As Levenson notes, by abstracting the *Akedah* from the Abraham story, and indeed from the Jewish tradition, Kant's account stands at the point of origin of a whole line of hostile readings, in which Abraham is the "model of the abusive father, the violent male," and indeed the "terrorist."[129] This then becomes an Abraham from whom we must "take leave."[130]

The *Akedah*'s challenge to theodicy was thus of no interest to Enlightenment writers. It was not read as a caution against fanaticism but as its purported justification. That it might lead to the thought that defending God is idle, because His actions are incomprehensible to us, that what we experience as unde-

served suffering may be a delight to Him, inflicted in consequence of some divine whim, his ways not being our ways, was
not entertained by the generality of Enlightenment thinkers.
Kant, one of the boldest among them, could only entertain the
thought in order to dismiss it; Edward Gibbon, one of the most
impious among them, floated it merely to rag the Protestants.[131]

In brief, Enlightenment readings of the Abraham story rarely
enhanced the Jews' good name. Abraham himself was given a
bad character. He was no longer to be revered as the Gentile
Abraham,[132] the model of the righteous believer, and in his readiness to sacrifice his beloved son, the type of God Himself. He
was instead to be deplored as the Jewish Abraham, the model of
the modern Jew, and in his self-interested misanthropy, the enemy
of humankind. Such was the implication of the Enlightenment
account. We must look to the post-Enlightenment German philosopher G. W. F. Hegel to find this implication drawn out—
specifically to Hegel's early essay "The Spirit of Christianity and
Its Fate" (1798), unpublished in the philosopher's lifetime.

Abraham left Haran to be a wholly self-subsistent, independent man, Hegel writes. He snapped the bonds of communal
life and love. His spirit of self-maintenance, in strict opposition
to everything, carried him through his life. He looked on the
world as sustained by a God who was alien to it. He wandered
hither and thither without cultivating or improving the land he
traversed. He was a stranger on Earth, a stranger to the soil and
to people alike. He remained a foreigner. He was cunning and
duplicitous when dealing with kings who intended him no evil.
With others, he carefully kept relations on a strictly legal footing. What he needed he bought; he shrank from all equal, loving relations. Love's presence troubled him. In the person of
Isaac, it invaded his heart. To calm himself, Abraham found the
readiness to slay the boy.[133] What the Jews suffered thereafter,
and continue to suffer, are the consequences and elaborations of
Abraham's own history.[134]

The Academic Challenge: Historicizing, Fragmenting, Aestheticizing

The academic challenge to the JR discourse derives from the radical Enlightenment Jewish philosopher Benedict de (formerly, Baruch) Spinoza. "I hold that the method of interpreting Scripture," he wrote, "does not differ from the method of interpreting nature, but rather is wholly consonant with it."[135] The interpretive methods of Scripture's ecclesiastically accredited interpreters were entirely misconceived. Scripture itself had to be disarmed. It was merely one ancient book among and comparable to others; its divine authorship was a fiction. There is no such thing as "sacred history." The Bible is not a privileged source of knowledge. Knowledge is knowledge, and only one authority presides over its domain: that of evidence and reasoned judgment. Spinoza created the Bible of modern academic scholarship, writes J. Samuel Preus, the Bible as investigated through historical and critical study.[136]

The academic challenge derives from the Enlightenment, then, but purged of much of its residually Christian elements. "Read the Bible as you would read Livy or Tacitus," Thomas Jefferson advised. "For example, in the book of Joshua, we are told, the sun stood still several hours. Were we to read that fact in Livy or Tacitus, we should class it with their showers of blood, speaking of statues, beasts, etc. But it is said that the writer of that book was inspired. Examine candidly what evidence there is of his having been inspired. . . . You must lay aside all prejudice, and neither believe nor reject anything because any other persons have rejected or believed it. Your own reason is the only oracle."[137] This advice, given to his nephew, is an early statement of the professional ethics of a university teacher. Academic discourse is severe in its judgments; objectivity, rigor, integrity are chief among its ideals.[138]

Pondering biblical academic scholarship, Jean-Gérard Bursztein characterizes this "university discourse" as concerned with only two questions: What is the historicity of the Torah? Out of what disparate materials is it composed?[139] From the perspective of a universal history, the *Tanakh* shrinks to a collection of parochial documents. It is an account of the Jews, written by Jews, across an extended, relatively early period of human history,[140] a sourcebook, not a textbook,[141] a patchwork of texts.[142] Traditional scholarship harmonizes textual difficulties, on the premise of a single author; critical scholarship interprets textual difficulties as proof of many authors.

Critical scholarship addresses date, authorship, and stratification of the various biblical books.[143] In consequence of heterogeneities of language and genre, oddities, discrepancies, and irregularities of various types, contradictions and inconsistencies between verses or passages, the text becomes a source of something beyond itself. This hypothesis, associated with the German Higher Criticism in the mid- to late nineteenth century, continues to exercise influence in the academy. "The evidence suggests a rather loose relation between books and traditions, not the tightly defined network of relations implied when an exactly demarcated 'scripture' comes into existence," writes a modern Bible scholar.[144] The tendency is to dispute any treatment of Abraham as a historical figure. Hardly anyone today would attempt to interpret the texts available to us in Genesis 12–25 as direct accounts of the life of the historical Abraham, notes one academic.[145]

Objections may be made to aspects of academic Bible discourse. In the nineteenth century, much of it comprised little more than "thin secularizations of calumnies that derived from the New Testament."[146] In its worst iterations, it is a hostile evaluation, diminishing the Hebrew Scriptures to a collection of inert shards;[147] it carries, when it does not advance, the legacy of antisemitism.[148] Some academic writing on Judaism is a tacit teaching of Christianity. Even when not acknowledged, a developmental account of religion, from early Israelite religion in an upward ascent to Christianity, is often assumed. The distinction between the teaching *of* religion and teaching *about* religion rarely holds.[149] Joseph Blenkinsopp's *Abraham: The Story of a Life* (2015) is a recent example of the instability of this distinction. Academic in orientation, Blenkinsopp nonetheless acknowledges that he writes "explicitly as a Christian devotee of Abraham."[150]

Furthermore, academic discourse, in its remoteness from traditional interpretive models, can accommodate the most sentimental maundering: "The heartrending grief of the father commanded to sacrifice his child with his own hand, and then his boundless gratitude and joy when God's mercy releases him from this grievous trial"; "Abraham from the depths of his breaking heart quiets the questioning of his unsuspecting child."[151] Thus Herman Gunkel (1862–1932), the German "Old Testament" scholar and theologian. This is the consequence among biblical scholars of a more general deficiency in grasp of the Scriptures' literary dimension.[152] They resist treating it, as literary critics by instinct *would* treat it, as a synchronous, systemic entity.[153] The concept of unity is a cornerstone of both poetics and rabbinic interpretation.[154]

And yet, these judgments and characterizations may be put to one side, as either mere surface phenomena or indicative of an earlier phase of Bible scholarship. Academic discourse has the resources to correct itself. It was a German Protestant theologian, no less, who insisted that Christian interpretation of something not Christian, that is, the Torah, is mere *pseudo*-interpretation.[155] Victor P. Hamilton's widely read volumes for the *New International Commentary on the Old Testament* distinguish commentary from "New Testament appropriations"; regarding the identification of Abraham's three visitors with the Trinity, for example, Hamilton writes, "[it] forces on the text an interpretation the text itself will not yield."[156] Levenson reports that Christians involved in the historical criticism of the Bible today no longer want their work to be considered distinctively Christian. They are Christians everywhere except in the classroom and at the writing table. Jews, Christians, and others can work in tandem; the broad ecumenical character of critical biblical scholarship is now an established fact.[157]

The academic contribution to the study of Torah, and therefore to the study of the Abraham story, is essential. It is not a mere contingency that the most important translation of *Tanakh* in modern times is the work of an accomplished academic literary critic, Robert Alter; his work has contributed to the liberation of English-language readers from dependence on the Authorized Version.[158] Literary critics, even (or perhaps especially) when outsiders to biblical scholarship,[159] enrich academic discourse on the Torah. They find common ground with the rabbis, indeed. The traditional doctrine of the unitary composition of the Torah[160] is for them the starting point of literary appreciation. Scholarship that interprets texts against the author's own preferences and traditions, in the interests of intellectual honesty,[161] is a praiseworthy, indispensable endeavor. First-class contributions are being made to the Jewish understanding of Jewish foundational texts, and of Judaism itself, by Jews who embrace the disciplines and values of academic discourse.[162]

The university is the institutional expression of academic discourse, even though much of what passes for academic discourse in universities is not worthy of the name, and intellectual life can flourish outside the academy.[163] Hannah Arendt correctly affirmed that the university is a "refuge of truth." It is among a limited class of "free speech institutions" in which "contrary to all political rules, truth and truthfulness have always constituted the highest criteria of speech and endeavor." The "chances for truth to prevail in public are greatly improved by the mere existence of such places and by the organization of independent, *supposedly* disinterested scholars associated with them." The adverb is Arendt's concession to the reality principle.[164] The Abraham story, a small masterpiece in Israel's ancient library of sacred texts,[165] is safe in the university.

IX

The destruction of the Temple and the arrival of modernity were two ruptures in Jewish history, eliciting responses from two cohorts of Jews, JR Jews and JX Jews, and leading to two sets of "takes" on the Abraham story.

Modernity

Let us imagine a modern Jewish intellectual, committed to his people, contemplating the course of Jewish Enlightenment and Emancipation, the one incomplete, the other ever at risk of repudiation, a very protracted process yet experienced as a "whiplash transition" by many Jews.[166] What kinds of writing would be appropriate to this new conjuncture?

It could not be just *one* kind. After the completion of the Talmud, Franz Rosenzweig wrote, there was a highway common to all Jews. To be sure, there were side roads, bridges, towns; but essentially there was only one main road. That common highway is no longer in existence. Its extension is at best one of many roads; it is no longer *the* way.[167]

JX Identities

JX writers self-define as Jews, in terms personal to each one among them—say, the splendid Hilary Putnam elaborating his "very own personal manifestation of Judaism."[168] They are very interested in Judaism as a "problem," in the nonpejorative sense of the word; correctly, they do not consider that this requires them to submit to any given routine of Jewish observance.[169] "There is no one today who is not alienated," wrote Rosenzweig. All maintain a certain distance from normative Judaism.[170] There has always been Jewish speculation on the dilemmas of Jewishness;[171] only among JX writers, however, is this speculation a distinct Jewish endeavor.

Take as an example *A Scholar's Tale* (2007), the autobiography of the literary critic and JX writer Geoffrey Hartman (1929–2016). He acknowledges that he has only a slight understanding of Hebrew and of Jewish ritual. He lacks childhood associations with prayer services or communal ceremonies. When other people pray, he fidgets; he cannot lose himself in Shabbat songs. And yet, he writes, he does not feel himself exiled from Jewishness. He defines himself as a "Jew of culture," or a "Jew, but not of the synagogue." Regarding literature and the arts, he finds no bright dividing line between the Jewish and the non-Jewish, the sacred and secular. In the preface to a book of essays on Jewish topics, he introduces himself: "I, the *am ha'aretz*."[172] In another, less self-chastising judgment, he describes himself as a "raider and explorer" of the Jewish tradition, which opened its riches to him through a belated intellectual acquisition.[173]

There are many instances in the JX canon of this engagement in alienation, affirmations of relation accompanied by acknowledgments of distance.[174] JX writers in general are "raiders and explorers" in their literary encounters with Judaism. In their most inventive endeavors, they formulate novel understandings of Judaism. In Kafka, it is an antitheology of inaccessible Law;[175] in Levinas, it is a reimagined tradition, constructed in part out of nontraditional sources.[176] In more everyday instances, the raiding and exploring flourishes as an amateur pursuit—"amateur," that is, in the sense Erich Auerbach gave the word, writing of Michel de Montaigne (1533–1592), that son of a Jewish mother, first in the line of writers to whom JX writers owe allegiance. All other great intellectual figures of the sixteenth century were *experts*, possessing at least one specialization, says Auerbach. But not Montaigne. There was no professional connection between his practical endeavors and his intellectual work. He was unsystematic and without method. He knew both more and less than the experts (Auerbach refers to them as "mere specialists"), a state of affairs that was the wellspring of his originality. He wrote for a community that his writing itself contributed to bringing into existence, an "educated public" of which he himself was an early member.[177] Thus the JX writer in relation to the rabbis and in relation to the Jewish public.

JX writers may not believe in an afterlife or in God as a supernatural helper who intervenes in the course of our lives to rescue us from disaster.[178] The content of their self-definition may even actively elude them (when they do not actively repudiate it). Some in consequence embrace a divided identity: "I am and am not a Jew."[179] Some others embrace a negative anthropology of the Jew, a self-definition *via negationis*.[180] Think of Philip Roth's Nathan Zuckerman: "A Jew without Jews, without Judaism, without Zionism, without Jewishness."[181] Kafka went even further: "What do I have in common with Jews? I have scarcely anything in common with myself."[182]

In consequence of this self-definition, which is typically a refusal to self-define, JX writers invented a new class of Jews. They asserted within Jewish life, and contrary to the standard rabbinic dichotomy of Talmud scholars and unlearned Jews (*amei ha'aretz*), the existence of a *third* class of Jew, neither rabbi nor *am ha'aretz* but secular and learned. (Maimonides was exceptional in anticipating this third class.)[183] Hannah Arendt, for example, described her "third class" as people of Jewish background, unaware of any Jewish substance in their lives but constituting a distinct element in society, generous in spirit, sensitive to injustices, lacking in prejudice, and respecting the life of the mind.[184] Members of this third class will have their own Jewish canon. "Jewish high culture," wrote Harold Bloom, identifying his version of it, "is now an amalgam of imaginative literature, psychoanalysis, and a kind of Kabbalah."[185]

JX writers operate within a literary culture, in Richard Rorty's strong meaning of the term. It is the fact that our culture does not stand in awe of God, he argues, that makes it "literary." Religion and philosophy appear as literary genres. We value above all the exercise of imagination, rather than self-examination; we are more occupied with inventing selves than with discovering one's self.[186] It is the Bible's "surpassing splendor & force" of speech and its "fathomless gulfs of meaning"[187] that appeal to this culture, not its theological authority. It was to no avail that Abraham Joshua Heschel protested, "Some people hail the Bible as 'literature,' as if 'literature' were the climax of spiritual reality. What would Moses, what would Isaiah, have said to such praise?"[188]

JX writers participate in this culture, while also interrogating it. Their participation has a certain quality of defiance. "The Scripture stories do not, like Homer's, court our favor, they do not flatter us that they may please us and enchant us," wrote Erich Auerbach. "They seek to subject us, and if we refuse to be subjected we are rebels."[189] Here is the true voice of the JX writer. "Jewish literature," writes Adam Kirsch, in a generous definition, "is what happens every time a writer tries to make a place for himself or herself" in the "ancient lineage" of Jewish texts.[190]

JX writers thus make free with the texts, authors, and traditions that had been the preserve of the rabbis. They find in *Tanakh* both a repository of stories and a model of literary accomplishment. Freud wrote, "My deep engrossment in the Bible story (almost as soon as I had learnt the art of reading) had, as I recognised much later, an enduring effect upon the direction of my interest" (20:8). "I acquired a great love and admiration for the stories told in Genesis," wrote Isaac Bashevis Singer. "I am still learning the art of writing from Genesis."[191] It is a commonplace that almost every poem written by the major modern-day Hebrew poets makes use of Scriptural words, phrases, and tropes.[192]

JX writers found other repositories to raid, of course. There were no "outside books" for them. Kafka wrote to his friend Max Brod, "In my first months here [in hospital] I read the Bible a great deal; that has stopped." In the same letter, he conjured up a story about "an anonymous Greek who comes to Troy without ever having intended to" and gets caught up in a battle.[193] JX writers resisted any imperative to choose between repositories, between Athens's dramas and Jerusalem's jeremiads, between European literary models and Jewish literary models. The peril in bowing to the imperative? A "rupture," a "tearing of the heart" into a "Jewish part" and a "humanist part."[194]

So much of the modern Jewish literary canon concerns sons in their relations with their fathers, related from the son's perspective. This is not just a *topic*. In another letter to Brod, Kafka wrote, "Psycho-analysis lays stress on the father-complex and many find the concept intellectually fruitful. In this case, I prefer another version, where the issue revolves not around the innocent father, but around the father's Jewishness. Most young Jews who began to write German wanted to leave Jewishness behind them, and their fathers approved of this, but vaguely (this vagueness was what outraged them). But with their posterior legs, they were still glued to their father's Jewishness, and with their waving anterior legs, they found no new ground. The ensuing despair became their inspiration."[195] This is a literature of recalcitrant, bound but struggling, Isaacs, a literature of sons.

This multilingual Jewish literature, another extraordinary intellectual achievement of the Jews (rivaling the rabbinic achievement but of an entirely different character), became a distinct object of study for Jews, and a focus for Jewish self-understanding, as Jewish identity itself splintered.[196]

However uneasy JX writers may be with traditional belief and practice,[197] most have a personal investment in Jewish life no less intense than the rabbis'. They regard their intellectual undertakings as (at the very least) no less challenging or important as the rabbis', and they relate to each other through informal networks as open textured and international as the rabbis'. For these reasons, as well as others, their relations with JR writers tend to be somewhat fraught. Even in the earliest years, when JX writers were ready to ventriloquize Jewish folk wisdom, relations with JR writers were rarely cordial.

In an eruption of rebellion and loathing, the fathers of modern Hebrew literature portrayed the orthodox eastern European Jewish world as a swamp, a heap of dead words and extinguished souls; they reviled it and at the same time immortalized it in their books, wrote Amos Oz.[198] Later on, as the shared space shrank, relations of any kind thinned, other than in exceptional cases.[199] Among the reasons to regret this process, the consequent neglect of rabbinic interpretation, as both a practice and a fund, is the greatest. The rabbis, writes Cynthia Ozick, are the muses of exegesis, where "exegesis" is understood as the exegete's ushering of his or her insights toward the formulation of principles.[200]

And what of the Abraham story? One has an immediate sense of antipathy to the Torah Abraham.[201] The man who always knew who he was, who always knew where he stood with God, the *ur*-father of all certainties! Writers alienated from traditional Judaism, with its idealization of Abraham; writers in revolt against fathers, in all their burdensome, benighted, and yet also disappointing presence; writers in recoil from the fanaticisms of their times; writers in quest for the meaning of Judaism by a reexamination of the Jewish past, in consequence of a radical break with that past[202]—what would these writers want with such a person?

To begin an answer to this question and investigate further the character of JX discourse, let me end the book with a brief review of three exemplary central European JX writers.

Kafka, Freud, Auerbach

Each one of the three was an immensely consequential writer, founding or transforming a field of humanistic endeavor (literary fiction, the science of the mind, comparative literature). Each explored Jewish themes in complex and fruitful ways. Each had a distinctive "take" on his own Jewishness. Each wrote in the mode of provocation, as interveners in their times and milieus.[203]

Franz Kafka (1883–1924) struggled with Hebrew. Though he intended to achieve fluency, he ended up achieving nothing, the language "strangely beyond his ability."[204] His knowledge of Kabbalah was "only second-hand."[205] These distances contributed to his distinct inventiveness. "I consider my true blood-relations," he wrote, "to be Grillparzer, Dostoevsky, Kleist and Flaubert."[206] His rejection of family in favor of literature, however, has an Abrahamic quality. The "penchant for depicting my dreamlike inner life has pushed everything else aside," he wrote.[207] He situated himself at an intersection of Western literature and the Jewish exegetical tradition; he was one of the keenest readers of the Hebrew Scriptures since the masters of the Midrash, writes one critic.[208] Kafka was haunted by his Jewishness; his *Jude sein*, his sense of Jewish being, was all his own, writes another critic.[209] Gershom Scholem looked on Kafka's writings "as possessing an almost canonical halo."[210]

Sigmund Freud (1856–1939) was born in Moravia, then part of the Austrian Empire, and he died in London. He disavowed all knowledge of Hebrew; he described himself as among the "poor in faith" (23:122); he is generally supposed to have had a vexed relation with Judaism.[211] Yet he once compared himself to Yohanan ben Zakkai, who rescued Judaism from the catastrophe of the destruction of the Temple, just as Freud himself would rescue psychoanalysis from the catastrophe of the nascent Shoah. He allowed himself a freedom of interpretation in relation to Moses's life that overran hitherto-thought limits. Deviations from the Scriptural text, he claimed, are allowed to artists (13:230, 232). In his writing on Jewish topics, Freud intended a major, public impact.

Erich Auerbach (1892–1957) was born in Berlin and died in Connecticut. He was dismissed from his university position in October 1935. He is known as the father of comparative literature.[212] He was ignorant of the tradition of rabbinic interpretation and knew no Hebrew.[213] Yet his masterpiece, *Mimesis* (1946), written when he was living in exile in Istanbul, restates the cultural centrality of the *Akedah* in the new register of literary history. It is in *Mimesis* that Auerbach's Jewishness spectacularly emerges; it is here that he discovers himself in his intellectual undertaking as a Jew. He wrote the book at a moment of crisis in which he confronted his Jewishness as he never had (or had to) before and as he never would again.[214] It is "defiantly and strategically Jewish in its response" to Nazi and Nazi-sympathizing efforts "to blot out the inheritance of Jewish thinking from the Western world."[215]

Still, why these three? They contribute toward a mapping of JX engagements with the Abraham story. There are other Abraham-related works by JX writers, of course. Among the strongest is A. B. Yehoshua's novel *Mr. Mani* (1990), which restates the *Akedah* in the register of protest and rejection. The persistence of the story in secular modern Hebrew and Israeli literature, indeed, has been said to "border on obsession."[216] Many further accounts of the Abraham story will doubtless be written. On the subject of Abraham, the modern Jewish canon is not closed.

Let me begin with Kafka. I will pass over *The Trial*, his novel about a man caught up in an incomprehensible process that ends in his death, even though its German title could also be translated as "The Test" and even though its Isaac-protagonist is dispatched "like a dog."[217] I will also pass over two of his short stories, "The Metamorphosis" and "In the Penal Colony," in both of which, as Saul Friedländer has pointed out, a son is driven to death by his father.[218] I want instead to survey one other short story and two letters.

The story, "The Judgment," was written the day after Yom Kippur 1912. It is in three parts. The first part establishes Georg

Bendemann's independence and maturity. The second part concerns his encounter with his father, when this independence is under attack. In the third part, the father passes judgment on Georg, who thereupon kills himself, jumping off a bridge into the motor traffic below. He is helpless before his father's lethal authority.[219] "The story came out of me," Kafka confided to his diary, "like a veritable birth covered with filth and slime." It is a story with "still unknown possibilities."[220]

"Can you discover any meaning in 'The Judgment,'—some straightforward, coherent meaning that one could follow?" he asked his fiancée, Felice Bauer. "I can't find any, nor can I explain anything in it." A week later, he wrote to her again: "'The Judgment' cannot be explained."[221] Not explained but commented on perhaps. Georg's surname, Bendemann, is derived from the German word *binden*, which means "to bind."[222] Not that it's a clue to the text's meaning. It's an allusion in the text. It prompts associations. It invites a reading of the story as a parable. But do we have the doctrine that Kafka's parables interpret? asked Walter Benjamin. No we do not, because the doctrine does not exist, he wrote, answering his own question.[223]

Several years later, Kafka wrote a long letter to his father but did not send it. The letter was written in November 1919, when Kafka was thirty-six years old, about the same age as Isaac when bound.[224] He began the letter, "You asked me recently why I maintain that I am afraid of you." The letter is the structural equivalent of the *Akedah*. When the son has been bound, God will know that the father fears Him; when the letter is read, the father will know that his son fears him. Kafka writes in the letter of the special pain of being threatened with a beating: "It is as if someone is going to be hanged. If he really is hanged, then he is dead and it is all over. But if he has to go through all the preliminaries to being hanged, and he learns of his reprieve only when the noose is dangling before his face, he may suffer from it all his life." This is Isaac's suffering. Near the end of the letter, Kafka writes despairingly of himself, "me, the thirty-six-year-old."[225]

Was there ever to be a retaliation by this powerless son?[226] In a June 1921 letter to his friend Robert Klopstock, Kafka wrote, "I can imagine another Abraham."[227] They had been corresponding about Kierkegaard. Kafka had of course *already* imagined Abrahams. In his letter, however, he proposes much smaller Abrahams, ignominious, not terrifying, cut down to a paltry size.

There is the Abraham, say, who is ready to carry out the orders for the sacrifice, as a waiter is ready to carry out *his* orders, but wouldn't be able to because he couldn't get away from home. There is another Abraham who wants to carry out the sacrifice properly, and senses what the whole thing is about, but cannot imagine that he is the one meant, this repulsive old man and his dirty boy. He is afraid that the world will laugh itself sick over the spectacle they make. And then there is the Abraham who is *not* the one summoned but who mishears the call, thinking that it is for him.

Part of the way through this riff, in which Kafka (a) multiplies and diminishes Abraham, binding him to domestic life, a Lot-like schlemiel; (b) asserts literature's privileges over Scripture,[228] substituting ridicule and bathos for fear and trembling; and (c) champions the relaxed, informal inventiveness of the merely human author against the Divine Author's own enterprises in writing, Kafka breaks off to observe, "[I] have been meditating a good deal about this Abraham, *but these are old stories, no longer worth discussing.*"[229]

And now Freud. His student-years letters to his friend Eduard Silberstein contain references to the Abraham story,[230] but then Abraham drops out. "Freud strangely ignores Father Abraham and his Covenant," wrote Phillip Rieff.[231] Not strange at all.

For one thing, Freud could never have played the part of the submissive, cooperative son of an overbearing, murderous father. Quite the contrary. He did not have such a father; he himself sought the hero's role (4:196–197). He was to be the anti-Isaac, who "has had the courage to rebel against his father and has in the end victoriously overcome him" (23:12). *Of course* he would find in Moses a certain commonality of ambition and achievement, both of them liberators, the one of the Jews from Egyptian bondage, the other of humankind from irrational fears, largely associated with the Church.[232]

More importantly, the character of Freud's "lifelong preoccupation"[233] with Moses drove away Abraham. This tendency reached its fullest expression in *Moses and Monotheism* (1938), which attributes to Moses, *not* Abraham, the introduction of monotheism and circumcision to the Jews.

In the story that Freud tells of the origins of human society, circumcision is the symbolic substitute for the castration that the Primal Father once inflicted on his sons, in the plenitude of his absolute power. To submit to that symbolic violence is to affirm submission to one's father's will, though it imposes a most painful sacrifice (23:121–122). For Freud, Abraham therefore could not be the founder of the Jews' monotheistic faith. He circumcised himself before he circumcised his son; he was both originator of the practice and its first subject. By implication, then, the Abraham figure is a retroactive fiction of continuity, and the covenant of circumcision is a "particularly clumsy invention" (23:45).[234]

Indeed, to assimilate Judaism to Freud's theory of religion, one must reject the Abraham story as its narrative of origins. No religion of which Abraham is the founder can be regarded as derived from a generalized submissiveness to fathers. That is, Judaism cannot be derived from a father-complex. Its independence from this complex is everywhere plain, even in the most minor of halakhic rulings. Concerning a detail of ritual slaughtering, Maimonides concludes, "My revered father belonged to those who declared it forbidden, while I am of those who declare it permitted."[235]

"There is an intimate connection between the father-complex and belief in the gods," wrote Freud in his 1911 Leonardo da Vinci essay. "A personal God is psychologically nothing other than an exalted father. Young people lose their religious beliefs as soon as their father's authority breaks down. The roots of the need for religion are in the parental complex; the Almighty and just God, and kindly Nature, appear to us as grand sublimations of father and mother, or rather as revivals and restorations of the young child's ideas of them" (11:122–123). If this is true generally, then Judaism is an exception. Judaism is a *rejection* of father-complexes. It stands fully outside Freud's account, with its *ur*-drama of an archaic father and master of the primeval horde killed by conspiring sons, who then restore paternal authority, seized with a sense of guilt, and so on.[236] Abraham does not defer to his father; he is helpless *as* a father to stop Sarah's cruelty to his son Ishmael; the will both to sacrifice and to desist from sacrificing Isaac is fully *not* Abraham's will but God's. So far from the *Akedah* functioning to establish the authority of the father, as has been argued,[237] it functions to hollow it out, leaving the paternal Abraham wholly bewildered.[238]

The strong wish to eliminate Abraham led Freud into considerable difficulties in the *Moses* book. Freud relates that the Jews who leave Egypt meet up with "closely related tribes" in Kadesh, "a well-watered locality." These tribes are worshipers of the "volcano god Yahweh" (23:61–63). They are *also* monotheist—or perhaps they are henotheist, worshiping one god but granting the existence of other gods, who nonetheless don't count.[239] (Freud equivocates: "we cannot suppose that it came into the head of a Yahweh worshipper of those days to deny the existence of the gods of Canaan"; 23:62.) The two combine, and they constitute the foundational generations of Jews. The question arises, From where did these other tribes get their Yahweh-worshiping attachment to one god, their monotheism (or henotheism)? Freud's answer is the general development of religion from the Primal Horde. But if that is so, why wasn't *everyone* monotheist? (Freud concedes that the world was not then monotheist.) There must have been some person who introduced monotheism to these tribes, and it could not have been the Egyptian Moses. Was it Abraham perhaps?[240]

Last, Auerbach. *Mimesis*'s opening chapter, "Odysseus's Scar," bears the tacit alternative title "Abraham's sacrifice." Auerbach contrasts in it Homeric epic and Jewish biblical narrative. The one is all surface, incapable of historical depth or truth; it is the stuff of myth and legend. The other is all depth and disturbing complication, even containing abysses, and is shaped by history and historical truth. Homer remains within the legendary with all his material, whereas the material of the Hebrew Scriptures comes closer and closer to history as the narrative proceeds. And the stories Auerbach explores, to make his argument, in all the richness of literary critical detail? From the *Odyssey*, the scene in which Odysseus's old nurse recognizes him by a scar on his thigh and, from the Hebrew Scriptures, the *Akedah*. Abraham's *Hineini* indicates his "moral position" in respect to God. The *Akedah* is a "homogeneous narrative," the work of a single author. His "relation . . . to the truth of his story [is] a far more passionate and definite one than is Homer's relation."[241]

Auerbach develops this argument in later chapters. He stages a confrontation between these two types, these two worlds of forms, which are versions of the figures Athens and Jerusalem. He gave the prize to Jerusalem, making the *Akedah* the foundational moment of Western literature and thereby asserting the "ineradicable persistence of a Jewish modality of thought . . . throughout the whole of Western literature."[242] Auerbach's reading is colored by an attachment to Jewish perspectives, tacitly correcting Christian, Enlightenment, and academic ones. I have drawn in these paragraphs on James I. Porter's account of Auerbach's "pointed and even strongly Jewish critical writing."[243] In brief, by treating him as a literary character, Auerbach overcomes the JX tendency to deprecate Abraham or push him to the margins.

Auerbach faced two antagonists. The first was mythical thinking. The mythical understanding of life is embedded in the cycle of nature. The gods have no special plan or destiny for humankind—still less any part of it. The universe must be kept on track; humans contribute to this undertaking by religious rites. In the historical understanding, the temporal has a strong role. The world was created from nothing; it was not eternal. It marked a distinct moment in time. God intervenes in history. Lives are lived across periods marked by those lives, and there are always new, unpredictable events. There are no returns to earlier conditions; there is no cycle.

Historical consciousness involves the overcoming of all magical thinking and the disenchantment of ritual. No sorcery, no superstition. The Jews inaugurated historical thinking. They have a historically mobilized consciousness. They constantly have to ask themselves, "What has God planned for us?" This is a God who surprises, a God with whom there is a relationship[244] or the possibility of a relationship.

The second antagonist was Christian typology and in particular the appropriations of the *Akedah* by that "member of the Jewish diaspora, the Apostle Paul," and the Church Fathers. "The Old Testament was played down as popular history and as the code of the Jewish people," Auerbach writes. It instead "assumed the appearance of a series of 'figures,' prophetic announcements and anticipations of Jesus."[245] Figural interpretation creates connections between two events or persons in which the event or person signifies not only itself but also another event or person, which encompasses or fulfills it. The purpose of the Old Testament is to reveal the New Testament by means of figures and prophecies; the purpose of the New Testament is to illuminate for the human mind the glory of eternal blessedness.[246]

Auerbach's argument can be unspooled. Christianity subjects the Hebrew Scriptures to a figural, typological reading; this reading is an "[in]adequate substitute for the lost comprehension of rational, earthly connections between things."[247] As Christianity establishes its ascendancy, figural reading becomes hegemonic. This Christian hegemony exacts a heavy price. Its exact quantum, and countervailing benefits, however, is not elaborated.

Momentous in its implications, founded on a strong, anti-typological reading of the *Akedah*, *Mimesis* itself now has to be protected from Christianizing appropriations.[248] Defending Jewish endeavor against depredation is work for every generation.

———

Preface

1. David N. Gottleib, *Second Slayings* (Piscataway, N.J., 2019), 4, 25 ("the defining moment, the 'chosen trauma' of Jewish identity").

2. William Blake, "The Marriage of Heaven and Hell," in *The Complete Poems*, ed. Alicia Ostriker (London, 2004), 181.

3. The scholarly literature on the topic is considerable, as one would expect. See, for example, John Van Seters, *Abraham in History and Tradition* (New Haven, Conn., 1975) and Thomas L. Thompson, *The Historicity of the Patriarchal Narratives: The Quest for the Historical Abraham* (Harrisburg, Pa., 2002). I have not read deeply into this literature. Ronald Hendel writes, "There is no clear evidence concerning the original Abraham. . . . We do not know when or if [he] ever existed in history. All we can say is that *traditions* about [him] existed, and we can date some aspects of these traditions." *Remembering Abraham* (Oxford, 2005), 47.

4. Leonard Woolley, *Ur of the Chaldees* (London, 1950), 112.

5. Martin Buber, "Abraham the Seer," in *On the Bible* (New York, 2000), 24, 36.

6. Michael Walzer, *The Struggle for a Decent Politics* (New Haven, Conn., 2023), 138.

7. Steven Nadler and T. M. Rudavsky, "Introduction," in *The Cambridge History of Jewish Philosophy*, Vol. 1, *From Antiquity through the Seventeenth Century*, ed. Steven Nadler and T. M. Rudavsky (Cambridge, 2009), 1–4. The ambition, in brief, is to write a Jewish book. See Nahum N. Glatzer, "Introduction to Rosenzweig's *Little Book of Common Sense and Sick Reason*," in *Essays in Jewish Thought* (Tuscaloosa, Ala., 1978), 250 ("[Rosenzweig] was convinced he had written a Jewish book").

8. Hilary Putnam, "Brains in a Vat," in *Reason, Truth and History* (Cambridge, 1981), 5.

9. James L. Kugel, "Early Jewish Biblical Interpretation," in *Early Judaism*, ed. John J. Collins and Daniel C. Harlow (Grand Rapids, Mich., 2010), 163.

10. In Guide, II.32, Maimonides identifies three opinions on prophecy: (1) God chooses whom He wishes from among men, turns him into a prophet, and sends him with a mission; (2) prophecy is a certain perfection in the nature of man; when a man achieves perfection in his moral and rational qualities, and therefore in his imaginative faculty, he will necessarily become a prophet; (3) as with the previous position, save that God can prevent a person from becoming a prophet, even though he is fit for prophecy. Opinion #1 is held by the multitude of pagans and some of the common people among the Jews; opinion #2 is held by the philosophers; opinion #3 is "the opinion of our Law." See Moshe Halbertal, *Maimonides* (Princeton, N.J., 2014), 326 ("Maimonides even argues that when Abraham saw the three angels at the entrance to his tent he was either in a dream state or one of wakeful vision"); Micah Goodman, *Maimonides and the Book That Changed Judaism* (Philadelphia, 2015), 29 ("the Rambam understood prophecy as natural, not miraculous; it is a human achievement, not a divine achievement"); José Faur, *Homo Mysticus* (New York, 1998), 73 ("This class of cognition is within the realm of natural, not the miraculous");

Howard Kreisel, *Maimonides' Political Thought* (New York, 1999), 31 ("Maimonides' naturalistic approach to revelation"); Dani Rabinowitz, "The Prophetic Method in the Guide," in *Maimonides' Guide of the Perplexed: A Critical Guide*, ed. Daniel Frank and Aaron Segal (Cambridge, 2021), 168 (a "graphic aid" to Maimonides's account of the prophetic method).

11. Isadore Twersky, *Introduction to the Code of Maimonides (Mishneh Torah)* (New Haven, Conn., 1980), 225.

12. Avivah Gottlieb Zornberg, *Moses* (New Haven, Conn. 2016), 1.

13. Each generation pours its yearnings into Elijah, writes Daniel C. Matt. He has an endless career; there is an aspect of Elijah in each of us. See *Elijah* (New Haven, Conn., 2022), 6–7.

14. Dan Jacobson, *The Story of Stories* (London, 1982), vii.

Chapter 1. Abraham 1's Life

1. See Michael Carasik, ed., *The Commentator's Bible: Genesis* (Philadelphia, 2018), 95.

2. See Susan A. Handelman, *Fragments of Redemption* (Bloomington, Ind., 1991), 267.

3. Leonard Woolley, *Ur of the Chaldees* (London, 1950), 78.

4. See Samuel Noah Kramer, "Poets and Psalmists: Goddesses and Theologians," in *Bibliotheca Mesopotamia: The Legacy of Sumer*, ed. Denise Schmandt-Besserat (Malibu, Calif., 1976), 6.

5. Leonard Woolley, *Abraham* (London, 1936), 16, 103–104; C. C. Lamberg-Karlovsky, "The Economic World of Sumer," in Schmandt-Besserat, *Bibliotheca Mesopotamia*, 59.

6. Denise Schmandt-Besserat, "Sumer—Art in an Urban Context," in Schmandt-Besserat, *Bibliotheca Mesopotamia*, 81.

7. Samuel Noah Kramer, *From the Poetry of Sumer* (Berkeley, Calif., 1979), 1.

8. Benjamin R. Foster, "A Religious World," in *Mesopotamia: Civilization Begins*, ed. Ariane Thomas and Timothy Potts (Los Angeles, 2020), 39.

9. Quoted in Joshua Cohen, *Attention* (London, 2013), 14.

10. Woolley, *Abraham*, 108–109.

11. Laerke Recht, *Human Sacrifice* (Cambridge, 2019), 9–10.

12. Franz Kafka, *The Zürau Aphorisms* (London, 2006), 68.

13. Jonathan Kirsch, *God against the Gods* (New York, 2004), 49.

14. Kramer, *From the Poetry of Sumer*, 20.

15. See Kramer, "Poets and Psalmists," 4–5.

16. Robert J. Braidwood, "The Background for Sumerian Civilization in the Euphrates-Tigris-Karun Drainage Basin," in Schmandt-Besserat, *Bibliotheca Mesopotamia*, 41.

17. Schmandt-Besserat, "Sumer," 79.

18. See Leonard Woolley, *Ur of the Chaldees* (London, 1950), 7.

19. W. W. Hallo, "Women of Sumer," in Schmandt-Besserat, *Bibliotheca Mesopotamia*, 32.

20. Kramer, *From the Poetry of Sumer*, 27.

21. Tikva Frymer-Kensky, *In the Wake of the Goddesses* (New York, 1992), 39, 41.

22. Kramer, *From the Poetry of Sumer*, 27–29; Kramer, "Poets and Psalmists," 1, 12–17. Kramer was born in Kiev in 1897 and died in Philadelphia in 1990. He taught in his father's Hebrew school before embarking on an academic career, one so distinguished that at the end of his life, he was recognized as among the greatest Assyriologists of his generation. And see too Tikva Frymer-Kensky, *In the Wake of the Goddesses* (New York, 1992), 5 ("marginalized"), 6 ("usurped"), 70 ("diminution," "supplanted"), 80 ("decline").

23. See Samuel N. Kramer, *Lamentation over the Destruction of Ur* (Chicago, 1940), 1–97.

24. See James L. Kugel, *The Bible as It Was* (Cambridge, Mass., 1997), 140–141.

25. Bertrand Russell, *The Problems of Philosophy* (Oxford, 1998), 65.

26. Alasdair MacIntyre, *Is Patriotism a Virtue?* (Lawrence, Kan., 1984), 1.

27. See Michèle Le Doeuff, *The Sex of Knowing* (London, 2003), 26, 32–33.

28. I borrow from Micah Joseph Berdichevsky, "On Sanctity" (1900–1903), in *The Zionist Idea*, ed. Arthur Hertzberg (Philadelphia, 1997), 299–300.

29. Kramer, *From the Poetry of Sumer,* 55.

30. See Alice Jardine, *At the Risk of Thinking* (London, 2020), 85.

31. See Cornelius Castoriadis, "The Psychical and Social Roots of Hatred," in *Figures of the Thinkable* (Stanford, Calif., 2007), 29.

32. See W. R. Bion, *Experiences in Groups and Other Papers* (London, 1961), 85.

33. See Isadore Twersky, *Introduction to the Code of Maimonides (Mishneh Torah)* (New Haven, Conn., 1980), 274.

34. Hélène Cixous, *Portrait of Jacques Derrida as a Young Jewish Saint* (New York, 2004), 74.

35. See Claire Tomalin, *Mary Wollstonecraft* (London, 1992), 32.

36. See Karen Horney, "The Flight from Womanhood," in *Feminine Psychology* (New York, 1993), 69.

37. Tomalin, *Mary Wollstonecraft,* 196.

38. See Søren Kierkegaard, *Fear and Trembling* (New York, 2022), 10.

39. See Thomas Nagel, *The View from Nowhere* (Oxford, 1986), 215; Tomalin *Mary Wollstonecraft,* 20–21, 49–50.

40. *Suffragette Manifestos* (London, 2020), 49, 73, 114; Tomalin *Mary Wollstonecraft,* 139.

41. Genevieve Lloyd, *The Man of Reason* (London, 1995), 107.

42. See Susanne Lettow, "Feminism and the Enlightenment," in *The Routledge Companion to Feminist Philosophy,* ed. Ann Garry, Serene J. Khader, and Alison Stone (New York, 2017), 94–105.

43. Mary Wollstonecraft, *A Vindication of the Rights of Women* (London, 2004), 3, 31.

44. Le Doeuff, *Sex of Knowing,* xvi.

45. Dominque Eddé, *Edward Said* (London, 2019), 3 (quoting the Muslim philosopher Ibn Khaldun); Edward Said, *Beginnings: Intention and Method* (London, 2012), 3, 6, 143, 316, 347, 350, 357.

46. René Char, *Hypnos* (London, 2014), 34.

47. See Jean-Paul Sartre, *Existentialism and Humanism* (London, 2007), 62.

48. Emmanuel Levinas, *Ethics and Infinity* (Pittsburgh, 1985), 21.

49. See Alasdair MacIntyre, *After Virtue* (London, 2011), 86.

50. See Matt Bower, "The Birth of the World: An Exploration in Husserl's Genetic Phenomenology" (PhD diss., University of Memphis, 2013), *Electronic Theses and Dissertations* 728:89, https://digitalcommons.memphis.edu/etd/728.

51. Edmund Husserl, "Philosophy and the Crisis of European Man," in *Phenomenology and the Crisis of Philosophy* (New York, 1965), 166.

52. Plato, *Republic,* 505d, in *Complete Works,* ed. John M. Cooper (Indianapolis, 1997), 1126.

53. Al-Ghazali, *Al-Ghazali's Path to Sufism,* trans. R. J. McCarthy, S.J. (Louisville, Ky., 2000), 18–20, 25, 31, 82, 85.

54. Benjamin Fondane, *Existential Monday* (New York, 2016), 29.

55. James Joyce, *A Portrait of the Artist as a Young Man* (Oxford, 2000), 70.

56. René Descartes, "Rules for the Direction of the Mind," *The Philosophical Writings of Descartes,* Vol. 1 (Cambridge, 1985), 16.

57. Ludwig Wittgenstein, *Philosophical Investigations* (Oxford, 1968), 49 (I.123). "Philosophy as I have understood it and lived it so far is a life lived freely and in ice and high mountains—visiting all the strange and questionable aspects of existence, everything banned by morality so far. My long experience from these wanderings in the forbidden has taught me to see the reasons why people have been moralizing and idealizing very differently than they might desire: the hidden history of philosophers, the psychology of its greatest names, came to light for me." Friedrich Nietzsche, "Ecce Homo," in *The Anti-Christ and Other Writings,* ed. Aaron Ridley and Judith Norman (Cambridge, 2005), 72.

58. Hannah Arendt, *Rahel Varnhagen* (New York, 2022), 17.

59. G. W. F. Hegel, *The Difference between Fichte's and Schelling's System of Philosophy* (New York, 1977), 130.

60. Edmund Husserl, "Philosophy and the Crisis of European Man," in *Phenomenology and the Crisis of Philosophy* (New York, 1965), 182.

61. See Michel Malherbe, "Reason," in *The Cambridge History*

of *Eighteenth Century Philosophy*, Vol. 1, ed. Knud Haakonssen (Cambridge, 2006), 320.

62. Immanuel Kant, *Critique of Pure Reason*, ed. and trans. Paul Guyer and Allen W. Wood (Cambridge, 1998), 579, 580.

63. Freud, 23:111–115.

64. Kant, *Critique of Pure Reason*, 578–579; Solomon Maimon, *The Autobiography of Solomon Maimon*, ed. Yitzhak Y. Melamed and Abraham Socher (Princeton, N.J., 2018), 14.

65. Kant, *Critique of Pure Reason*, 99, 584. See Voltaire, *Philosophical Dictionary* (London, 2004), 499.

66. Elliot Sober, *The Design Argument* (Cambridge, 2019), 36–38.

67. Chaïm Perelman, *An Historical Introduction to Philosophical Thinking* (New York, 1965), 194.

68. Roland Barthes, "The Last Happy Writer," in *A Roland Barthes Reader*, ed. Susan Sontag (London, 1993), 153.

69. Ludwig Wittgenstein, *Tractatus-Logico-Philosophicus* (New York, 1963), 149 (6.432).

70. See Micah Goodman, *Maimonides and the Book That Changed Judaism* (Philadelphia, 2015), 8.

71. Kant, *Critique of Pure Reason*, 582.

72. Immanuel Kant, *Anthropology from a Pragmatic Point of View* (Carbondale, Ill., 1996), 206–207.

73. Kant, *Anthropology from a Pragmatic Point of View*, 207.

74. Husserl, "Philosophy and the Crisis of European Man," 177, 178.

75. Kant, *Critique of Pure Reason*, 499.

76. See Voltaire, *Philosophical Dictionary*, 206.

77. See Cora Diamond, *Reading Wittgenstein with Anscombe, Going On to Ethics* (Cambridge, Mass., 2019), 228, 237, 269, 272, 293, 304.

78. Wittgenstein, *Tractatus-Logico-Philosophicus*, 49 (4.112).

79. William Wordsworth, *The Prelude: The Four Texts*, ed. Jonathan Wordsworth (London, 1995), 378, 402, 414, 430 (Bk. IX, l. 586; Bk. X, ll. 76–77, 285, 539).

80. Midrash Ha-Gadol, Genesis 12:1, quoted in Avivah Gott-

leib Zornberg, *Genesis: The Beginning of Desire* (Philadelphia, 2010), 83–84.

81. Plato, *Laws*, in *Complete Works*, ed. John M. Cooper (Indianapolis, 1997), 1547 (890a).

82. I have borrowed from Pierre Hadot's accounts of ancient philosophy as a way of life. See *The Selected Writings of Pierre Hadot* (London, 2020), 49, 75.

83. Nietzsche, "Ecce Homo," 115.

84. Samson R. Hirsch, *The Hirsch Chumash* (Jerusalem, 2002), 458.

85. Julian E. Zelizer, *Abraham Joshua Heschel* (New Haven, Conn., 2021), 212.

86. Russell, *Problems of Philosophy*, 87.

87. G. W. F. Hegel, *Aesthetics*, Vol. 1 (Oxford, 1975), 152.

88. Iris Murdoch, *Living on Paper: Letters from Iris Murdoch 1934–1995*, ed. Avril Horner and Anne Rowe (London, 2015), 439.

89. John Locke, "Epistle to the Reader," in *Essay Concerning Human Understanding* (London, 1997), 7.

90. Colin McGinn, *The Making of a Philosopher* (London, 2003), 35, 54.

91. Plato, *Letter VII*, in *Complete Works*, 1661 (344c).

92. Husserl, "Philosophy and the Crisis of European Man," 178.

93. See Friedrich Nietzsche, *Ecce Homo* (London, 1992), 16–17.

94. Simone de Beauvoir, "Pyrrhus and Cineas," in *What Is Existentialism?* (London, 2020), 31.

95. Wordsworth, *Prelude*, 400 (Bk. X, l. 38).

96. Isadore Twersky's characterization of Maimonides, which is no less applicable to Abraham, his philosophical hero. See *Introduction to the Code of Maimonides (Mishneh Torah)* (New Haven, Conn., 1980), 3, 406 ("the reciprocity of the *vita contemplativa* and *vita activa*").

Chapter 2. Abraham 1's Crisis

1. Beverley Clack, "Feminist Engagement with Judeo-Christian Traditions," in *The Routledge Companion to Feminist Philosophy*,

35. Braude and Kapstein, *Tanna Debe Eliyyahu*, 63, 484.

36. See Philo, "On Abraham," in *The Works of Philo* (Peabody, Mass., 1993), 417.

37. Cf. William Wordsworth, *The Prelude: The Four Texts*, ed. Jonathan Wordsworth (London, 1995), 414–415 (Bk. X, ll. 284, 286).

38. "The Royal Tombs at Ur present some of the earliest secure evidence of human sacrifice." Laerke Recht, *Human Sacrifice* (Cambridge, 2019), 8.

39. Samuel Noah Kramer, *From the Poetry of Sumer* (Berkeley, Calif., 1979), 57–59, 65–70.

40. Samuel R. Hirsch, *The Pentateuch* (New York, 1997), 52.

41. Alenka Zupančič, *Why Psychoanalysis?* (Helsinki, 2014), 55.

42. John Milton, *Paradise Lost*, ed. Alastair Fowler (London, 2013), 124 (II.307–308).

43. Moses Mendelssohn, *Jerusalem* (Hanover, N.H., 1983), 43, 63, 81, 85.

44. See Friedrich Nietzsche, *Ecce Homo* (London, 1992), 21.

45. Novalis, "Christianity or Europe: A Fragment," and Friedrich von Schlegel, "Ideas," in *The Early Political Writings of the German Romantics*, ed. Frederick C. Beiser (Cambridge, 1996), 62–63, 69–75, 127.

46. Cf. William Shakespeare, *Hamlet*, ed. Ann Thompson and Neil Taylor (London, 2016), 208 (1.2.150).

47. Aristotle, *Nicomachean Ethics* (1143b).

48. See George Bataille, *Essential Writings*, ed. Michael Richardson (London, 1998), 112.

49. See John Wisdom, "Philosophy and Psychoanalysis," in *Philosophy and Psychoanalysis* (Berkeley, Calif., 1995), 170.

50. Freud, "Delusions and Dreams in Jensen's *Gradiva*," 9:7 (on dream interpretation).

51. See Immanuel Kant, *Groundwork for the Metaphysics of Morals* (Oxford, 2019), 20.

52. Thomas Nagel, *The View from Nowhere* (Oxford, 1986), 4, 5, 6, 7, 9, 10.

53. Breyten Breytenbach, "The Writer and Responsibility," in *End Papers* (London, 1986), 100.

54. Mary Lefkowitz, *Greek Gods, Human Lives* (New Haven, Conn., 2003), 239.

55. Plato, *Laws*, in *Complete Works*, ed. John M. Cooper (Indianapolis, 1997), 1404 (718a).

56. Joseph de Maistre, *Considerations on France* (Cambridge, 2006), xvii, xviii, 31.

57. Thomas Paine, *Age of Reason* (1794), in *Selected Writings of Thomas Paine*, ed. Ian Shapiro and Jane E. Calvert (New Haven, Conn., 2014), 373.

58. Freud, 22:171.

59. Voltaire, *Treatise on Toleration* (London, 2016), 114.

60. Milton, *Paradise Lost*, 61 (I.39).

61. Friedrich Nietzsche, *The Gay Science* (Cambridge, 2001), 127–128 (Bk. 3, para 143).

62. Berlin, *Magus of the North*, 32, 50.

63. Isaiah Berlin, "From Hope and Fear Set Free," in *Concepts and Categories* (Oxford, 1980), 194–195.

64. J. G. Hamann, "Aesthetica in nuce," in *Writings on Philosophy and Language* (Cambridge, 2007), 63.

65. Friedrich Nietzsche, *Human, All Too Human* (Cambridge, 1986), 343.

66. "The substitution of poetry for religion as a source of ideals, a movement that began with the Romantic, [is] a return to polytheism." Richard Rorty, "Pragmatism as Romantic Polytheism," in *The Rorty Reader*, ed. Christopher J. Voparil and Richard J. Bernstein (Chichester, U.K., 2010), 445.

67. William Hazlitt, "Coriolanus," in *The Fight and Other Writings* (London, 2000), 51–52.

68. Friedrich Nietzsche, *On the Genealogy of Morals* (Oxford, 1996), 75 (2.24).

69. Cf. "The Jews emerge as the eternal critics, the detached, uncommitted judges of the Christian world." Berlin, *Magus of the North*, 52.

70. Hilary Putnam, "Mind and Body," in *Reason, Truth and History* (Cambridge, 1981), 5.

71. See Berlin, *Magus of the North*, 84, 97, 68; G. W. F. Hegel,

Lectures on the Philosophy of World History: Introduction (Cambridge, 1980), 81.

72. See Arthur Schopenhauer, "Religion: A Dialogue," in *Essays* (London, 1951), 19–22.

73. Ludwig Wittgenstein, *Tractatus-Logico-Philosophicus* (New York, 1963), 79 (5.136).

74. José Ortega y Gasset, *What Is Philosophy?* (New York, 1964), 92.

75. Lev Shestov, *All Things Are Possible* (London, 1920), 174.

76. Mill, "Subjection of Women," 169.

77. Plato, *Laws*, 1403–1404 (717c–e).

78. See Samuel Noah Kramer, "Poets and Psalmists: Goddesses and Theologians," in *Bibliotheca Mesopotamia: The Legacy of Sumer*, ed. Denise Schmandt-Besserat (Malibu, Calif., 1976), 4.

79. Freud, *The Interpretation of Dreams*, 4:217, fn. 1.

80. Plato, *Euthyphro*, in *Complete Works*, 4 (4e).

81. See Plato, *Laws*, 1544–1545 (887d).

82. See James A. Diamond, *Maimonides and the Hermeneutics of Concealment* (New York, 2002), 63.

83. "The liberation of an individual, as he grows up, from the authority of his parents is one of the most necessary, though one of the most painful results brought about by the course of his development. It is quite essential that that liberation should occur and it may be presumed that it has been to some extent achieved by everyone who has reached a normal state. . . . On the other hand, there is a class of neurotics whose condition is recognizably determined by their having failed in this task." Freud, "Family Romances," 9:237.

84. Mendelssohn, *Jerusalem*, 49.

85. See Helena Rosenblatt, *Liberal Virtues* (Cambridge, 2008), 132.

86. See Bruce Baugh, "Introduction," in *Existential Monday*, by Benjamin Fondane (New York, 2016), xxix.

87. The commentator Nachmanides (1194–1270) makes a distinction between "open" and "hidden" miracles. All miracles that a person can deny, contending that they are instead a part of the

natural order, are "hidden" miracles. All those miracles that cannot be denied, and are clearly the consequence of God's intervention, are "open." If Abraham's release was a miracle, it was a hidden one. See *Commentary on the Torah: Genesis* (New York, 1971), 158–159, 215.

88. "The God of Israel does not take man by surprise. Rather, He responds to man's fervid plea." Joseph B. Soloveitchik, *Fate and Destiny* (Hoboken, N.J., 2000), 57.

Chapter 3. Abraham 2's Life

1. See Walter Brueggemann, *The Prophetic Imagination* (Minneapolis, 2018), 21.

2. William G. Braude and Israel J. Kapstein, trans., *Tanna Debe Eliyyahu* (Philadelphia, 1981), 486.

3. Howard Jacobson, "Pseudo-Philo, Book of Biblical Antiquities," in *Outside the Bible*, ed. Louis H. Feldman, James L. Kugel, and Lawrence H. Schiffman (Philadelphia, 2013), 486.

4. I have revised Braude and Kapstein, *Tanna Debe Eliyyahu*, 486.

5. Ari Ackerman, "Miracles," in *The Cambridge History of Jewish Philosophy*, Vol. 1, *From Antiquity through the Seventeenth Century*, ed. Steven Nadler and T. M. Rudavsky (Cambridge, 2009), 364.

6. H. Freedman, trans., *Midrash Rabbah: Genesis* (London, 1983), 313 (XXXIX.3).

7. See Anthony Flew, "Divine Omnipotence and Human Freedom," and Anthony Flew and D. M. MacKinnon, "Creation," both in Anthony Flew and Alasdair MacIntyre, eds., *New Essays in Philosophical Theology* (London, 1972), 164, 171, 172.

8. See Ludwig Wittgenstein, *Movements of Thought: Ludwig Wittgenstein's Diary 1930–1932 and 1936–1937*, ed. James C. Klagge and Alfred Nordmann (London, 2023), 93.

9. Harry Austryn Wolfson, *From Philo to Spinoza* (New York, 1977), 28–30, 45.

10. Michah Gottlieb, "Mysticism and Philosophy," in Nadler and Rudavsky, *Cambridge History of Jewish Philosophy*, 125.

11. See Judah Halevi, *The Kuzari* (New York, 1964), 36, 200.

12. See Alasdair MacIntyre, "Visions," in Flew and MacIntyre, *New Essays in Philosophical Theology*, 260.

13. See Nahum Sokolow, *Zionism in the Bible* (London, 1918). He reads "go to the land I will show you" (12:1) as "give you" (1–2). Sokolow dismisses a "denationaliz[ed] Judaism" as "thoroughly pagan." Indeed, "no matter whether Jews call themselves religious or nationalist; the Jewish religion cannot be separated from nationalism unless another Bible is invented" (7, 8).

14. "The Bible . . . does not consider beauty a power or strategy of women. The beauty of Sarah and Bathsheba make them objects of attention, victims of the superior male. Sarah and Bathsheba do not consciously use their beauty to attract: their beauty is their vulnerability rather than their power." Tikva Frymer-Kensky, *In the Wake of the Goddesses* (New York, 1992), 206.

15. Josephus, *Jewish Antiquities*, trans. H. St. J. Thackeray (Cambridge, Mass., 1998), 83.

16. "He is a man of peace, he represents the arts of peace, the diplomacy required to perpetuate a relationship, the avoidance of trouble before it begins, the reluctance to turn friction into violence. In the next three generations the same will be true of Isaac, Jacob and Joseph. Bursting with seed, they will be fathers and family men. Not one of them will be a warrior." Alicia Suskin Ostriker, *The Nakedness of the Fathers* (New Brunswick, N.J., 1994), 56.

17. Samson R. Hirsch, *The Hirsch Chumash* (Jerusalem, 2002), 372.

18. Franceska Stavrakopoulou identifies "connection[s] between the circumcision rite and the sacrifice of the firstborn," amounting to a "close affiliation." *King Manasseh and Child Sacrifice* (Berlin, 2004), 200, 282.

19. Rabbi Eliezer, *Pirke de Rabbi Eliezer*, trans. and ed. Gerald Friedlander (London, 1916), 72, 204. It relates that the circumcision took place on Mt. Moriah, which was the place where the Temple was built. The Midrash thereby establishes the chain: (1) circumcision to (2) *Akedah* to (3) Temple sacrifices. See also Shaye J. D. Cohen *Why Aren't Jewish Women Circumcised?* (Berkeley, Calif., 2005), 31–32.

20. See Cohen, *Why Aren't Jewish Women Circumcised?*, xii, xiii, xiv, 12 ("the word *brit* appears thirteen times in Genesis 17, but not once is the word or concept associated with Sarah"), 136.

21. Piero Boitani, *The Bible and Its Rewritings* (Oxford, 1999), 2.

22. Emmanuel Levinas, "Kierkegaard: Existence and Ethics," in *Proper Names* (London, 1996), 74.

23. Cf. "Abraham loses his battle." Harris Bor, *Staying Human* (Eugene, Ore., 2021), 143. "[Abraham's response to God's announcement regarding Sodom shows] that people can argue with God and win." Jon D. Levenson, *Creation and the Persistence of Evil* (Princeton, N.J., 1988), 149. I am with Levenson on this point.

24. Anson Laytner, *Arguing with God: A Jewish Tradition* (Lanham, Md., 2004). Hillel Halkin, "Introduction," in *Tevye the Dairyman and the Railroad Stories*, by Sholem Aleichem (New York, 1987), xxiv–xxv.

25. A Midrash has Abraham remonstrating with God in the ruins of the temple. See Alexander Altmann, "Epilogue," in *The Meaning of Jewish Existence* (Hanover, N.H., 1991), 134.

26. Laytner, *Arguing with God*, xv.

27. See Ilona N. Rashkow, "Daddy-Dearest and the 'Invisible Spirit of Wine,'" in *Genesis*, ed. Athalya Brenner (Sheffield, U.K., 1998), 99.

28. Matthew J. Lynch, *Portraying Violence in the Hebrew Bible* (Cambridge, 2020), 156.

29. See Lyn M. Bechtel, "A Feminist Reading of Genesis 19.1–11," in Brenner, *Genesis*, 124.

30. Y. Aharoni, "The Land of Gerar," *Israel Exploration Journal*, 1956, Vol. 6, No. 1, 26–32.

31. See John Rawls, *The Law of Peoples* (Cambridge, Mass., 1999), 59–62 (§ 7).

32. Malbim, *Commentary on the Torah: The Patriarchs* (Jerusalem, 1982), 13.

33. Joseph B. Soloveitchik, *Abraham's Journey* (New York, 2008), 199 (after Rashi).

34. Samuel A. Berman, *Midrash Tanhumma-Yelammedenu* (Hoboken, N.J., 1996), 538.

35. Melanie Klein, "Weaning," in *Love, Guilt and Reparation and Other Works 1921–1945* (London, 1998), 300.

36. Robert Alter, *The Hebrew Bible: The Five Books of Moses* (New York, 2019), 69, fn. 9.

37. See Steven Connor, *Styles of Seriousness* (Stanford, Calif., 2023), 5.

38. Jeremy Dauber, *Jewish Comedy* (New York, 2017), 174.

39. Ruth Wisse, *No Joke* (Princeton, N.J., 2013), 22.

40. "Oh that men / (Canst thou believe?) should be so stupid," is the general sentiment. John Milton, *Paradise Lost*, ed. Alastair Fowler (London, 2013), 652 (XII.115–120). All mockery is forbidden, rules the Talmud, except for mockery of idol worshiping (Sanhedrin 63b).

41. See Theodor Herzl, "The Jewish State," in *Zionist Writings*, Vol. 1 (New Milford, Conn., 2023), 463.

42. See Mark Harman, "Torturing the Gordian Knot," in *Kafka for the Twenty-First Century*, ed. Stanley Corngold and Ruth V. Gross (Rochester, N.Y., 2011), 54.

43. Devorah Baum, *The Jewish Joke* (London, 2017), 40.

44. Hillel Halkin, "Introduction," in *Tevye the Dairyman and the Railroad Stories*, by Sholem Aleichem (New York, 1987), xvi.

45. Albert S. Lindemann, *Esau's Tears* (Cambridge, 1997). I do not admire this book. See Alan E. Steinweis's review, published on H-Antisemitism (October 1997), https://www.h-net.org/reviews/showpdf.php?id=1399.

46. There is a related story later on in tractate Sanhedrin 107b. Jesus studied with Yehoshua ben Perachya. He did something that caused his teacher to reproach him. On several occasions, Jesus came to offer repentance, but ben Perachya took no notice of him. Then Jesus came when the teacher was praying. On this occasion, ben Perachya intended to hear him, but only after he had finished praying. He signaled Jesus with his hand to wait. Jesus did not understand the signal and thought, "He is driving me away." He repudiated Judaism, inciting Jews to engage in idolatry and leading Israel astray. "Had Yehoshua ben Perachya not caused him to despair of atonement, he would not have taken the path of evil," the tractate concludes.

47. Jon D. Levenson, *The Death and Resurrection of the Beloved Son* (New Haven, Conn., 1993), 85.

48. See my *Trials of the Diaspora: A History of Anti-Semitism in England* (Oxford, 2012), ch. 1.

49. Thomas Mann, "Freud and the Future," in *Essays of Three Decades* (London, 1947), 420.

50. Jean-Gérard Bursztein, *A Psychoanalytic Commentary on the Hebrew Bible* (Paris, 2015), 11–13.

51. On "converting," see Stanley Cavell, *Conditions Handsome and Unhandsome* (Chicago, 1990), 47.

52. Moses Maimonides, *A Maimonides Reader*, ed. Isadore Twersky (West Orange, N.J., 1972), 477 ("Letter to an Inquirer").

53. Maimonides, *Maimonides Reader*, 474–476 ("Letter to Obadiah the Proselyte"); Menachem Kellner, *Maimonides on Judaism and the Jewish People* (New York, 1991), 5, 51, 55–56, 60, 94.

54. Aharon Agus, *The Binding of Isaac and Messiah* (New York, 1988), 3; James Goodman, *But Where Is the Lamb?* (New York, 2013), 13.

Chapter 4. Abraham 2's Crisis

1. Franz Kafka, describing himself. See *Letters to Felice* (London, 1999), 204.

2. E. A. Speiser, *Genesis* (New York, 1964), 161.

3. See Ephraim ben Jacob of Bonn, "The *Akedah*," in *The Last Trial*, by Shalom Spiegel (Woodstock, Vt., 1993), 147 ("When the one whose life was bound up in the lad's").

4. "I began my labors in the philosophy of love at a time when hardly any reputable philosophers in the Anglo-Saxon world considered that subject professional or even respectable." "I was cautioned to avoid it because—I was told—I would ruin my career. . . . I would be ostracized by the American Philosophical Association." Irving Singer, *Philosophy of Love* (Cambridge, Mass., 2011), xvi, 109.

5. See Georges Bataille, *George Bataille: Essential Writings*, ed. Michael Richardson (London, 1998), 61–79.

6. John Milton, *Paradise Lost*, ed. Alastair Fowler (London, 2013), 84–85, 89 (I.390–395, 456–457).

7. See Michel de Montaigne, "Of the Affection of Fathers for Their Children," in *Essays* (London, 2003), 353.

8. Albert van der Heide, *"Now I Know": Five Centuries of Aqedah Exegesis* (Leiden, 2017), 16; Samuel A. Berman, *Midrash Tanhumma-Yelammedenu* (Hoboken, N.J., 1996), 143; Wendy Zierler, "In Search of a Feminist Reading of the *Akedah*," *Nashim: A Journal of Jewish Women's Studies & Gender Issues*, Spring 5765/2005, No. 9, "Jewish Women's Spirituality," 13.

9. See William Shakespeare, *Antony and Cleopatra* (London, 2005), 13 (1.2.138–141 (Antony/Enobarbus).

10. Alicia Suskin Ostriker, *Feminist Revision and the Bible* (Cambridge, Mass., 1993), 39.

11. D. H. Lawrence, "England, My England," in *Selected Stories* (London, 2007), 168. Lawrence wrongly reads this claim of father-right as implicit in Abraham's readiness to sacrifice Isaac: "fatherhood that had even the right to sacrifice the child to God, like Isaac."

12. Berman, *Midrash Tanhumma-Yelammedenu*, 146–147.

13. Berman, *Midrash Tanhumma-Yelammedenu*, 146.

14. Berman, *Midrash Tanhumma-Yelammedenu*, 147.

15. "Art not thou our God, who didst drive out the inhabitants of this land before thy people Israel, and gavest it to the seed of Abraham thy friend for ever?" (2 Chronicles 20:7).

16. Cf. "the great friendship between God and Abraham." Joseph B. Soloveitchik, *Abraham's Journey* (New York, 2008), 146.

17. Cf. Isaiah 55:8–9.

18. "The word *hasachta* is . . . used to refer to circumstances in which someone (or something) has been spared or saved by being withheld from danger. Here, however, the verb is employed in the negative, meaning that Isaac is *not* spared or saved as a result of Abraham's holding him back from danger. . . . By the time God intervenes, it is already too late. Isaac will live, but he has not been spared or saved." Yoram Hazony, *The Philosophy of Hebrew Scripture* (Cambridge, 2012), 120.

19. Lionel Trilling, *The Liberal Imagination* (New York, 2008), 105.

20. Van der Heide, *"Now I Know,"* 15.
21. Milton, *Paradise Lost*, 120 (II.226–227).
22. Adin Steinsaltz, *Biblical Images* (Jerusalem, 1994), 23–24.
23. Steinsaltz, *Biblical Images*, 26.
24. See Karen Horney, *Self-Analysis* (London, 1999), 55.
25. Freud, "'Civilized' Sexual Morality and Modern Nervous Illness" (9:195).
26. Karen Horney, "The Problem of the Monogamous Ideal," in *Feminine Psychology* (New York, 1993), 98.
27. Cf. Freud's letter to his then fiancée, Martha Bernays: "everything that fell before the decisive break in my life, before our coming together and my choice of calling, I have put behind me." Quoted in Ernest Jones, *The Life and Work of Sigmund Freud* (New York, 1953), xii–xiii (28 April 1885).
28. Berman, *Midrash Tanhumma-Yelammedenu*, 136–137.
29. See Bataille, *George Bataille: Essential Writings*, 115.
30. Yvonne Sherwood, "Textual Carcasses and Isaac's Scar," in *Sanctified Aggression*, ed. Jonneke Bekkenkamp and Yvonne Sherwood (London, 2004), 42.
31. See Stephen Greenblatt, *Tyrant* (London, 2018), 119 (said of King Lear).
32. Karen Armstrong, *In the Beginning* (New York, 1996), 67.
33. Jonathan Lear, *A Case for Irony* (Cambridge, Mass., 2011), 12–13.
34. Compare Milton, *Paradise Lost*, 673 (XII.558–564).
35. Lear, *Case for Irony*, 18, 19, 27, 31.
36. See Menachem Kellner, *Must a Jew Believe Anything?* (Oxford, 2006), 21.
37. Joseph B. Soloveitchik, *The Emergence of Ethical Man* (Jersey City, N.J., 2005), 156, n. 2.
38. Howard Wettstein strikes a speculative, tentatively hopeful note that I reject. "To withstand any such an experience must be transformative. And *sometimes* as the text perhaps suggests, one comes out the other end having survived that ordeal, loves intact, having grown in ways otherwise unavailable." "God's Struggles,"

in *Divine Evil?*, ed. Michael Bergmann, Michael J. Murray, and Michael C. Rea (Oxford, 2011), 329.

39. Cf. "Be not a terror unto me: thou art my hope in the day of evil" (Jer. 17:17).

40. Cora Diamond, *Reading Wittgenstein with Anscombe, Going On to Ethics* (Cambridge, Mass., 2019), 261.

41. Hilary Putnam, *Jewish Philosophy as a Guide to Life* (Bloomington, Ind., 2008), 27.

42. Ludwig Wittgenstein, *Culture and Value* (Chicago, 1984), 64.

43. Louis Ginzberg, *The Legends of the Jews*, Vol. 1 (Baltimore, 1998), 291.

44. Judith N. Shklar, *Legalism* (Cambridge, Mass., 1986), 30.

45. Jonathan Lear, *Imagining the End* (Cambridge, Mass., 2022), 12–13.

46. Joseph B. Soloveitchik, "Confrontation," in *"Confrontation" and Other Essays* (Jerusalem, 2015), 112.

47. See Immanuel Kant, "On the Miscarriage of All Philosophical Trials in Theodicy," in *Religion and Rational Theology*, ed. Allen W. Wood and George di Giovanni (Cambridge, 1996), 24.

48. "With the other prophets, God broke off His discourse, but with Moses, He never broke off his discourse." S. M. Lehrman, trans., *Midrash Rabbah: Exodus* (London, 1983), 56 (II.6).

49. "Rabbi Bena'a was marking burial caves for the purpose of helping to prevent the contracting of ritual impurity. When he arrived at the cave of Abraham, i.e., the Cave of Machpelah, he encountered Eliezer, the servant of Abraham, who was standing before the entrance. Rabbi Bena'a said to him: What is Abraham doing at this moment? Eliezer said to him: He is lying in the arms of Sarah, and she is examining his head" (Baba Batra 58a).

50. Søren Kierkegaard, *Fear and Trembling* (New York, 2022), 13.

51. "After Abraham's death, God blessed Isaac" (Genesis 25:11). According to Bereishit Rabba 61:5, Abraham withholds the blessing. "If I bless Isaac now, the sons of Ishmael and Keturah will be

included. And if I don't bless them, how can I bless Isaac?" See Avivah Gottlieb Zornberg, *Genesis: The Beginning of Desire* (Philadelphia, 2010), 137.

52. See G. W. F. Hegel, *Lectures on the Philosophy of World History: Introduction* (Cambridge, 1980), 82–89.

53. See William Wordsworth, "Resolution and Independence," in *Poetical Works* (Oxford, 1950), 155 (ll. 246–248).

54. Dante Gabriel Rossetti, "The Woodspurge," in *The Pre-Raphaelites from Rossetti to Ruskin*, ed. Dinah Roe (London, 2010), 110.

55. Alicia Suskin Ostriker, *The Nakedness of the Fathers* (New Brunswick, N.J., 1994), 65.

56. William Shakespeare, *Cymbeline* (London, 2017), 303 (4.2.272).

57. It is only in this limited sense, then, that Abraham dies "in a good old age, old and satisfied" (Genesis 25:8). Given the multiple alienations and deaths that attended on his life, no deeper satisfaction was available to him. That his son lives is doubtless a relief to Abraham, though not a source of satisfaction, given his readiness to slaughter his son. Emil L. Fackenheim thinks otherwise, however. See *The Jewish Bible after the Holocaust* (Manchester, U.K., 1990), 93.

58. See Emmanuel Levinas, *Ethics and Infinity* (Pittsburgh, 1985), 23. "The modern Jew is daily reviving the ancient text." Ruth Kartun-Blum, *Profane Scriptures* (Cincinnati, 1991), 17.

59. On this and on what follows, see Immanuel Kant, *Critique of Judgment*, ed. Nicholas Walker (Oxford, 2007), 142–144 (§49).

60. Sanhedrin 34a, glossing "Once did God speak, twice did I hear" (Psalms 62:12); Judah J. Slotkin, trans., *Midrash Rabbah: Numbers II* (London, 1983), 534 (13:15–16).

61. Emmanuel Levinas, "On the Jewish Reading of Scriptures," in *Levinas and Biblical Studies*, ed. Tamara Cohn Eskenazi, Gary A. Phillips, and David Jobling (Atlanta, 2003), 17.

62. James L. Kugel, *Traditions of the Bible* (Cambridge, Mass., 1998), 15; Marc Zvi Brettler, *How to Read the Jewish Bible* (Oxford, 2005), 1.

63. Michael Fishbane, *The Exegetical Imagination* (Cambridge, Mass., 1998), 2.

64. Erich Auerbach, *Mimesis* (Princeton, N.J., 2003), 15.

65. Abraham Socher, "Take Your Son . . . ," in *Liberal and Illiberal Arts* (Philadelphia, 2022), 21. Michael J. Harris gets at the same point when he writes, "[the Akedah] is open to . . . a wide spectrum of reasonable interpretations." *Divine Command Ethics* (London, 2003), 129.

66. Slotkin, *Midrash Rabbah: Numbers II,* 534 (13:16); James A. Diamond and Menachem Kellner, *Reinventing Maimonides in Contemporary Jewish Thought* (London, 2019), 126.

67. Emmanuel Levinas, "Means of Identification," in *Difficult Freedom* (London, 1990), 52.

68. Shoshana Lepon, *The Ten Tests of Abraham* (New York, 1986), 29.

69. See Northrop Frye, *The Great Code* (London, 1982), 221.

70. This reading is not to be muddled with the *Pirke Avot* reading—see the coda.

71. "[Against Leibowitz,] I prefer an understanding of the covenantal relationship between God and Israel in which the fullness of the human person is affirmed. In contrast to choosing the Akedah as the paradigm of faith in God, I choose the story of Abraham arguing with God for the people of Sodom, in which God is expected to act in accordance with Abraham's understanding of justice and morality." David Hartman, *Israelis and the Jewish Tradition* (New Haven, Conn., 2000), 140–141. He "prefers" the Sodom Abraham to the Moriah Abraham.

72. Wendy Zierler, "In Search of a Feminist Reading of the *Akedah,*" *Nashim: A Journal of Jewish Women's Studies & Gender Issues,* Spring 5765/2005, No. 9, "Jewish Women's Spirituality," 21. According to Martin S. Bergmann, the *Akedah* "became a source of embarrassment" to "the modern religious conscience." And so, "efforts were made to interpret the myth as a renunciation of infanticide." *In the Shadow of Moloch* (New York, 1992), 100.

73. Gershom Scholem, "With Gershom Scholem: An Interview," in *On Jews and Judaism in Crisis* (New York, 1976), 5.

74. Daniel R. Schwartz, *Judeans and Jews* (Toronto, 2014), 46.

75. The most famous occasion? Perhaps in 1913, when the young Franz Rosenzweig, born into an assimilated German-Jewish family ("we are Christians in every respect"), pulled back from the brink of affirming a full Christian identity and instead decided to become/remain a Jew. See Eugen Rosenstock-Huessy and Franz Rosenzweig, *Judaism Despite Christianity* (New York, 1971), 29–30, 36–37, 39, 74.

76. Benjamin Fondane, *Existential Monday* (New York, 2016), xxiii.

77. See Bruce Baugh, "Introduction," in *Existential Monday*, by Benjamin Fondane (New York, 2016), xxiii.

78. See Steven Greenberg, *Wrestling with God and Men* (Madison, Wisc., 2004). In a private communication, Rabbi Greenberg tells me that homosexuality was (absurdly) described to him as his "*Akedah.*"

79. Medieval commentators read the Hebrew word *nes* not as "tested" but as "presented" or "exhibited"—not "God tested Abraham" but "God presented Abraham as a model." See Omri Boehm, *The Binding of Isaac* (New York, 2007), 121.

80. On Maimonides's reading of the *Akedah* as a parable, see James A. Diamond, *Maimonides and the Shaping of the Jewish Canon* (Cambridge, 2014), 133 (fn. 64), 270–273; and Diamond, *Maimonides and the Hermeneutics of Concealment* (New York, 2002), 147. On Maimonides's reading of the *Akedah* as a prophetic vision, see Menachem Kellner, *Maimonides' Confrontation with Mysticism* (Oxford, 2006), 110, fn. 81. Of course, it could be *both* parable *and* vision: a parable about one of Abraham's prophetic visions.

81. Louis MacNeice, *Varieties of Parable* (London, 2008), 2, 7.

82. Frank Kermode, *The Genesis of Secrecy* (Cambridge, Mass., 1979), 47.

83. For example, imagine a machine that could give you any experience you might desire. You can program your experiences for tomorrow or this week or even for the rest of your life. You can live your fondest dreams "from the inside." Would you choose to

107. Haym Soloveitchik, *Rupture and Reconstruction* (London, 2021), 11.

108. Micah Goodman, *The Wondering Jew* (New Haven, Conn., 2020), 2.

109. And then there is the nontrivial matter of the forgotten laws. The Talmud (Temurah 16a) reports that three thousand *halakhot* were forgotten during the days of mourning for Moses. The Jewish people said to Joshua, Ask for guidance from Heaven so that you can reacquire the forgotten *halakhot*. Joshua said to them, "It is not in heaven." Once the Torah was given on Sinai, the Sages of each generation must determine the halakha.

110. Carlos Alós-Ferrer and Federica Farolfi, "Trust Games and Beyond," *Frontiers in Neuroscience*, Sept. 2019, Vol. 13, Art. 887.

111. See Ludwig Wittgenstein, *Movements of Thought: Ludwig Wittgenstein's Diary 1930–1932 and 1936–1937*, ed. James C. Klagge and Alfred Nordmann (London, 2023), 107.

112. See Norman Lamm, "Putting a Bad Conscience to Good Use," in *Derashot Lederot* (Jerusalem, 2012), 67–70.

113. Howard Wettstein, "The Fabric of Faith," in *Jewish Philosophy in an Analytic Age*, ed. Samuel Lebens, Dani Rabinowitz, and Aaron Segal (Oxford, 2019), 186, 187 (here quoting John Dewey).

114. Rashi, commentary on Exodus 30:15.

115. See Green, "Fear and Awe in Maimonides' Thought," 55.

116. A. J. Heschel, "Reflections on Being a Jew," in *Modern Jewish Thought*, ed. Nahum Glatzer (New York, 1977), 204; Heinrich Graetz, "The Structure of Jewish History," in *"The Structure of Jewish History" and Other Essays* (New York, 1975), 63; Ostriker, *Nakedness of the Fathers*, xii.

117. For an exploration of this theme, see Rachel S. Mikva, *Dangerous Religious Ideas* (Boston, 2020).

118. When Job says to his friends, "*These ten times* have ye reproached me," we think of Abraham's ten tests. Associating Abraham and Job became standard—not least because the author of Job invited the association. See Dale C. Allison Jr., *Testament of Abraham* (New York, 2003), 308, 317–318; Judy Klitsker, *Subversive Sequels in the Bible* (Philadelphia, 2009), xx–xxiii. Job takes the

form of a thought experiment, a philosophical fiction, incorporated in the canon to give people an occasion for arguing about God's providence, suggested Spinoza: in *Theologico-Political Treatise* (1670), ch. X, in *The Collected Works of Spinoza*, Vol. 2, ed. Edwin Curley (Princeton, N.J., 2016), 230. In Job's prose sections, Job accepts his suffering; in the poetry, he protests and holds God to account. That is, Job 1 is patient with God; Job 2, impatient. See Marc Zvi Brettler, *How to Read the Jewish Bible* (Oxford, 2005), 245–251; Martin Buber, "Job," in *On the Bible* (New York, 2000), 192.

119. An incomplete list: (a) the story of Pinchas—a warning against zealotry (see Anthony Julius, "A Few Thoughts on Fanaticism and Zealotry," *Marom Journal*, 2017, Vol. 2, 46–49); (b) the story of Korach—a warning against legalism (see J. Sanhedrin 10:1: "Korah was an Epicurean.... He went and made togas completely out of blue wool. He came before Moses and asked, does a toga made completely out of blue wool need *tzitzit*?"); (c) Ecclesiastes— a warning against theological complacency; (d) Job—a qualified warning against theodicies; (e) the story of Daniel the Tailor—a warning against Halakhic injustice (see Leviticus Rabbah 38.8, regarding *mamzerim*).

120. Barry W. Holtz, *Textual Knowledge* (New York, 2003), 147. Holtz's chapter "The Pedagogical Challenge of Difficult Texts" comprises a thorough, sophisticated alternative to my sixth reading.

121. See Walter Brueggemann, "Foreword," in *A Whirlpool of Torment*, by James L. Crenshaw (Atlanta, 2008), vii. My argument in this section runs in company with Phillis Trible's feminist reading of the Hagar and Ishmael story. Trible reinterprets the "use, abuse, and rejection" of Hagar in order to "shape a remnant theology that challenges the sexism of scripture." *Texts of Terror* (Minneapolis, 2022), 3, 9. I have also had in mind Ilana Pardes, *Countertraditions in the Bible* (Cambridge, Mass., 1992).

122. Emmanuel Levinas, "*A Propos* of 'Kierkegaard *Vivant*,'" in *Proper Names* (London, 1996), 77.

123. For example, Hazony, *Philosophy of Hebrew Scripture*, 116 ("[it] emphasizes that the universe is ruled by a God who has no

of God's power." "The Impious Impatience of Job," in *Letters of Intent* (London, 2017), 244, 246.

Chapter 5. "Abraham, Abraham"

1. Edmund Leach, "Genesis as Myth," in *"Genesis as Myth" and Other Essays* (London, 1969), 9.
2. Philo: Adam 1, created in the image of God, incorporeal, neither male nor female, imperishable by nature; Adam 2, perceptible to the external senses, consisting of body and soul, man or woman, by nature mortal. "On the Creation," in *The Works of Philo* (Peabody, Mass., 1993), 19 (XLVI). Levinas: First, the coexistence of "male" and "female" in each person; second, the separating of the sexes. *Ethics and Infinity* (Pittsburgh, 1985), 68–69. Soloveitchik: The distinction between Adam 1 and Adam 2 in *The Lonely Man of Faith* (New York, 1965). See also Eruvim 18a–18b.
3. "God" demands the sacrifice (Genesis 22:1). "The Lord" stays Abraham's hand (22:11), saying, "Now I know you fear *God*" (22:12); He does *not* say, "Now I know you fear *Me*." Abraham names the place *"the Lord* will see" (22:14), not *"God* will see." David N. Gottlieb writes of "God's double identity" manifesting itself here, "a profound distinction within the divine itself." There is "the one who demands human sacrifice and the one who takes pity on man and forbids [it]." *Second Slayings* (Piscataway, N.J., 2019), 173.
4. David Biale, "Historical Heresies and Modern Jewish Identity," in *Jewish Culture between Canon and Heresy* (Stanford, Calif., 2023), 117.
5. Heinrich Graetz, "The Structure of Jewish History," in *"The Structure of Jewish History" and Other Essays* (New York, 1975), 96.
6. Heinrich Graetz, "Introduction to Vol. 4 of the *History of the Jews*," in *"Structure of Jewish History" and Other Essays*, 125–126.
7. Yosef Haim Yerushalmi, *Zakhor* (Seattle, 1989), 81, 97. Yerushalmi writes, "the traditions and memories of many peoples are in disarray." The Jewish experience is an instance of "a universal and ever-growing dichotomy." However, those Jews who are still "within the enchanted circle of tradition," "find the work of

the historian irrelevant. They seek, not the historicity of the past, but its eternal contemporaneity" (93, 96).

8. In addition to Adam 1/Adam 2 (see earlier), there is his influential, interesting binarism, in several formulations: Covenant at Sinai/Covenant in Egypt; Covenant of Fate/Covenant of Destiny; camp/congregation; circumcision/immersion. See Joseph B. Soloveitchik, *Fate and Destiny* (Hoboken, N.J., 2000), 42–63.

9. Martin Buber, *On Judaism* (New York, 1972), 24, 88; Gershom Scholem, "Martin Buber's Conception of Judaism," in *On Jews and Judaism in Crisis* (New York, 1976), 144, 141. Less comfortable with the thought of inner conflict, Herman Cohen preferred to write of "the duality of the undivided national spirit." *Religion of Reason out of the Sources of Judaism* (Atlanta, 1995), 27.

10. Yosef Haim Yerushalmi, *Freud's Moses* (New Haven, Conn., 1991), 29.

11. Jacques Lacan, *The Ethics of Psychoanalysis* (New York, 1992), 214.

12. Philip Rieff, *Freud: The Mind of the Moralist* (Chicago, 1979), x. We can add the more biographically conditioned dichotomies, such as his affective investment in Rome (love object, hate object). See Carl E. Schorske, *Fin-de-Siècle Vienna* (New York, 1981), 191–193.

13. Gershom Scholem's formulation. See Alan L. Mittleman, *Between Kant and Kabbalah* (New York, 1990), 2.

14. Emmanuel Levinas, "Assimilation and New Culture," in *Beyond the Verse* (London, 1994), 197; Arthur Hertzberg, *The French Enlightenment and the Jews* (New York, 1970), 360.

15. Emmanuel Levinas, "Means of Identification," in *Difficult Freedom* (London, 1990), 50.

16. On dichotomies as institutions, see Hilary Putnam, "Fact and Value," in *Reason, Truth and History* (Cambridge, 1981), 127; on how dichotomies become "outdated," see Putnam, "Preface," in *Reason, Truth and History*, x–xi.

17. Gershom Scholem, *Major Trends in Jewish Mysticism* (New York, 1961), 322. Gnosticism was always anti-Jewish, even when it

arose among Jews: Harold Bloom, *Kabbalah and Criticism* (New York, 1984), 20.

18. Jonathan Sacks, "Alienation and Faith," *Tradition*, Spring–Summer 1973, Vol. 13, No. 4, and Vol. 14, No. 1, 140, 143, 150. Sacks restates the dividedness at the metalevel. There are "two readings of the inner possibilities of the Jew": "empathy" with alienation or dividedness and the "healing" of dividedness (160–161).

19. Elias Canetti, *The Human Province* (London, 1985), 51; Jean-Christophe Attias, *The Jews and the Bible* (Stanford, Calif., 2015), 135–136.

20. Harry Austryn Wolfson, "Maimonides and Halevi: A Study in Typical Jewish Attitudes towards Greek Philosophy in the Middle Ages," *Jewish Quarterly Review*, Jan. 1912, Vol. 2, No. 3, 304 ("the intrusion of Greek philosophical ideas into Jewish thought . . . gave rise to the need of a new reconciliation between Judaism and Hellenism"), 306.

21. Scholem, "Martin Buber's Conception of Judaism," 168; Menachem Kellner, *Maimonides on Jews and the Jewish People* (New York, 1991), 6.

22. See Hilary Putnam, "The Collapse of the Fact/Value Dichotomy," in *"The Collapse of the Fact/Value Dichotomy" and Other Essays* (Cambridge, Mass., 2002), 2–3, 7, 8–9, 10, 11, 19.

23. "Scholem . . . dichotomized the intellectual currents of mysticism and philosophy in too simplistic a fashion. . . . It is impossible to disentangle the threads of philosophy and mysticism when examining the texture of medieval Jewish mysticism in any of its major expressions." Elliot Wolfson, "Jewish Mysticism: A Philosophical Overview," in *History of Jewish Philosophy*, ed. Daniel H. Frank and Oliver Leaman (London, 1997), 452–453.

24. Levinas, *Ethics and Infinity*, 23.

25. Isadore Twersky, *Introduction to the Code of Maimonides (Mishneh Torah)* (New Haven, Conn., 1980), 220.

26. David Hartman, *The God Who Hates Lies* (Woodstock, Vt., 2011), 154. Elsewhere, Hartman implies that we must also choose between "the two very different forms" of the "God of Abraham,"

the "God who demands total surrender to His command" and the "God who invites independent moral critique." Hartman, *A Heart of Many Rooms* (Woodstock, Vt., 1999), 14.

27. Abraham Joshua Heschel, *God in Search of Man* (New York, 1976), 201. Heschel adds Isaac and Jacob too.

28. John Wisdom, "Gods," in *Philosophy and Psychoanalysis* (Berkeley, Calif., 1969), 164–165.

29. Micah Goodman, *Maimonides and the Book That Changed Judaism* (Philadelphia, 2015), 3.

30. "Anyone who denies the worship of false gods acknowledges the entire Torah in its totality, all the works of the prophets, and everything that has been commanded to the prophets from Adam, [the first man,] until eternity."

31. James A. Diamond, *Maimonides and the Hermeneutics of Concealment* (New York, 2002), 159–160.

32. Ernst Cassirer, "Judaism and the Modern Political Myths," *Contemporary Jewish Record*, 1 Apr. 1944, 117–118.

33. Theodor W. Adorno, "Why Still Philosophy," in *Critical Models* (New York, 1998), 10.

34. Solomon Maimon, *The Autobiography of Solomon Maimon*, ed. Yitzhak Y. Melamed and Abraham Socher (Princeton, N.J., 2018), xx, xxxvii, 123, 202, 209, 215, 223; Abraham P. Socher, *The Radical Enlightenment of Solomon Maimon* (Stanford, Calif., 2006), 114, 125, 158 ("a wrenching move").

35. Hannah Arendt, "The Jew as Pariah: A Hidden Tradition," in *The Jewish Writings* (New York, 2007), 276–297. To this type, Arendt gave the misleading name "pariah." It has limited, if any, utility and can be safely disregarded. But for identifying the type and for delineating its features, we must give her credit.

36. Philo, "The Worse Attacks the Better," in *Works of Philo*, 129 (XLIV).

37. Geoffrey D. Claussen, comp., *Modern Musar* (Lincoln, Neb., 2022), 69–70.

38. Claussen, *Modern Mussar*, 264; Maimonides, *Commentary on Pirke Avot*, 5:20; Yevamot 79a.

39. Judah Halevi, *The Kuzari* (New York, 1964), 168–169.

40. Adam Shear, *The Kuzari and the Shaping of Jewish Identity 1167–1900* (Cambridge, 2008), ix, 3–4 ("this dichotomy"); H. Wolfson, "Maimonides and Halevi," 304 ("the intrusion Greek philosophical ideas into Jewish thought . . . gave rise to the need of a new reconciliation between Judaism and Hellenism"), 316 ("Diametrically opposed to Maimonides, in insight, in conception of life and destiny, is Judah Halevi").

41. Micah Gottlieb, "Mysticism and Philosophy," in *The Cambridge History of Jewish Philosophy*, Vol. 1, *From Antiquity through the Seventeenth Century*, ed. Steven Nadler and T. M. Rudavsky (Cambridge, 2009), 130.

42. Halevi, *Kuzari*, 92.

43. Halevi, *Kuzari*, 206–207.

44. Halevi, *Kuzari*, 92.

45. Halevi, *Kuzari*, 161–162.

46. Lenn E. Goodman, *Judaism* (London, 2017), 179.

47. Halevi, *Kuzari*, 53–54.

48. Halevi, *Kuzari*, 223, 239; Hillel Halkin, *Yehuda Halevi* (New York, 2010), 156–157.

49. Hilary Putnam, *Jewish Philosophy as a Guide to Life* (Bloomington, Ind., 2008), 19; Putnam, *Philosophy as Dialogue* (Cambridge, Mass., 2022), 291; Franz Rosenzweig, *Understanding the Sick and the Healthy* (Cambridge, Mass., 1999), 40, 41, 42, 59.

50. Franz Rosenzweig, *The Star of Redemption* (London, 1971), 3, 176. For a gloss on "In Philosophos," see Leora Batnitzky, *Idolatry and Representation* (Princeton, N.J., 2000), 246–247, fn. 45.

51. Michael Wyschogrod, *The Body of Faith* (Lanham, Md., 1996), xxxv, 26–27, 33, 73, 84, 99. But compare: "At its best, this parochial identification [with Jewish life] exists as a tie of memory through pity; at its worst, it may be the continuity of appetite—the lox, cream cheese, and bagel combinations; or through comedians' jokes." Daniel Bell, "Reflections on Jewish Identity," *Commentary*, June 1961, 22. I am grateful to Chloë Julius for this reference.

52. Franz Rosenzweig, *Understanding the Sick and the Healthy* (Cambridge, Mass., 1999), 56–57. Cf. "The Star of Redemption is an inspired book. Yet its inspiration did not prevent it from re-

maining a book of theories, speculations, doctrines." Nahum N. Glatzer, "Franz Rosenzweig's Conversion," in *Essays in Jewish Thought* (Tuscaloosa, Ala., 1978), 238.

53. Wyschogrod, *Body of Faith*, 173.

54. Emmanuel Levinas, "The Temptation of Temptation," in *Nine Talmudic Readings* (Bloomington, Ind., 1990), 34.

55. Wyschogrod, *Body of Faith*, 55.

56. Yaakov Medan, "From Babel to Berit bein HaBetarim—The Early Life of Abraham," in *Torah MiEtzion—New Readings in Tanach: Bereishit* (Jerusalem, 2011), 109.

57. Nachmanides, *Commentary on the Torah*, Vol. 1, *Genesis* (New York, 1971), 167–168. The Hebrew University scholars Avigdor Shinan and Yair Zakovitch give a militant edge to Nachmanides's explanation. The purpose of the *Tanakh*, they argue, was to teach Jews about themselves. It aimed to persuade them of the existence of one god and their relationship with Him. The Jewish nation was to be educated, its beliefs purified, cleansed of the dust of idolatry and myth. The *Tanakh* does not argue openly against unwanted traditions, however. The battle it wages is instead a covert one. It takes reprobated traditional stories and substitutes new versions of them. In these versions, one can detect traces of the original stories. The authors term this work of detection "literary archaeology"; they are engaged in the reconstruction of prebiblical traditions. Regarding the story of Abraham's life in Ur, then, the authors infer that the Torah's "stunning silence" reflects an anxiety that stories of Abraham's heroic battles against idol worship would jeopardize the idea that he lived a life untouched by idolatry. Traces of the story can be found in the *Tanakh*, however, and the story itself returned in post-*Tanakh* texts—e.g., in Jubilees. Shinan and Zakovitch, *From Gods to God* (Lincoln, Neb., 2004), 1, 7, 147–148, 268, 269.

58. "And Rabbi Ami bar Abba said: Abraham recognized his Creator at the age of three years, as it is stated: 'Because [*ekev*] Abraham hearkened to My voice' (Genesis 26:5). The numerical value of the letters of the word *ekev* is 172, indicating that he observed the halakha for this many years. If Abraham lived until 175 then his first recognition of the Creator must have been at the age

of three." Hasdai Crescas followed the Talmud but insisted that at three, Abraham had already "attained to reason." *Light of the Lord (or Hashem)* (Oxford, 2018), 17.

59. Edmund Husserl, *The Idea of Phenomenology* (Dordrecht, 1990), 1, 14–15, 19; Husserl, *The Crisis of European Sciences and Transcendental Phenomenology* (Evanston, Ill., 1970), 75, 143–147, 197 (§§ 17, 38, 56); Dermot Moran and Joseph Cohen, *The Husserl Dictionary* (London, 2012), 139, 216–218, 254, 292; Barry Smith, "Common Sense," in *The Cambridge Companion to Husserl*, ed. Barry Smith and David Woodruff Smith (Cambridge, 1995), 394, 415, 426.

60. Hannah Arendt, *The Origins of Totalitarianism* (New York, 1976), 473.

61. See G. W. F. Hegel, *Phenomenology of Spirit* (Oxford, 1977), 344 (§ 564).

62. Putnam, *Philosophy as Dialogue*, 283.

63. See Simone de Beauvoir, "Pyrrhus and Cineas," in *What Is Existentialism?* (London, 2020), 35.

64. Husserl, *Idea of Phenomenology*, 15; Smith, "Common Sense," 396, 426.

65. Bertrand Russell's definition of faith. See G. E. M. Anscombe, "Faith," in *Ethics, Religion and Politics* (Oxford, 1981), 115.

66. Søren Kierkegaard, *Fear and Trembling* (New York, 2022), 5.

67. Augustine, *De praedestinatione sanctorum*, ch. 2, n. 5. Quoted in Peter Gay, *The Enlightenment*, Vol. 1 (New York, 1995), 230. I have revised the translation.

68. Sam Lebens, *The Principles of Judaism* (Oxford, 2020), 278.

69. See Lebens, *Principles of Judaism*, 189, 275.

70. Martin Buber, "The Man of Today and the Jewish Bible," in *On the Bible* (New York, 2000), 1, 5.

71. See my *Trials of the Diaspora* (Oxford, 2012), 36–37.

72. See Kellner, *Maimonides on Judaism and the Jewish People*, 10, 14, 97.

73. See Michael A. Shmidman, "An Anti-Maimonidean on Philosophy and Aggadah," in *"In the Dwelling of a Sage Lie Precious Treasures,"* ed. Yitzhak Berger and Chaim Milikowsky (New York, 2020), 211.

74. See Beauvoir, "Pyrrhus and Cineas," 26.

75. Jonathan Sacks, "The Eighth Day," in *Covenant and Conversation: Leviticus* (Jerusalem, 2015), 135–141.

76. See Geoffrey Hartman's poem "The Eighth Day," in *The Eighth Day* (Lubbock, Tex., 2013), 85. I have made a slight modification to the quoted lines.

77. Nathan Rotenstreich, *The Recurring Pattern* (London, 1963), 18.

78. Judah Halevi, "Song," in *Three Jewish Philosophers*, ed. Hans Lewy, Alexander Altmann, Isaak Heinemann (New York, 1974), 137.

79. Loren T. Stuckenbruck, "Apocrypha and Pseudepigrapha," in *Early Judaism*, ed. John J. Collins and Daniel C. Harlow (Grand Rapids, Mich., 2010), 190.

80. Emmanuel Levinas, "Dialogue with Richard Kearney," quoted in Gillian Rose, *The Broken Middle* (Oxford, 1992), 248.

81. Levinas, "Temptation of Temptation," 34–35.

82. Emmanuel Levinas, "The Pact" and "Revelation in the Jewish Tradition," in *Beyond the Verse*, 78, 146.

83. James A. Diamond, *Jewish Theology Unbound* (Oxford, 2018), 101.

84. See Yerushalmi, *Freud's Moses*, 29, 35, 89–90.

85. John Updike, "Bech Noir," quoted in Adam Kirsch, "Who Wants to Be a Jewish Writer?," in *"Who Wants to Be a Jewish Writer?" and Other Essays* (New Haven, Conn., 2019), 8.

86. Beauvoir, "Pyrrhus and Cineas," 17.

87. See Gershom Scholem, "Letter to Hannah Arendt," in *On Jews and Judaism in Crisis*, 300–306.

88. Hannah Arendt, "A Letter to Gershom Scholem," in *Jewish Writings*, 466.

89. Yeshayahu Leibowitz, *The Faith of Maimonides* (Tel Aviv, 1989), 22.

90. Samuel A. Berman, *Midrash Tanhumma-Yelammedenu* (Hoboken, N.J., 1996), 81.

91. See Putnam, "Collapse of the Fact/Value Dichotomy," 2–3, 7, 8–9, 10, 11, 19.

92. Martin Jay, "Walter Benjamin and Isaiah Berlin," in *Genesis and Validity* (Philadelphia, 2022), 77.

93. Nachmanides, *Commentary on the Torah*, 169.

94. Even Aristotle was not an "authority" in this strong, conclusive sense. See Maimonides, Guide, II.15 ("Most of the people who believe themselves to philosophize follow Aristotle as an authority"). And yet to Maimonides, Aristotle's mind was "the finality of the human mind"—other than the mind of a person in a state of prophecy, for as long as that state lasts. See José Faur, *Homo Mysticus* (New York, 1998), 98–99, 106.

95. J. Y. Gellman, *This Was from God* (Brighton, Mass., 2016), 185, cited in Lebens, *Principles of Judaism*, 217.

96. Émile Perreau-Saussine, *Alasdair MacIntyre* (Notre Dame, Ind., 2022), 40.

97. See Yerushalmi, *Freud's Moses*, 10–11.

98. Compare William Wordsworth, *The Prelude: The Four Texts*, ed. Jonathan Wordsworth (London, 1995), 408 (Bk. X, ll. 172–175).

99. Friedrich Nietzsche, *The Gay Science* (Cambridge, 2001), 199 (§ 343). Some phrases in my next paragraph are taken from 200 (§ 344).

100. Alexis de Tocqueville, *Democracy in America* (London, 2003), 493–494 (Bk. 2, S. 1, ch. 1).

101. See Willi Goetschel and Gilad Sharvit, "Introduction," in *Canonization and Alterity*, ed. Gilad Sharvit and Willi Goetschel (Berlin, 2020), 3.

102. See Yehuda Gellman, "The *Akedah* in the Thought of David Hartman," in *Judaism and Modernity: The Religious Philosophy of David Hartman*, by Jonathan W. Malino (Burlington, Vt., 2004), 174.

103. Mittleman, *Between Kant and Kabbalah*, 33, 46.

104. See Mittleman, *Between Kant and Kabbalah*, viii, 9, 30, 35 (Breuer's *The New Kuzari*), 46, 176.

105. See Jonathan Z. Smith, *Relating Religion* (Chicago, 2004), 103.

106. "At any given time, the committed Jew is faced with the

task of finding a reflective equilibrium between the demands of Jewish law, as it is in their day and age, and their own ethical intuitions. . . . The equilibrium pulls in multiple directions." Lebens, *Principles of Judaism*, 218. This reminds me of William Empson's remark that ostensibly "profound paradoxes" often turn out on scrutiny to be no more than "contradictions" "jammed together." See *Milton's God* (London, 1965), 253.

107. Diamond, *Maimonides and the Hermeneutics of Concealment*, 144.

108. See Sarah Stroumsa, *Maimonides in His World* (Princeton, N.J., 2009), 186, where the point is made more cautiously.

109. Halevi, *Kuzari*, 142.

110. Maimon, *Autobiography of Solomon Maimon*, 124. Maimonides, writes Micah Goodman, considered our preconceptions to be the greatest obstacle to intellectual development. *Maimonides and the Book That Changed Judaism* (Philadelphia, 2015), 17.

111. "Maimonides' opposition to this kind of popular religion [writing names of angels etc. on *mezuzahs*] was uniform and uncompromising." Twersky, *Introduction to the Code of Maimonides*, 480, 502.

112. Abraham Joshua Heschel, *Maimonides* (New York, 1982), 24, 144–145, 209.

113. Lenn E. Goodman, "Creation and Emanation," in Nadler and Rudavsky, *Cambridge History of Jewish Philosophy*, 607.

114. Moses Maimonides, *Epistles of Maimonides: Crisis and Leadership*, trans. Abraham Halkin (Philadelphia, 1985), 211.

115. Walt Whitman, *Leaves of Grass* (Oxford, 2009), 78.

116. David Hartman, *Israelis and the Jewish Tradition* (New Haven, Conn., 2000), 27–28. Yeshayahu Leibowitz, on the other hand, insists that even the "distinction" between Maimonides the halakhist and Maimonides the philosopher is "artificial." *Faith of Maimonides*, 107.

117. See James A. Diamond and Menachem Kellner, *Reinventing Maimonides in Contemporary Jewish Thought* (London, 2019), 20; H. Wolfson, "Maimonides and Halevi," 327 ("Maimonides' condemnation of excessive prayer"); James A. Diamond, *Maimonides*

and the Shaping of the Jewish Canon (Cambridge, 2014), 215 ("Maimonides envisions a time when it will be surpassed by a far more advanced form of silent meditation"); Faur, *Homo Mysticus*, 6 ("the Maimonidean doctrine of silence").

118. Emily Dickinson, *The Complete Poems* (London, 2016), 275 (564).

119. Marvin Fox, *Interpreting Maimonides* (Chicago, 1990), 78–83. See also Diamond, *Maimonides and the Hermeneutics of Concealment*, 28 ("balancing act"), 54 ("the inconsistency defies resolution").

120. Kenneth Seeskin, "Introduction," in *The Cambridge Companion to Maimonides* (Cambridge, 2005), 2.

121. Leon Roth, *Is There a Jewish Philosophy?* (London, 1999), 11.

122. As charged by the Talmudist Jacob Fromer (1865–1938). See Alberto Manguel, *Maimonides* (New Haven, Conn., 2023), 170. "The question of contradictions, real or alleged, central or peripheral, has been a pivot of modern Maimonidean scholarship. The unity or duality of Maimonides, the esoteric versus the exoteric teaching, the Talmudist versus the philosopher, or the Rabbi versus the Aristotelian, the native and traditional authentic doctrine, vis-à-vis the extraneous, foreign, spurious doctrine, the author of 'intentional perplexities,' or the constructor of a tense yet unified system—such formulations and/or evaluations continue to bestir or to bedevil scholars." Twersky, *Introduction to the Code of Maimonides*, 447–448.

123. See Leo W. Schwarz, *Wolfson of Harvard* (Philadelphia, 1978), 53–54 (Wolfson on Crescas).

124. Putnam, *Jewish Philosophy as a Guide to Life*, 107.

125. Manguel, *Maimonides*, xi.

126. "Maimonides' harmonization of philosophy and Torah was impossible to sustain. In the hands of his successors, his philosophy shattered the 'unity of the Jewish philosophy.'" See Mittleman, writing of Isaac Breuer, in *Between Kant and Kabbalah*, 27.

127. Hilary Putnam, *Renewing Philosophy* (Cambridge, Mass., 1992), 1.

128. Putnam, *Jewish Philosophy as a Guide to Life*, 5.

129. Putnam, *Jewish Philosophy as a Guide to Life*, 7–8.

130. See Alasdair MacIntyre, "Visions," in *New Essays in Philosophical Theology*, ed. Anthony Flew and Alasdair MacIntyre (London, 1972), 254–260.

131. Hélène Cixous, *Portrait of Jacques Derrida as a Young Jewish Saint* (New York, 2004), 122.

132. L. Goodman, *Judaism*, 63.

133. Benjamin Fondane, *Existential Monday* (New York, 2016), 39.

Coda

1. Michael Wyschogrod, *The Body of Faith* (Lanham, Md., 1996), xxxii.

2. Isadore Twersky, *Introduction to the Code of Maimonides (Mishneh Torah)* (New Haven, Conn., 1980), 337.

3. Betty Rojtman, *Black Fire on White Fire* (Berkeley, Calif., 1998), 7.

4. See Frank Kermode, "The Uses of Error," in *The Uses of Error* (London, 1990), 431. "The Bible has no rivals when it comes to the art of omission, of not saying what everyone would like to know." Robert Calasso, *The Book of All Books* (London, 2021), 296.

5. Erich Auerbach, *Mimesis* (Princeton, N.J., 2003), 15.

6. For example, when the three men appear to Abraham (Genesis 18), he addresses them as '*dny*, which, according to the vowels added, can mean *adoni* (my lord), *adonay* (my lords), or *adonai* (my Lord). See Piero Boitani *The Bible and Its Rewritings* (Oxford, 1999), 3. "Devoid of vowel points, punctuation, cantillation marks, and accents—the insertion of which renders a Torah scroll ritually unfit for religious purposes—the strings of consonants that constitute the bare and partial syntax of the Hebrew Scriptures are unreadable. In other words, some initial interpretive act of elucidation is required in order to render the primordial text even *potentially* meaningful." Menachem Fisch, *Rational Rabbis* (Bloomington, Ind., 1997), 56.

7. James L. Kugel, *Traditions of the Bible* (Cambridge, Mass., 1998), 4.

8. *Zohar*, Vol. 3, 149b, in *The Kabbalistic Tradition*, ed. Alan Unterman (London, 2008), 32.

9. John Donne, "The first alteration, the first grudging of the sickness," in *Devotions upon Emergent Occasions* (New York, 1999), 12 ("Prayer").

10. Fisch, *Rational Rabbis*, ix.

11. "Biblical texts fall almost completely silent on the great trial after its appearance in Genesis: the *Akedah* receives no further mention until it becomes the object of considerable interpretive attention in the first centuries of the Common Era." David N. Gottlieb, *Second Slayings* (Piscataway, N.J., 2019), 104.

12. See Harold Bloom, "Pragmatics of Jewish Culture," in *Post-Analytic Philosophy*, ed. John Rajchman and Cornel West (New York, 1985), 118, 126.

13. Seth Schwartz, *The Ancient Jews from Alexander to Muhammad* (Cambridge, 2014), 66, 67, 68, 88.

14. James C. Vanderkam, "Judaism in the Land of Israel," in *Early Judaism*, ed. John J. Collins and Daniel C. Harlow (Cambridge, 2012), 76.

15. Jacob Neusner, *Three Questions of Formative Judaism* (Boston, 2002), 4.

16. Benjamin Sommer, *Revelation and Authority* (New Haven, Conn., 2015), 250, cited in Sam Lebens, *The Principles of Judaism* (Oxford, 2020), 187.

17. James L. Kugel, "Early Jewish Biblical Interpretation," in Collins and Harlow, *Early Judaism*, 151–178.

18. James C. Vanderkam, "Judaism in the Land of Israel," and Eibert Tigchelaar, "The Dead Sea Scrolls," in Collins and Harlow, *Early Judaism*, 84–88, 216. James Kugel identifies three distinct activities: (a) editing and reediting the Torah (including adding to it), (b) writing new versions of Torah narratives (e.g., Jubilees), and (c) writing commentaries on the Torah. They are "really all part of a single mentality." "The Descent of the Wicked Angels and the Persistence of Evil," in *The Call of Abraham*, ed. Gary A. Anderson and Joel S. Kaminsky (Notre Dame, Ind., 2013), 216, 231 ("Scripture was changed again and again").

19. Erich S. Gruen, "Judaism in the Diaspora," in Collins and Harlow, *Early Judaism*, 103.

20. See James L. Kugel, "Jubilees," in *Outside the Bible*, ed. Louis H. Feldman, James L. Kugel, and Lawrence H. Schiffman (Philadelphia, 2013), 335–359.

21. James L. Kugel, "Pseudo-Jubilees," in Feldman, Kugel, and Schiffman, *Outside the Bible*, 466–468.

22. Philo, "On Abraham" and "On the Migration of Abraham," in *The Works of Philo* (Peabody, Mass., 1993), 274, 417, 420, 423; Ellen Birnbaum, "On the Life of Abraham," in Feldman, Kugel, and Schiffman, *Outside the Bible*, 939, 943, 944.

23. Josephus, *Jewish Antiquities*, trans. H. St. J. Thackeray (Cambridge, Mass., 1998), 79, 81, 83, 95, 113–117.

24. David A. de Silva, "4 Maccabees," in Feldman, Kugel, and Schiffman, *Outside the Bible*, 2387.

25. Robert Eisen, *Judaism and Violence* (Cambridge, 2021), 27–28.

26. Seth Schwartz, *The Ancient Jews from Alexander to Muhammad* (Cambridge, 2014), 15, 63, 66, 77, 86, 87.

27. See Wyschogrod, *Body of Faith*, 15.

28. See Emmanuel Levinas, "Preface," in *Beyond the Verse* (London, 1994), xi.

29. See Schwartz, *Ancient Jews from Alexander to Muhammad*, ch. 5.

30. Neusner, *Three Questions of Formative Judaism*, xv, 2–3, 27.

31. Leo Baeck, "The Pharisees," in *"The Pharisees" and Other Essays* (New York, 1966), 47.

32. Kugel, *Traditions of the Bible*, 22 ("a sagely construct").

33. See Roland Barthes, *The Pleasure of the Text* (New York, 1975), 54; Barthes, *Writing Degree Zero* (New York, 1975), 75; Jonathan Culler, *Structuralist Poetics* (London, 1975), 107; Culler, *Barthes* (Oxford, 2002), 21, 43–44, 115–116; Randolph Bourne, "Traps for the Unwary," in *The Radical Will* (Los Angeles, 1995), 483; Ernest Jones, *Free Associations* (London, 1990), 197. Freud wrote of "these shallow or high-handed attempts at reinterpretation," the work of "critics" who thereby "ward off the objectionable novelties" in psy-

following the destruction of the Alexandrian Jewish community in 115–117 CE. Gregory E. Sterling, David T. Runia, Maren R. Niehoff, and Annewies van den Hoek, "Philo," in Collins and Harlow, *Early Judaism*, 253.

73. See Dale C. Allison Jr., *Testament of Abraham* (New York, 2003), ch. 4 ("Jewish or Christian?"). There may be differences in this respect between the lost original texts and the surviving recensions.

74. Allison, *Testament of Abraham*, 63.

75. For early examples, see Kugel, *Traditions of the Bible*, 306–307.

76. "The Index of Christian Art at Princeton gives no less than 1,450 entries for Genesis 22:1–19." Judah Goldin, "Introduction," in *The Last Trial*, by Shalom Spiegel (Woodstock, Vt., 1993), xv.

77. Daniel C. Harlow, "Early Judaism and Early Christianity," in Collins and Harlow, *Early Judaism*, 405.

78. Frank Kermode, *The Genesis of Secrecy* (Cambridge, Mass., 1979), 18.

79. Erich Auerbach, "Symbolism in Medieval Literature," in *Selected Essays of Erich Auerbach* (Princeton, N.J., 2014), 119.

80. "The whole mythology of the Hebraic household was *nothing but* a type of a more transcendent history, the horoscope of a heavenly hero, by whose appearance everything is already concluded and will be yet" (italics added). Johann Georg Hamann, "Golgotha and Sheblimini!," in *Writings on Philosophy and Language* (Cambridge, 2007), 188–189.

81. Piero Boitani, *The Bible and Its Rewritings* (Oxford, 1999), 10.

82. Mishael M. Caspi and John T. Green, "Prolegomenon," in *Unbinding the Binding of Isaac*, ed. Mishael M. Caspi and John T. Greene (Lanham, Md., 2007), xiv.

83. St. Augustine, *Reply to Faustus* (n.p., 2014), 57 (ch. 4).

84. Maxwell Staniforth and Andrew Louth, eds., *Early Christian Writings* (London, 1987), 167. The second-century Church Father Melito wrote, "Christ suffered, whereas Isaac did not suffer." See Jeremy Cohen, *Sanctifying the Name* (Philadelphia, 2004), 171, fn. 33.

85. "The difference is significant. Judaism *emphasizes* that the

sacrifice did not take place." Martin S. Bergmann, *In the Shadow of Moloch* (New York, 1992), 116.

86. See Levenson, *Inheriting Abraham*, 102–103.

87. Levenson, *Death and Resurrection of the Beloved Son*, x, 69, 70.

88. Edward Kessler, *Bound by the Bible* (Cambridge, 2004), 85.

89. Justin Martyr, quoted in David Nirenberg, *Anti-Judaism* (London, 2015), 103.

90. Irenaeus, *Against Heresies*, in *The Ante-Nicene Fathers*, Vol. 1, ed. Alexander Roberts and James Donaldson (Peabody, Mass., 2004), 467, 469.

91. Susan A. Handelman, *The Slayers of Moses* (New York, 1982), 15, 86, 107.

92. Peder Gorgen, "In Accordance with the Scriptures," in *Early Christian Thought in Its Jewish Context*, ed. John Barclay and John Sweet (Cambridge, 1996), 201, 204.

93. Shalom Spiegel, *The Last Trial* (Woodstock, Vt., 1993), 85.

94. Erich Auerbach, "Figura," in *Selected Essays of Erich Auerbach*, 94.

95. Pseudo-Gregory of Nyssa, quoted in Kessler, *Bound by the Bible*, 66.

96. Kessler, *Bound by the Bible*, 133.

97. *The Vision of Paul*, in *The Ante-Nicene Fathers*, Vol. 9, ed. Allan Menzies (Peabody, Mass., 2004), 164.

98. Jon D. Levenson, *The Hebrew Bible, the Old Testament, and Historical Criticism* (Louisville, Ky., 1993), 15, 26, 58, 104. See also Robert Chazan, *From Anti-Judaism to Anti-Semitism* (Cambridge, 2016), 29–33.

99. See Leo W. Schwarz, *Wolfson of Harvard* (Philadelphia, 1978), xxv.

100. Dan Jacobson, *The Story of Stories* (London, 1981), 177–178.

101. Jody L. Vaccaro, "Abraham," in *Augustine through the Ages*, ed. Allan D. Fitzgerald (Grand Rapids, Mich., 1999), 2.

102. Augustine, *The City of God* (Cambridge, 2017), 735, 745, 747 (Bk. XVI, chs. 25, 32).

103. Augustine, *Reply to Faustus*, 216, 234–242 (ch. 22).

104. Israel Shahar, *The Judensau: A Medieval Anti-Jewish Motif and Its History* (London, 1974), 26–72.

105. See Colum Hourihane, ed., *Abraham in Medieval Christian, Islamic and Jewish Art* (Princeton, N.J., 2013), 66, 97.

106. Jeffrey S. Siker regards *Trypho* as the terminal point in the working out of the Christian appropriation of Abraham. "Justin's use of Abraham marks the final stage of development in Christian use of Abraham against non-Christian Judaism. The many centuries of Christian controversy with Judaism following Justin simply restate in various ways the Christian conclusion that Abraham is the father of Christians and not of Jews." *Disinheriting the Jews* (Louisville, Ky., 1991), 193.

107. Such readings tend to neglect an Augustinian aspect of this "telos." Augustine writes, "Even if his son was slain, one ought to believe that Abraham believed that he would soon be returned to him by being raised from the dead." *The Retractions* (Washington, DC, 2017), 165. Augustine cites Hebrews 11:17–19. See note 110 below.

108. Harold Bloom, *Jesus and Yahweh* (New York, 2005), 163.

109. Gillian Rose, *The Broken Middle* (Oxford, 1992), 15. See also Levenson, *Death and Resurrection of the Beloved Son*, 130 ("the profound Pauline-Lutheran wellsprings of Kierkegaard's interpretation").

110. "By faith Abraham, when God tested him, offered Isaac as a sacrifice. He who had embraced the promises was about to sacrifice his one and only son, even though God had said to him, 'It is through Isaac that your offspring will be reckoned.' Abraham reasoned that God could even raise the dead, and so in a manner of speaking he did receive Isaac back from death" (Heb. 11:17–19).

111. Their understanding of *Fear and Trembling* is one-eyed. See Aharon Lichtenstein, *By His Light* (Jerusalem, 2016), 108, 109; Wyschogrod, *Body of Faith*, 20, 22; Joseph B. Soloveitchik, *Abraham's Journey* (New York, 2008), 97, 190 (Abraham is a "Knight of Faith"); Soloveitchik, *The Lonely Man of Faith* (New York, 1965), 2, 50 ("Abraham the knight of faith"); Soloveitchik, *The Emergence of*

Ethical Man (Jersey City, N.J., 2005), 156 ("knight of faith"). As to Koller as an exception, see *Unbinding Isaac* (Lincoln, Neb., 2020), chs. 3–4; and Chaim Navon, *Genesis and Jewish Thought* (Jersey City, N.J., 2008), 330, fn. 3 ("operative here is the Christian motif of faith in the absurd").

112. On Levinas, see Samuel Moyn, *Origins of the Other* (Ithaca, N.Y., 2005), 165, 186–187 ("Opposing the solitary—and in his view, narcissistic and melodramatic—quest of the knight of faith, Levinas recommended the calm and healthy solicitude of interpersonal morality"). While Kafka's "studies of Kierkegaard . . . grew deeper and deeper," he kept his distance from Kierkegaard's "Abraham conception." Max Brod, *Franz Kafka: A Biography* (New York, 1973), 164, 170–171, 184. Theodor Adorno develops the point: "In Kafka, unlike *Fear and Trembling*, ambiguity and obscurity are attributed not exclusively to the Other as such but to human beings and to the conditions in which they live." "Notes on Kafka," in *Prisms* (London, 1967), 259. Ritchie Robinson is clear: "Kafka disagreed radically with the message of *Fear and Trembling* and . . . regarded Kierkegaard . . . with a mixture of fascination and scepticism." *Kafka: Judaism, Politics, and Literature* (Oxford, 1985), 194.

113. Yeshayahu Leibowitz, *Judaism, Human Values, and the Jewish State* (Cambridge, Mass., 1992), 259. Leibowitz "reduces . . . theological discourse to the brute act of obedience to divine will." James A. Diamond, *Jewish Theology Unbound* (Oxford, 2018), 1.

114. "Towards Judaism in its entirety and towards the Old Testament," wrote the German-Jewish philosopher Ernst Cassirer (1874–1945), "Kant had all along so strongly subjective a prejudice that he could see in the religion of the prophets and in the psalms nothing more than a collection of statutory laws and usages." *Kant's Life and Thought* (New Haven, Conn., 1981), 388. For an instance of this "subjective prejudice," see the footnote on "the Palestinians" in Kant's *Anthropology from a Pragmatic Point of View* (Carbondale, Ill., 1978), 101–102.

115. Ritchie Robertson, *The Enlightenment* (London, 2022), 189–190.

116. Russell Goulbourne, "Voltaire's Socrates," in *Socrates from*

Antiquity to the Enlightenment, ed. Michael Trapp (London, 2007), 229–231.

117. Werner Schneiders, "Concepts of Philosophy," in *The Cambridge History of Eighteenth Century Philosophy,* Vol. 1, ed. Knud Haakonssen (Cambridge, 2006), 27.

118. Pierre Bayle, *The Dictionary Historical and Critical,* Vol. 1 (London, 1734), 44.

119. See Kugel, *Traditions of the Bible,* 246–247 (quoting Josephus, *Jewish Antiquities:* "[Abraham] became the first person to argue there is a single God who is the creator of all things").

120. Richard H. Popkin, "Introduction," in *Historical and Critical Dictionary,* by Pierre Bayle (Indianapolis, 1991), xxvi.

121. Bayle, *Dictionary Historical and Critical,* 44.

122. Isaiah Berlin, *The Age of Enlightenment* (Oxford, 1979), 113.

123. Guy G. Stroumsa, *The Idea of Semitic Monotheism* (Oxford, 2021), 53.

124. See Adam Sutcliffe, *Judaism and Enlightenment* (Cambridge, 2003), 236.

125. Voltaire, *Philosophical Dictionary* (London, 2004), 16–20.

126. See Arthur Hertzberg, *The French Enlightenment and the Jews* (New York, 1970), 302–303; Peter Gay, *The Enlightenment,* Vol. 1 (New York, 1995), 396. This contempt seeped through into the nineteenth century. The philosopher Arthur Schopenhauer, for example, writes of Abraham's "villainy," holding him to be an "outrageous and ruthless model" for Jews, and cites the expulsion of Ishmael and Hagar. "On Religion," *Parerga and Paralipomena,* Vol. 2 (Cambridge, 2015), 341.

127. Immanuel Kant, *Religion within the Limits of Reason Alone* (1793) and *The Conflict of the Faculties* (1798), in *Religion and Rational Theology,* ed. Allen W. Wood and George di Giovanni (Cambridge, 1996), 124, 203–204, 275–276, 283. Michel Malherbe, "Reason," in Haakonssen, *Cambridge History of Eighteenth Century Philosophy,* 322.

128. Or at least the Three Monotheisms. See Richard Dawkins, *The God Delusion* (London, 2006), 243 ("deplorable tale"); Chris-

topher Hitchens, *God Is Not Great* (London, 2007), 206 ("frightful story").

129. Levenson, *Inheriting Abraham*, 107–108.

130. See Troels Nørager, *Taking Leave of Abraham* (Aarhus, Denmark, 2008). For the author, this is a *Christian* move. "We should embrace the possibility of conceptualizing Christian soteriology *not* in sacrificial terms but by seeing God as someone who 'gives' his son freely as a spiritual gift to be enjoyed by all those who come to believe in the kingdom of God" (241). See also Carol Delaney, "Abraham and the Seeds of Patriarchy," in *Genesis*, ed. Athalya Brenner (Sheffield, U.K., 1998), 149: "Why is the willingness to sacrifice the child at God's command the model of faith, rather than the passionate protection of the child? What would be the shape of our society if that had been the model of faith?"

131. Kant dismissed it as a "vindication worse than the complaint." "On the miscarriage of all philosophical trials in theodicy," in *Religion and Rational Theology*, 27. Gibbon teased, "many a sober Christian would rather admit that a wafer is God, than that God is a cruel and capricious tyrant." Edward Gibbon, *The History of the Decline and Fall of the Roman Empire*, Vol. 3, ed. David Wormsley (London, 1995), 437 (ch. 54). Playwrights of the period, however, were readier to explore the topic of divine evil, on occasion using the *Akedah* as the proof text. See Robertson, *Enlightenment*, 242.

132. See Anders Gerdmar, *Roots of Theological Anti-Semitism* (Leiden, 2010), 208.

133. G. W. F. Hegel, *Early Theological Writings* (Philadelphia, 1996), 182–191; see also Yirmiyahu Yovel, *Dark Riddle* (Cambridge, 1998), 35–38. The Hegelian, Kierkegaardian Soloveitchik echoes Hegel: "The interpenetration of faith and loneliness . . . goes back to the dawn of the Judaic covenant." *Lonely Man of Faith*, 6. See also Soloveitchik, *Fate and Destiny* (Hoboken, N.J., 2000), 43–44.

134. See Nirenberg, *Anti-Judaism*, 399. "[Abraham's] wandering meant a new relationship with 'true.' This nomadic movement revealed itself not as the eternal privation of sojourn, but as a genuine way of residing. As if the truth itself were necessarily seden-

tary!" Marc-Alain Ouaknin, *The Burnt Book* (Princeton, N.J., 1995), 153 (text slightly revised).

135. Benedictus de Spinoza, *Theological-Political Treatise* (Cambridge, 2007), 98 (ch. 7 [2]).

136. J. Samuel Preus, *Spinoza and the Irrelevance of Biblical Authority* (Cambridge, 2001), 1, 2, 3, 4, 25, 31, 33, 157, 182, 203.

137. Thomas Jefferson, *The Life and Selected Writings of Thomas Jefferson*, ed. Adrienne Koch and William Peden (New York, 2004), 399–400.

138. Anthony Julius, "Willed Ignorance: Reflections on Academic Free Speech, Occasioned by the David Miller Case," *Current Legal Problems*, 2022, Vol. 75, No. 1, 18.

139. Jean-Gérard Bursztein, *A Psychoanalytic Commentary on the Hebrew Bible* (Paris, 2015), 14.

140. See Jonathan Z. Smith, *Relating Religion* (Chicago, 2004), 314.

141. Brettler, *How to Read the Jewish Bible*, 280.

142. Harvey Cox, *How to Read the Bible* (New York, 2015), 14; J. P. Fokkelman, "Genesis," in *The Literary Guide to the Bible*, ed. Robert Alter and Frank Kermode (London, 1989), 36, 40.

143. John Barton, *The Nature of Biblical Criticism* (Louisville, Ky., 2007), 2.

144. James Barr, *Holy Scripture: Canon, Authority, Criticism* (Oxford, 1983), 9.

145. Rolf Rendtorff, *The Covenant Formula* (Edinburgh, 1998), 6.

146. Levenson, *Hebrew Bible, the Old Testament, and Historical Criticism*, 41.

147. See Barton, *Nature of Biblical Criticism*, 3, 4.

148. Carol Smith, "Challenged by the Text," in *A Feminist Companion to Reading the Bible: Approaches, Methods and Strategies*, ed. Athalya Brenner and Carole Fontaine (London, 1997), 122.

149. "The Court would recognize the propriety of . . . the teaching about religion, as distinguished from the teaching of religion, in the public schools." Justice Arthur Goldberg, concurring in *Abington School District v. Schempp*, 374 U.S. 203, 306 (1963).

150. Joseph Blenkinsopp, *Abraham: The Story of a Life* (Grand Rapids, Mich., 2015), 201.

151. Herman Gunkel, *The Legends of Genesis* (Eugene, Ore., 2003), 11, 14, 62, 69, 75.

152. Robert Alter, *The Art of Biblical Translation* (Princeton, N.J., 2019), 12 ("attention to the literary aspects . . . plays no role in [their] training," "blindness to the literary dimension").

153. Levenson, *Hebrew Bible, the Old Testament, and Historical Criticism*, xiv.

154. See Geoffrey Hartman, *The Third Pillar* (Philadelphia, 2011), 87.

155. Friedrich Baumgärtel (1888–1981), quoted in Levenson, *Hebrew Bible, the Old Testament, and Historical Criticism*, 29.

156. Victor P. Hamilton, *The Book of Genesis: Chapters 18–50* (Grand Rapids, Mich., 1995), 8. "All of the NICOT volumes combine superior scholarship, an evangelical view of Scripture as the Word of God, and concern for the life of faith today. . . . Readers who want to hear God's voice anew through Scripture will find the NICOT series to be a faithful, trustworthy guide for helping them navigate the strange other country we call the Old Testament." Best Commentaries, "New International Commentary on the Old Testament," accessed 18 April 2024, https://bestcommentaries.com /series/new-international-commentary-on-the-old-testament -nicot/.

157. Levenson is a Harvard Jewish studies professor and an "observant Jew." See *Hebrew Bible, the Old Testament, and Historical Criticism*, 29, 34, 80.

158. Adam Kirsch, "The Book of Psalms," in *"Who Wants to Be a Jewish Writer?" and Other Essays* (New Haven, Conn., 2019), 22–24.

159. Kermode, *Genesis of Secrecy*, viii–ix ("The linguistic requirement is formidable, and I myself had better say at once that I have no Aramaic or Hebrew, only enough Greek, and German so enfeebled that whenever possible I use translations"); Kermode, "Deciphering the Big Book," in *Uses of Error*, 28 ("outsider").

160. Levenson, *Inheriting Abraham*, 86–87.

161. See Levenson, *Death and Resurrection of the Beloved Son*, 3.

162. See, for example, Lebens, *Principles of Judaism*; and Harris Bor, *Staying Human* (Eugene, Ore., 2021). I instance these two works because the writers are known to me personally. Many other works, similarly possessing the academic virtues, could be cited.

163. Julius, "Willed Ignorance," 18–19.

164. Hannah Arendt, "Truth and Politics," in *Between Past and Future* (London, 2006), 255–256.

165. Kugel, *Traditions of the Bible*, 38.

166. Ruth Wisse, *Free as a Jew* (New York, 2021), 209 ("whiplash transition from tradition to modernity").

167. Quoted in Samuel Hugo Bergman, *Faith and Reason* (New York 1963), 77–78.

168. Hilary Putnam, *Philosophy as Dialogue* (Cambridge, Mass., 2022), 287.

169. Gershom Scholem, *On Jews and Judaism in Crisis* (New York, 1976), 10, 173.

170. Nahum Glatzer, *Franz Rosenzweig: His Life and Thought* (New York, 1953), 231. "Like Bialik, Berdichevsky wished to explore . . . the national spirit of folk, but that meant the spirit which was not subjugated to the pressures of 'normative Judaism.'" Shachar M. Pinsker, *Literary Passports* (Stanford, Calif., 2011), 285.

171. See Harold Bloom, "Foreword," in Yerushalmi, *Zakhor*, xiv.

172. Hartman, *Third Pillar*, 5.

173. Geoffrey Hartman, *A Scholar's Tale* (New York, 2007), 115, 146–150.

174. Dan Jacobson explains that his book about the Bible "is an attempt by the writer to make contact with a tradition from which he has always felt himself sundered, and which has yet affected his life." *Story of Stories*, 2.

175. David Biale, "Gershom Scholem's Ten Unhistorical Aphorisms on Kabbalah," in *Gershom Scholem: Modern Critical Views*, ed. Harold Bloom (New York, 1987), 101, 114–115, 121–122.

176. Moyn, *Origins of the Other*, 16, 17, 18, 201, 207.

177. Erich Auerbach, "Montaigne the Writer," in *Selected Essays of Erich Auerbach*, 202–205, 213.

178. Hilary Putnam, *Jewish Philosophy as a Guide to Life* (Bloomington, Ind., 2008), 102. Putnam writes, "I don't believe in 'miracles' in that sense. But spirituality—in my case, that means praying, meditating, putting myself in touch with the ideals, rituals, ancient texts, that the Jewish people have passed down for more than two millennia, and undergoing the experiences that go with all of these—is miraculous and natural at the same time."

179. Alicia Suskin Ostriker, *The Nakedness of the Fathers* (New Brunswick, N.J., 1994), 5.

180. Yosef Hayim Yerushalmi, *Transmitting Jewish History* (Waltham, Mass., 2021), 42, 48.

181. Philip Roth, *The Counterlife* (London, 2016), 328.

182. Franz Kafka, *Diaries* (New York, 2022), 327.

183. My reasoning is as follows: (i) Maimonides explains that the *Guide* is not for "those who have not engaged in any study other than the science of the Law—I mean the legalistic study of the Law" (I.Introduction)—that is, the ordinary run of rabbis; (ii) in his parable of the king's palace, such individuals do not secure access to the inner chamber (III.51); (iii) "can there be any doubt that Maimonides assigned Aristotle a portion in the world to come?" Menachem Kellner, *Maimonides on Judaism and the Jewish People* (New York, 1991), 77; (iv) philosophers, Gentile and Jews alike, constitute the third class.

184. Hannah Arendt and Karl Jaspers, *Correspondence 1926–1969* (New York, 1992), 199–200 (July 9, 1952). This third class tends to share the rabbinic conception of *amei ha'aretz*, however, regarding them as subsisting in their Judaism without effort, understanding, or misery (to adapt another remark of Kafka's; see *Diaries*, 29).

185. Harold Bloom, *The Strong Light of the Canonical*, City College Papers, no. 20 (New York, 1987), 77, quoted in Geoffrey Hartman, "Who Is an Educated Jew?," in *Third Pillar*, 155.

186. Richard Rorty, "Philosophy as a Transitional Genre," in *Philosophy as Cultural Politics* (Cambridge, 2007), 89–104.

187. Undated letter from Emily Dickinson to Joseph Lyman: "Dickinson/Lyman Correspondence," letter 3, www.emilydickinson .org.

188. Abraham Joshua Heschel, *God in Search of Man* (1955), quoted in Jean-Christophe Attias, *The Jews and the Bible* (Stanford, Calif., 2015), 70.

189. Auerbach, *Mimesis*, 15.

190. Adam Kirsch, "Who Wants to Be a Jewish Writer?," in *"Who Wants to Be a Jewish Writer?" and Other Essays*, 1–2, 15.

191. See David Norton, *A History of the English Bible as Literature* (Cambridge, 2000), 395.

192. Caspi and Green, "Prolegomenon," xxiii.

193. Franz Kafka, *Letters to Friends, Family, and Editors* (New York, 2016), 270–271 (mid-April 1921).

194. In the words of M. Y. Berdichevsky (1865–1921). See Pinsker, *Literary Passports*, 282.

195. Kafka, *Letters to Friends, Family, and Editors*, 288–289 (June 1921).

196. "Jewish identity devolved into a state of confusion, veering between waning tradition . . . and secularization, whose openness posed multiple and conflicting options." Eyal Chowers, *The Political Philosophy of Zionism* (Cambridge, 2012), 6.

197. Adam Kirsch, "Preface," in *"Who Wants to Be a Jewish Writer?" and Other Essays*, xi.

198. Amos Oz, *In the Land of Israel* (New York, 1993), 6.

199. For example, the Buber/Rosenzweig Bible translation, on which their "fidelity to the rabbinic exegetical tradition . . . left an indelible mark." Orr Scharf, *Thinking in Translation* (Berlin, 2021), 154.

200. Cynthia Ozick, "Ruth," in *Letters of Intent* (London, 2017), 257.

201. Not true of the Yiddish writers, however. There's something both of the sentimental, folk-rabbinic practice of invoking Abraham's name and the relating of episodes in his life to the writer's own times in Sholom Aleichem and in Isaac Bashevis Singer. See Sholem Aleichem, "Lekh-Lekho," in *Tevye the Dairyman and the Railroad Stories* (New York, 1987), 116–131; and Singer, "The Little Shoemakers," in *A Treasury of Yiddish Stories*, ed. Eliezer Greenberg and Irving Howe (New York, 1989), 555 ("He often thought

that if the Almighty were to call on him to sacrifice his eldest son, Gimpel, he would rise early in the morning").

202. See Yosef Haim Yerushalmi, *Freud's Moses* (New Haven, Conn., 1991), 2.

203. It is only with Auerbach that the point needs references. See James I. Porter, "Auerbach and Philology," *Critical Inquiry*, Autumn 2008, Vol. 35, 127 ("he uses the words *Jewish* or *Israel* and their equivalents nearly a dozen times, casually but insistently—and now we can see, provocatively, in a kind of 're-Jewification' of the biblical text"). Porter, "Old Testament Realism in the Writings of Erich Auerbach," in *Jews and the Ends of Theory*, ed. Shai Ginsburg, Martin Land, and Jonathan Boyarin (New York, 2019), 202.

204. Dan Miron, *The Animal in the Synagogue* (London, 2019), 94, 107–108.

205. Robert Alter, "Kafka as Kabbalist," *Salmagundi*, Spring–Summer 1993, Vol. 98/99, 86.

206. Franz Kafka, *Letters to Felice* (London, 1999), 355.

207. Kafka, *Diaries*, 286.

208. Alter, "Kafka as Kabbalist," 93.

209. Miron, *Animal in the Synagogue*, 1, 18.

210. Gershom Scholem, "A Candid Letter about My True Intentions in Studying Kabbalah" (1937), in *On the Possibility of Jewish Mysticism in Our Time* (Philadelphia, 1997), 4.

211. Harold Bloom, *Take Arms against a Sea of Trouble* (New York, 2020), 561, 562.

212. Daniel Mendelsohn, *Three Rings* (London, 2020), 31.

213. Porter, "Auerbach and Philology," 126.

214. Porter, "Auerbach and Philology," 116.

215. Porter, "Old Testament Realism in the Writings of Erich Auerbach," 189, 202 (Auerbach's account of Dante in both *Mimesis* and *Dante: Poet of the Secular World* is "an act of intellectual revenge" in response to "the attempt to drain the Old Testament of its reality and historical validity").

216. Ruth Kartun-Blum, *Profane Scriptures* (Cincinnati, 1991), 18.

217. From *The Trial*'s last sentence. See Franz Kafka, *The Complete Novels* (London, 2019), 198.

218. Saul Friedländer, *Franz Kafka: The Poet of Shame and Guilt* (New Haven, Conn., 2013), 30–31 ("the fathers hound the sons to their death"), 36–37.

219. Erich Heller, *Kafka* (London, 1974), 23.

220. Kafka, *Diaries*, 257, 258.

221. Kafka, *Letters to Felice*, 295, 297.

222. See the account of this Bohemian name at www.houseof names.com. Kafka told Brod, "In 'Bendemann,' the 'mann' is there only to strengthen the syllable 'Bende' in case of any unforeseen possibilities in the story." "Unforeseen possibilities"! Brod, *Franz Kafka*, 130.

223. Walter Benjamin, "Franz Kafka," in *Illuminations* (London, 2015), 119.

224. Sarah was 90 when Isaac was born (Gen. 17:17) and 127 (Gen. 23:1) when she died. See Kugel, *Traditions of the Bible*, 320. The rabbis disagreed on Isaac's age at the time of the *Aqedah*. Some said 36, others said 37, and still others proposed younger ages. See Kessler, *Bound by the Bible*, 108.

225. Franz Kafka, *Letter to His Father* (New York, 1966), 1, 47, 107.

226. Of "Metamorphosis" (1915), Cynthia Ozick writes, "In Kafka's myth, it is the powerless son who turns into a cockroach." *Letters of Intent*, 169.

227. See Kafka, *Letters to Friends, Family, and Editors*, 285–286.

228. See Chris Danta, *Literature Suspends Death* (London, 2011), 6.

229. Kafka, *Letters to Friends, Family, and Editors*, 285 (italics added).

230. Sigmund Freud, *The Letters of Sigmund Freud to Eduard Silberstein*, ed. Walter Boelich (Cambridge, Mass., 1990), 21, 70.

231. Phillip Rieff, *Freud: The Mind of the Moralist* (Chicago, 1979), 284. "Freud seems to have been determined to make Moses, with whom he thoroughly identified, the father of the Jewish people, rather than Abraham." Emanuel Rice, *Freud and Moses* (Albany, N.Y., 1990), 161.

232. Wyschogrod, *Body of Faith*, 50.

233. Mary Bergstein, *Mirrors of Memory* (Ithaca, N.Y., 2010), 100.

234. Jan Assmann, *The Price of Monotheism* (Stanford, Calif., 2010), 93. Richard Bernstein describes Freud's own account of Abraham as "tortuous." *Freud and the Legacy of Moses* (Cambridge, 1998), 11.

235. See Twersky, *Introduction to the Code of Maimonides*, 117.

236. Julia Kristeva's summary. See *Powers of Horror* (New York, 1982), 56. "There can be no doubt that Freud could not identify with Isaac. Nor could he have identified with Abraham in [the *Akedah*], for he was just as 'bound' by his heavenly father as Isaac was." Yael S. Feldman, "And Rebecca Loved Jacob," in *Freud and Forbidden Knowledge*, ed. Peter L. Rudnytsky and Ellen Handler Spitz (New York, 1994), 8.

237. See Carol Delaney, "The Legacy of Abraham," in *Beyond Androcentrism*, ed. Rita M. Gross (Missoula, Mont., 1977), 231.

238. Rembrandt's Abraham, as interpreted by Bergmann, *In the Shadow of Moloch*, 114.

239. Jacques Lacan, *The Ethics of Psychoanalysis* (New York, 2008), 222.

240. There was a second, less consequential but still odd "Abraham" suppression. In 1912, Freud's colleague the psychoanalyst Karl Abraham published a paper crediting Amenhotep IV's cult as the precursor of Mosaic monotheism. "Amenhotep IV (Ikhnaton)—A Psychoanalytic Contribution to the Understanding of his Personality and the Monotheistic Cult of Aton," *Psychoanalytic Quarterly*, 1935, Vol. 4, 537–569. "One could reproach Freud for not quoting Abraham's essay, which had undoubtedly inspired him to write his book." Isabel Sanfeliu, *Karl Abraham* (London, 2014), 65. Abraham's surname played an obscure part in Freud's decision. Writing to Jung before he met Abraham, Freud asked, "Is he a descendent of his eponym?" To this awkwardly collusive question, Jung replied, "[He] is what his name implies," and added, "[he] often has mild ideas of persecution about me." See Sigmund Freud and Carl Jung, *The Freud/Jung Letters*, ed. William McGuire (Cambridge, Mass., 1974), 80, 81 (27, 29 August 1907); Yerushalmi, *Freud's*

Moses, 42–43. See also Joel Whitebook, "*Geistigkeit:* A Problematic Conception," in *Freud and Monotheism,* ed. Gilad Sharvit and Karen S. Feldman (New York, 2018), 60 ("There is a double Abrahamic repression in *Moses and Monotheism*").

241. Auerbach, *Mimesis,* 8, 14.

242. Porter, "Old Testament Realism in the Writings of Erich Auerbach," 208–209.

243. Porter, "Auerbach and Philology," 117, 125, 137.

244. Jürgen Habermas, *Also a History of Philosophy* (Cambridge, 2023), 223–228; Jan Assmann, *The Invention of Religion* (Princeton, N.J., 2018), 2.

245. Auerbach, *Mimesis,* 48.

246. Auerbach, "Figura," 96.

247. Auerbach, *Mimesis,* 75.

248. For example, Edward Said, "Introduction," in Auerbach, *Mimesis,* xxiv ("Christianity shatters the classical balance between high and low styles"); Terry Eagleton, "Pork Chops and Pineapples," *LRB,* 23 October 2003 ("Behind this realist mingling of styles lies the influence of Christianity"); and Kermode, *Genesis of Secrecy,* 104 ("He greatly admired the realism of the gospels, . . . the origin of . . . later realism"). See Porter, "Old Testament Realism in the Writings of Erich Auerbach," 219, fn. 37.

INDEX

INDEX

Abraham (*continued*)
Canaan, 91–92; in Jubilees, 243; leaving Haran, xiv, 88–91, 205, 243, 263; leaving Ur, xiv, 78–79; marriage to Keturah, 164; marriage to Sarah, xiv, 82–83, 87–88, 122, 126, 153, 160, 161, 307n86; meaning of name, 1–4; miracle of the furnace, xiv, 76–78, 81–84, 86–88, 90, 109, 129, 176, 208, 236; mother of, 12, 204; pausing, 30–32; Philo's interpretation of, 244; as philosopher, xviii; prayer for deliverance, 76–77, 81; preaching in Haran, 83–88, 92; preparation for the sacrifice, xiv, 140–142, 177; quarrel with Lot, 96–99; reasoning by, 23–28; rescuing Lot, 99–100, 175; and Sarah's death, 160–164; self-possession of, 32–35; serving God, 195; Terah's betrayal of, 53–55, 57–58; trying to persuade Chaldean society, 41–50; two lives of, 203–227; in Ur Kasdim, xiii, xv, 211, 225, 228; visions of, 90–91, 101–105, 107, 109, 110; wandering, 21–22, 129–133, 340–341n134. See also *Akedah*
Abraham, Karl, 348–349n240
Abraham: The Story of a Life (Blenkinsopp), 266
Abram, 2, 203
actual design question, 26, 27
Adam and Eve, 211, 218, 317n2, 320n30
Adorno, Theodor, 338n112
Aggadah, 199, 202
Akedah: Abraham and, xiv, 236, 314n139; arrival, 142–147; Christian conscription of, 259–260; circumcision as allusion to, 228; contestation vs. submission, 187–192; as decision, 170–173; ethics of, 194–196; as failure, 179–182; as family story, 3; God's call to Abraham, 136–140; and the issue of trust, 182–186; journey, 142; in

Jubilees and Pseudo-Jubilees, 243–244; in literature, 275, 276, 282; as miracle, 150, 158; as "patch-up," 176–179; polysemous texts, 168–170; and the principle of scission, 173–175; rabbis' interpretation of, xvi, 246–253; sacrifice of the ram, 145–146, 177–179; Sarah and, 140–142; self-reliance vs. reliance, 192–194; as self-sacrifice, 314n137; as test of faith, 249–250, 260, 305n71, 337n110, 340n130; theories of, xvi, 167–196; as warning, 186–187
Akiva, Rabbi, 193–194
Aleichem, Sholem, 193, 345–346n201
Al-Ghazali, 20–21
altars, 65, 68, 91–92, 93, 96, 99; Isaac as sacrifice on, 141–146, 153, 191, 243, 250, 255, 332n46
Alter, Robert, 267
Amalek, 127, 128
Amalekites, 128, 252
Amenhotep IV (Ikhnaton), 348–349n240
Ami, Rav, 192
Amtilai, 204
ancestor veneration, 6, 69–70, 92
Antigone, 180
antisemitism, 127, 128
Arendt, Hannah, 208, 215, 221, 267, 270, 320n35
Aristotle, 211, 325n94, 344n183
Athanasius, 257
Atudai, 204
Auerbach, Erich, 257, 269–270, 271, 273, 274–275, 280–282, 346n203
Augustine of Hippo (saint), 217, 258, 337n107
authority: of Abraham, 41, 53, 56, 87, 215, 222–223, 248; acceptance of, 10; Aristotle as, 325n94; claims to, 236; collapse of, 154; divine, 56, 103, 112, 146, 205, 236; male, 37; of Nimrod, 57, 59, 61; paternal, 39, 58, 72, 141, 276, 279, 295n83; political, 180; rabbinic, xix, 241,

Maimonides, Moses (*continued*)
205–206, 222, 223, 227, 229–235,
261, 270, 278, 327n122; *Mishne
Torah*, xv, 188, 213, 234; on perfection, 181–182, 218; on prophecy,
xviii, 205, 284–285n10
Mamre, 119
Mann, Thomas, 132
marriage: of Abraham and Sarah,
87–88, 122, 126, 153, 160, 161,
307n86; of Isaac, 164, 307n86
materialism, 16, 235
Medan, 173
Melito of Sardis, 255
Mendelssohn, Moses, xviii, 198, 200
Mesopotamia, 8–9
Micah (prophet), 189, 190
Midian, 173
Midrashim, 169, 194, 222, 246, 252,
315n149
Milcah, 12–13
Mimesis (Auerbach), 275, 280–282,
346n215
miracles: 85, 210, 227, 230, 295–296n87,
344n178; and the *Akedah*, 150,
158; Isaac's conception as, 119,
123; miracle of the furnace, xiv,
76–78, 81–84, 86–88, 90, 109,
129, 176, 208, 236
Mishnah, 219, 240, 246, 250
Mishne Torah (Maimonides), xv, 188,
213, 234
mitzvoth, 195
monotheism, xiii, 24, 30, 36–37, 46–47,
63–64, 66–67, 278; critical, 76, 81;
Ur, 84
Montaigne, Michel de, 269–270
Moritz, Karl Phillip, 207
Moses, xviii, 193–194, 210, 211, 220,
225, 227, 243, 278, 347n231
Moses and Monotheism (Freud), 199,
278–280
Moyn, Samuel, 196
Mr. Mani (Yehoshua), 275
Mt. Moriah, 3, 81, 151, 166, 190, 191,
194, 297n19
mysticism, 199, 319n23

Nachmanides, 213, 222, 322n57
Nahor, 12–13, 39–41, 90, 173
Nazism, 206
Nechayev, Sergey, 175
NICOT (New International Com-
mentary on the Old Testament),
342n156
Nimrod, 83, 86, 119, 139, 205;
Abraham's conversation with,
59–78, 114; as ruler of Ur, 55–57,
59–78; sentencing Abraham to
death, 76–78
Noah, 201, 211
Noahide laws, 132

Odyssey, 280
one-godism. *See* monotheism
Oz, Amos, 273
Ozick, Cynthia, 273, 316–317n166

paganism, 32, 227
Pagels, Elaine, 309n94
parables, 172–173
parenthood, 51, 52, 64, 72–73, 205,
252, 295n83, 313n135
Patriarchs, 253
Paul of Tarsus, 253–254, 256, 281
Perizites, 104
Pharaoh, 95–96, 119, 161, 252
phenomenology, 214
philistinism, 212–213
Philo of Alexandria, 208, 243, 244, 254,
261, 317n2
philosophy: of Abraham, 42–44, 52;
of Bacon, 42; as criticism, 32–34,
225; Greek, 211, 220, 229,
319n20; Jewish, xviii; of Maimonides, 326n126; and mysticism, 319n23; myth of, 210;
naturalistic, 235; Nimrod on,
70; of Singer, 300n4; of Wittgenstein, 228n57
Pikhol, 128, 129
Pirke Avot, 217, 220, 250
Pirke de Rabbi Eleazer, 204
Plato, 133
poetry, 67

JEWISH LIVES is a prizewinning series of interpretative biography designed to explore the many facets of Jewish identity. Individual volumes illuminate the imprint of Jewish figures upon literature, religion, philosophy, politics, cultural and economic life, and the arts and sciences. Subjects are paired with authors to elicit lively, deeply informed books that explore the range and depth of the Jewish experience from antiquity to the present.

Jewish Lives is a partnership of Yale University Press and the Leon D. Black Foundation. Ileene Smith is editorial director. Anita Shapira and Steven J. Zipperstein are series editors.

Ayn Rand: Writing a Gospel of Success, by Alexandra Popoff
Walther Rathenau: Weimar's Fallen Statesman, by Shulamit Volkov
Man Ray: The Artist and His Shadows, by Arthur Lubow
Sidney Reilly: Master Spy, by Benny Morris
Admiral Hyman Rickover: Engineer of Power, by Marc Wortman
Jerome Robbins: A Life in Dance, by Wendy Lesser
Julius Rosenwald: Repairing the World, by Hasia R. Diner
Mark Rothko: Toward the Light in the Chapel,
    by Annie Cohen-Solal
Ruth: A Migrant's Tale, by Ilana Pardes
Menachem Mendel Schneerson: Becoming the Messiah,
    by Ezra Glinter
Gershom Scholem: Master of the Kabbalah, by David Biale
Bugsy Siegel: The Dark Side of the American Dream,
    by Michael Shnayerson
Solomon: The Lure of Wisdom, by Steven Weitzman
Steven Spielberg: A Life in Films, by Molly Haskell
Spinoza: Freedom's Messiah, by Ian Buruma
Alfred Stieglitz: Taking Pictures, Making Painters, by Phyllis Rose
Barbra Streisand: Redefining Beauty, Femininity, and Power,
    by Neal Gabler
Henrietta Szold: Hadassah and the Zionist Dream, by Francine
    Klagsbrun
Leon Trotsky: A Revolutionary's Life, by Joshua Rubenstein
Warner Bros: The Making of an American Movie Studio,
    by David Thomson
Elie Wiesel: Confronting the Silence, by Joseph Berger

FORTHCOMING TITLES INCLUDE:

Hannah Arendt, by Masha Gessen
The Ba'al Shem Tov, by Ariel Mayse